KU-022-922

Contents

The National Trust and Industrial Archaeology

The National Trust became almost inadvertently the owner of a large number of industrial monuments. Wind- and water mills, lime kilns, mines, quarries, brickworks, turbines and others were acquired by the Trust in its early years either because they happened to be situated on land acquired for other reasons or because of their aesthetic value in the landscape. Few were considered on the grounds of their industrial archaeological value.

Styal, Cheshire, with its textile mill and village of workers' cottages, was accepted in 1939 as much because it was even then recognized as a rare surviving example of an eighteenth-century industrial complex still in use, as for the natural beauty of the Bollin Valley and the architectural distinction of the buildings.

It was accepted, tenanted but without endowment, a situation almost inevitable in the offer of any sizable industrial monument or complex. When after twenty years the mill itself came in hand, the Trust was unsure to what use to put it. As late as the 1950s the looms had been broken up with the help of government grants available for the destruction of obsolete machinery.

A shift of emphasis occurred in the early 1960s, with the fast-growing appreciation by the public of the importance of our industrial past. The Trust's first responsibility, it was felt, was to maintain and where necessary restore to a proper standard the industrial monuments already in its ownership. This more positive attitude was encapsulated in the June 1964 Executive Committee minutes: 'the Trust should continue to preserve industrial monuments, provided that the highest possible standards – aesthetic, historic and financial – were preserved.' At the same time an Honorary Industrial Archaeology Adviser was appointed.

In the ensuing nineteen years the Trust's progress in preserving industrial monuments has been steady but slow. It has been wary of venturing too fast into unfamiliar territory. Moreover, the outstanding contributions to industrial archaeology have come from independent self-generating bodies of enthusiasts. The Trust has felt that it should take second place to such groups. If it tried to shoulder the foremost national responsibility in this field, it might act as a disincentive to others. Its role continues to be that of the last option, while at the same time forging stronger links with the industrial heritage.

The case of Styal is instructive. Since 1959 the Trust has spent nearly £300,000 on putting the building into proper repair, and expenditure continues. Day-to-day management and fundraising have recently been handed over to a specially constituted and independent charitable trust by whom expertise can be harnessed and effort directed in a single-minded way and with an intensity that the Trust's own resources do not permit. The cost has been great, but the success of Styal and the broadening of the Trust's appeal to potential members who might otherwise not see the Trust's interests as theirs have been valuable.

Much credit for the Trust's improved presentation of its industrial monuments must go to the invaluable volunteers and experts who have made it possible to restore buildings and put machinery back into working order. In a similar way to the work carried out by the Quarry Bank Mill Development Trust at Styal, volunteer work on industrial monuments allows the Trust to use its financial and manpower resources elsewhere.

The only monuments so far acquired by the Trust for preservation solely on grounds of historic and engineering interest have been the Cornish Beam Engines, given in 1967. The historic metal-working site at Aberdulais (West Glamorgan), in the heart of industrial South Wales, was accepted for its historic interest, but it also happens to have been admired since the eighteenth century as a beautiful place.

Much larger industrial complexes may be offered to the National Trust in the future, but since they are unlikely to be accompanied by endowment funds, co-operation with national and other museums and local authorities will inevitably have to be sought.

The success of the lease of the mill at Dunster in

THE NATIONAL TRUST GUIDE TO OUR INDUSTRIAL PAST

Including full gazetteer to sites and monuments in the British Isles

THE NATIONAL TRUST GUIDE TO

Our Industrial Past

Anthony Burton

GEORGE PHILIP . THE NATIONAL TRUST
THE NATIONAL TRUST FOR SCOTLAND

British Library Cataloguing in Publication Data

Burton, Anthony
    The National Trust guide to our industrial past.
    1. Great Britain—Industries—History
    1. Title
    388′.0941   HC253

ISBN 0 540 01072 3

© Anthony Burton 1983

Published by George Philip, 12–14 Long Acre, London
WC2E 9LP, in association with The National Trust and
The National Trust for Scotland.

Filmset in Great Britain by Tameside Filmsetting Ltd,
Ashton-under-Lyne. Printed in Great Britain by
Butler & Tanner Ltd, Frome and London.

END-PAPERS *The bridges across the Tyne at Newcastle.
The swing bridge, originally powered by Armstrong's
hydraulic engine, has a central turret; Stephenson's High
Level Bridge has a train crossing it.*

HALF-TITLE PAGE *The late eighteenth century saw a huge
expansion in mill building, partly as a result of the invention
of the spinning mule.*

TITLE PAGE *The replica of* Locomotion, *built to celebrate
the 150th anniversary of the opening of the Stockton and
Darlington Railway.*

ILLUSTRATION ACKNOWLEDGMENTS
Aerofilms p 96; *J. Allan Cash* p 171; *The Bass Museum of
Brewing* p 192; *Beamish North of England Open Air Museum*
pp 30–1, p 167 (*above and below*), pp 215–15 (*below*);
Blackgang Sawmill Museum p 190; *The Bluebell Railway* p 142;
J. & C. Bord pp 26–7, p 97, p 98, p 156 (*below*), p 199, p 202
(*below*), p 209; *Bord Fáilte* p 22; *The British Library* p 20;
John Cornwell p 26, pp 74–5, p 76, p 82, p 83, p 89, p 197,
p 202 (*above*); *Mary Evans Picture Library* Half-title, p 51;
Exeter Maritime Museum p 113; *Timothy Hackworth Museum*
p 204; *Howarth-Loomes Collection* pp 106–7 (*right*); *Illustrated
London News* p 147, p 165, p 169; *Ironbridge Gorge Museum
Trust* p 212; *Ironbridge Gorge Museum Trust: Brian Bracegirdle*
pp 116–17; *Ironbridge Gorge Museum Trust: Elton Collection*
p 43, p 104, p 136 (*above*), p 146, p 222 (*above*); *Ironbridge
Gorge Museum Trust: Telford Collection* p 125; *Leicestershire
Museum of Technology* p 164; *Manchester City Council, Cultural
Services Department* p 58 (*left*); *The Mansell Collection* pp 40–1,
p 78; *The Museum of London* p 122; *National Monuments
Record* p 128; *National Museum of Wales* p 33, p 181; *National
Railway Museum* p 139, p 141; *The National Trust* p 16
(*above and below*), p 18, p 21 (*left*), p 56, p 57, pp 58–9
(*right*), p 67; *The National Trust for Scotland* p 223; *Northern
Ireland Tourist Board* p 13; *Oxford Central Library Local
History Collection* p 112 (*above*); *Derek Pratt* p 100, p 114,
pp 118–19, p 121, p 127, p 150, p 156 (*above*), p 187, p 191;
Quarry Bank Mill Trust p 52, p 55; *Royal Institution of Cornwall*
p 38, p 200 (*below*); *The Science Museum, London* p 29, p 35,
p 71, p 131, p 136 (*below*); *Scottish Development Department*
p 222 (*below*); *The Scottish Tourist Board* p 85 (*below*);
Somerset Levels Project p 94; *Severn Trent Water Authority* p 162;
Talyllyn Railway p 157; *Truro Pottery* p 200 (*above*); *Welsh
Industrial and Maritime Museum* pp 132–3 (*below*); *Colin
Westwood* p 23, p 37 (*right*), pp 48–9, p 65, pp 80–1, p 95,
p 149, pp 178–9 (*below*), p 180, pp 216–17; *Wetheriggs
Country Pottery* p 183; *Derek Widdicombe* Title-page, p 32,
p 42, p 53, p 54, p 61, p 66 (*above and below*), p 68 (*above and
below*), p 70, p 85 (*above*), p 86, p 87, p 88 (*above*), p 88
(*below*) – facilities granted by the Welsh Slate Museum
(Welsh Industrial and Maritime Museum), pp 90–1, p 109,
p 134, p 153, p 154, p 155, p 173, p 174, p 175 (*above and
below*), p 176 (*above and below*), p 179 (*above*), p 185, p 208,
p 215 (*above*), p 218, p 225, end-papers; *Derek Widdicombe/
Lancashire County Council – Higher Mill Museum* p 47; *Ulster
Museum* p 172, p 220.

Somerset to a tenant who has on his own initiative raised funds for its restoration is an encouraging success amongst smaller industrial monuments. Elsewhere, as at Shalford Mill near Guildford, Surrey, primarily interesting for its architecture, the building can be preserved by occupation by tenants and the cost of maintenance defrayed.

A great many of the Trust's properties stand in remote places, where its first duty is the preservation of solitude. Nevertheless, repairs, often increased by vandalism, must be undertaken, and the remoteness, together with the need for construction in traditional materials, adds to the cost of maintenance. The National Trust has embarked on the compilation of an inventory of the industrial sites and monuments in its care. This is an essential aspect of curatorship. Progress is now being made in transferring on to computer the information already painstakingly gathered while further sites are being methodically identified and recorded.

From relics of the pilchard fishing industry in Cornwall to the complexities of Styal, the Trust is now fully aware of its responsibilities for the sites it owns and is learning how it can best preserve them to the highest standards – aesthetic, historical and financial.

Author's Note

Throughout this book, units have been quoted in the old imperial measures, rather than metric. This is not an example of die-hard conservatism, but an attempt to rationalize a somewhat anarchic situation. A great many of those measurements relate to engineering dimensions and, as we are dealing with machinery built a century or more ago, we are dealing with a time when, in Britain, imperial measures were paramount. Thus, it would be quite wrong to describe a steam engine cylinder as having been bored to a diameter of 121.92 centimetres, for it most certainly was not: it was bored, with a good deal of precision, to a diameter of 48 inches. So, the original measures have been retained, and to avoid needless confusion all other measurements have been kept in line with the significant measures set by the early engineers. The author has no wish to be haunted by the irate ghost of George Stephenson who would doubtless insist that he never built a 143.51 cm gauge railway in his life.

Introduction

Interest in the remains of the industrial past has increased at an incredible rate in recent years, and with that increased interest has come a change in attitudes. The romanticization of the industrial landscape would have been inconceivable a generation or so ago when a Lancashire cotton town, for example, was regarded as at best an unfortunate reminder of the necessities that underlay prosperity; at worst, as an ugly blot, an excrescence on the fair face of the land. Today, when that same town echoes to the sound of clogs on cobbled streets, the clogs are no longer those of textile workers but of film crews on location. The old streets and the terraces are shot in soft focus to the accompaniment of bland band music in order to advertise the delights of wholemeal bread. The hard edges of the world's first industrial communities are being blurred behind veils of nostalgia. Look, for example, at how views of that great moving force of the Industrial Revolution, the steam engine, have changed. It drove the railway train and the ship, powered the mill and factory. Now that its day seems done, we have come to view it with delight, and hundreds of volunteers give up their leisure hours to bring the old dragons back into fire-breathing life. Yet how different attitudes were in the middle of the last century when this poem appeared in the *Northern Star* of 1843:

> *There is a King, and a ruthless King,*
> *Not a King of the poet's dream;*
> *But a tyrant fell, white slaves know well,*
> *And that ruthless King is Steam.*

How can we begin to reconcile these different views of our industrial past? One answer must surely lie in combining the study of the physical remains of the Industrial Revolution with a concern for the views of those who lived through those times. This need not lessen our appreciation of the remains themselves. In an age faced with the technology of the microchip, which to the great majority remains an incomprehensible mystery, the earlier machines offer a blissful, robust and even beautiful simplicity. Even the seemingly grim terraces of the early industrial towns seem somehow less grim when compared with the monstrous inhumanity of the tower block. And there is, perhaps, also an inevitably nostalgic attachment to an age when Britain led the world, when today we palpably do not hold any such position in the affairs of nations. So we look back with a certain pleasure to a time when engineers seemed giants in the land, to an age when there were great, dramatic changes which produced what we now begin to perceive as a kind of beauty. There is, however, that ever present danger that this view will blind us to the very real miseries of the changes wrought by industrialization. The poem quoted earlier could scarcely put it more forcibly:

> *Those hells upon earth, since the Steam King's birth,*
> *Have scatter'd around despair;*
> *For the human mind for Heav'n design'd,*
> *With the body is murdered there.*

We need, if we are to make sense of the past, both to understand the significance of the physical remains and to place them in a social context. Happily, those who have control of the more important industrial monuments are becoming increasingly aware of this need. A good example of a site where technical and social change are given equal weighting is the cotton mill and mill village of Styal (NT). Here we can appreciate the buildings and restored machinery, while at the same time we are never allowed to forget the often grim conditions under which the men, women and children who tended the machines worked. Such awareness of the social implications of technological change is not merely necessary as a correction to the trend towards a somewhat naively nostalgic view of the past, it is also necessary if the past is to be seen as having any relevance to the present and the future. Styal also serves to highlight another problem facing those who study this area of history. It is, like the great majority of the structures, buildings and machines we shall be looking at in this book, a product of the Industrial Revolution of the late eighteenth and early nineteenth centuries. Because the changes brought about in that period were so dramatic, it can seem that industry was actually born at that time, a ready formed and remarkably lusty infant striding straight out on to the stage of history. Just such a simile was, in fact, used by a writer in 1725, who described, in creaking verse, the instantaneous birth of the first steam engine:

> *I sprang, like Pallas, from a fruitful Brain,*
> *About the time of Charles the Second's Reign.*

Stories of invention are, in practice, never that simple, and industrial development can be traced back many centuries before the period we know as the Industrial Revolution. The physical remains available for study, however, tend to be of comparatively recent date, simply because the old has been changed, absorbed into later works, or has just decayed and disappeared. So, this volume is not being presented as any kind of comprehensive industrial history, but rather as a frame of reference within which what has survived can be understood. And, as a starting point, we shall look at a topic which lies at the very heart of all industrial development – power.

1 Natural Power

For many, many centuries the only power sources available to man were those provided by Nature – wind, water and, from the earliest times, animals. One of the first applications of power was its use in the grinding of grain into flour. At its simplest, this involved little more than one person operating a small pair of stones by hand, using devices of varying degrees of complexity and sophistication. Grain can be crushed by simply putting it on top of one stone and hitting it with another, although this could scarcely be described as very satisfactory. The saddle quern was an improvement over this basic method. Here the grain was placed in the hollow of a saddle-shaped stone and crushed not by pounding but by rubbing another stone backwards and forwards across the saddle. The rotary quern was an even better device in which the base stone was round, with the upper stone mounted above it on a central pivot, so that it could be swung backwards and forwards over the base. This rotary quern soon found widespread use, but it still represented a simple tool to be used by a single worker. However, at some time in the distant past man began to realize that it might be possible to make what would be, in effect, a very large rotary quern, which could be moved either by using several workers or by harnessing animals, such as oxen or asses. The household unit thus became an industrial unit, a commercial mill, grinding corn for a large population. When Milton described the blinded Samson as working 'Eyeless in Gaza at the mill with slaves', it was just such a mill that he was describing.

Animal-powered grain mills are mostly known from archaeological excavations and are rare in Britain. There are, however, a few examples, such as that at Woolley Manor, Chaddleworth, Berkshire. This is a comparatively late device, having been built into an older barn in the middle of the eighteenth century. Two horses were used to turn two pairs of grindstones. If such examples are rare, other uses of man and animal power are widespread. One of the most common applications was for winding, where a rope or cable wrapped round a turning drum could be used to raise or lower a bucket in a well or a man in a mine shaft. A fine example of the bucket in the well device can be seen at Greys Court (NT) at Rotherfield Greys in Oxfordshire. Early in the twelfth century, a well was sunk 200 foot down into the chalk, and water was laboriously hauled up for domestic use. The Tudor householders either took pity on their servants or demanded a better water supply, for they built a two-storey well house and in it they installed a donkey wheel. The wheel is 19 foot in diameter and almost 4 foot wide. The donkey walked inside the vertical wheel, and it turned a shaft which worked a two-bucket system, one bucket being at the top when the other was at the bottom, so that they balanced each other. As each loaded bucket reached the surface, the donkey was turned round and set off walking in the opposite direction, to bring up the next full bucket. It was a very efficient one-horse-power engine, and remained in use right up to the beginning of the twentieth century.

In many treadmills, the human animal took the place of the donkey. A particularly well-preserved example can be seen at Beaumaris Gaol on the Island of Anglesey. Again the wheel was used to raise water, but in this case the prisoners (who had been sentenced to hard labour) walked on the outside of the wheel to turn it. The treadmill was considered more as a punishment than as a useful device. Indeed, when enough water had been raised to fill the water tank for the gaol, the overflow was passed back into the well and the unhappy prisoners just kept on trudging. Historically, the use of human beings in this way was limited to slaves and prisoners, and in the case of the former the Romans considered the use of the treadmill as particularly beneficial to the community as a whole, simply because it provided employment for the large slave population. In fact, this appears to represent one of the earliest recorded examples of a government deliberately holding back advances in technology in favour of full employment – though the policy was largely governed by fear of the mischief that might be caused by underemployed slaves rather than by any concern for worker welfare. For the Romans could, if they had so wished, have replaced animal power by an alternative source of power – the power of water, harnessed through the water wheel. When they invaded and colonized Britain, they brought this new device with them.

Physical remains of Roman water wheels in Britain are, to say the least, somewhat scarce. There are indications that a water wheel was in use at Chesters on Hadrian's Wall where, beneath a tower on the bridge across the North Tyne, there was a special channel cut to divert water to turn the wheel. Roman mill sites have been unearthed and remains of a wheel were found in the River Witham at Lincoln. We learn rather more about Roman use of water power from other parts of the huge empire, and what we know suggests that the Romans had some quite sophisticated machines. This comes as no surprise, since they were renowned as the foremost hydraulic engineers of the ancient world, famous for their superb aqueducts. Yet in fact it was later invaders and settlers of this country, the Norsemen, who produced the simplest, most direct application of water power in Britain. They, too, brought the water wheel, and the device they used can still be seen in the northern isles, where Norse influence remained at its strongest. Perhaps the finest example of a Norse mill is to be found at Dounby on Mainland, Orkney.

The animal-powered wheels that we have already looked at are mechanically simple in that the shaft, turning with the wheel, powered the device directly – in the case of the grain mill, by turning the grindstones. This is precisely what we find at the Dounby Click Mill, which is built very much in the style of the oldest Norse mills. The building itself is crudely constructed of rough stone and covered by a turf roof. There are no windows, the only light being admitted through the open doorway. It is set directly over a small stream. The wheel itself consists of a vertical axle, on which is mounted a drum with two rows of curved blades, known as the tirl. The tirl stands directly in the mill stream, so that as the water strikes the blades, they move and turn the axle which passes up through the mill floor to the millstones above. The stones are cut with a pattern of grooves, and as the upper stone rotates over the lower, grain is fed in through a hopper and the criss-crossing grooves slice the grain finer and finer until it emerges under the stones as flour. The flour then falls into a box set in a trench below the mill. This is the water-powered mill at its very simplest. The Romans used a quite different type of wheel, much more efficient in use, but involving the millwrights in the construction of some much more complex machinery.

The Roman wheel is also known as the Vitruvian wheel, after the architect Vitruvius who wrote detailed descriptions of the different types of water wheels and their uses. In the Vitruvian wheel, the wheel itself is vertical, mounted on a horizontal axle. This arrangement produces both a complication and an advantage. The water wheel turns in a vertical plane but must move grindstones turning in a horizontal plane, so that to transmit the power from wheel to stones the millwright has to introduce gearing. A vertical gear wheel, the pit wheel, moving with the water wheel engages with a horizontal

Wellbrook Beetling Mill, Co. Tyrone (NT), showing the breastshot water wheel. The mill houses seven beetling machines which pounded the finished linen cloth to give it a sheen.

gear wheel, the wallower, mounted on a vertical shaft. The great advantage of introducing gears is that they need not be provided on a one-to-one basis. It is not necessary for the stones to make a single revolution for every revolution of the water wheel as was usual with the Norse mill. If the ratio of the number of teeth in one gear is changed in respect to the number of teeth in the other, then the stones can be made to move either slower or faster than the water wheel. In practice, the Romans favoured a system in which each turn of the wheel resulted in five turns of the stones. The same turning motion of wheels and shafts could also be adapted to help out with other jobs around the mill, such as raising and lowering sacks of grain.

The water mill preserved a certain unity through the centuries, though there were numerous small alterations and refinements. For a start, there were many different ways of supplying the water to the wheel. The essential elements were continuity of supply and consistency of flow. The miller could, for example, build a weir across the river to create a deep pool, from which water could be led away, controlled by sluice gates, eventually to reach the mill. Alternatively, water could be diverted into an artificial lake, the millpond, set above the level of the mill, from which water could again be released in a controlled manner through sluices. A third solution to the problem of water supply would be to construct an aqueduct, or launder, to carry the water to the wheel. The actual method adopted depended on the particular circumstances and the physical environment of the mill.

There were variations, too, in the water wheels themselves. The simplest type is the *undershot wheel* set, as with the Norse mill, directly

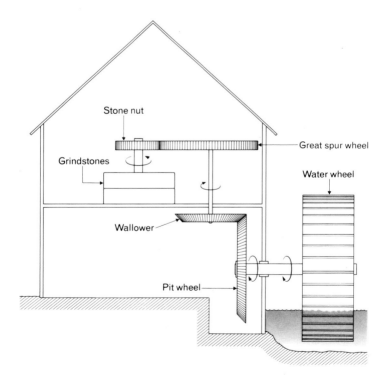

Types of water wheel (RIGHT) *and a typical water-powered grain mill* (LEFT).

Tirl

Horizontal or Norse mill

Undershot

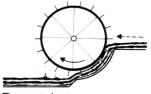

Breastshot

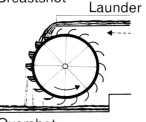

Launder

Overshot

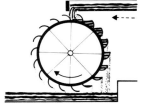

Pitchback

in the flow of the mill stream. Power is obtained by the force of the water hitting the paddles and forcing the wheel round. At the opposite extreme is the *overshot wheel*. In this case the rim of the wheel is fitted with 'buckets'. Water falls from a launder to fill the buckets, and the weight of the water carries each bucket downwards, turning the wheel and carrying the bucket on until eventually it becomes inverted and empties. So a continuous motion is set up, caused by the imbalance between the full buckets on one side of the wheel and the empty buckets on the other. Usually, the water drops into buckets forwards of a vertical line through the axle; when it falls on to the opposite side the wheel is known as a *pitchback wheel*. There is an intermediate position, where the water meets the paddles half way up the wheel, and this is known as the *breastshot wheel*. The overshot wheel is, in theory, the most efficient, but the extra expense involved in raising the water to a point high above the top of the wheel might be excessive. The breastshot wheel is a compromise, in many cases, between efficiency and expense. There is no perfect answer in mill design: each mill must be adapted to a particular set of circumstances, and each mill depends ultimately for its success on the skill and judgement of the millwright.

Today, we tend to regard the water mill as a quaint, romantic bygone, forgetting that it was once crucial to the economic life of the country. As far back as the eleventh century, *Domesday Book* could list over five thousand grain mills, the vast majority of which were water powered. The miller, indeed, had a uniquely important place in the community for a very long time. Throughout the Middle Ages, the Lord of the Manor could and did demand 'soke rights', by which all the grain grown in the manor had to be ground at the lord's mill, a privilege for which a toll was exacted, usually around a sixteenth of the flour produced. Bread was the great staple of the poor so that the mill was quite literally of vital importance, and the dishonest miller who cheated the poor of their due became one of the stock figures of medieval writing, culminating in Chaucer's portrait in *The Canterbury Tales*. As no one but the miller knew how much flour was produced from a given quantity of grain, there were ample opportunities for fraud. A popular saying of the time had it that the honest miller could be recognized by the tuft of hair growing in the palm of his hand. In practice, there was probably as much dishonesty among millers as there was in the rest of the community, neither more nor less. But their monopoly did breed mistrust and that, combined with the lonely siting of many mills, must have set the miller apart from his neighbours. Even as the mill's importance declined, it still remained within living memory as one of the fixed points of the rural scene. So that, today, there are still many mills standing, several of which have been lovingly restored and some of which still work at the task for which they were built – grinding grain.

The very many mills which are open to the public are listed in the

Nether Alderley Old Mill, Cheshire (NT), a water-powered grain mill dating back to the fifteenth century. Two reservoirs were constructed to provide water for the mill and the back wall of the mill building forms part of the dam of the lower one.

BELOW *The interior of Nether Alderley Old Mill (NT), showing the drive mechanism from the water wheel to the grindstones on the floor above. Flour passes down the chute on the left to the sack.*

gazetteer at the end of this book, but here we can look at a few in more detail. One of the oldest, and certainly one of the most attractive, is at Nether Alderley in Cheshire. Alderley Old Mill (NT) was originally built in the fifteenth century, and is especially interesting in that it shows some very sophisticated arrangements of machinery. Water is stored up in a millpond, and the mill itself is built into the dam wall. Its steep, stone-tiled roof running almost down to the ground gives it a most unusual appearance, but it is the placing of the two water wheels that makes it unique. They are both wooden, overshot wheels, but arranged in tandem, so that water first falls on to the larger of the two, 13 foot diameter by 4 foot width, and then passes on to the smaller, 12 foot by 3 foot. The arrangement may be somewhat odd, but it is undeniably effective as evidenced by the fact that the mill continued working right up to 1939 and now, after restoration, is back in full working order again. Elsewhere there are mills of almost equal antiquity still working for a living, a fine example being the seventeenth-century Felin Geri Mill at Newcastle Emlyn, Dyfed, which started work in 1604 and is still working in precisely the same manner today.

In many places, the centuries of change can be seen recorded in the very fabric of the building. Worsbrough Mill, near Barnsley in South Yorkshire, incorporates three quite different phases of building within the one structure. The oldest part is a water mill dating back to the early seventeenth century built of local stone with the typical mullioned windows of the period, and there is some evidence that the miller once lived in the mill itself before the mill house was built in the eighteenth century. Water was originally supplied directly from the River Dove, along a very lengthy channel or head race. This arrangement was changed in 1804, when the newly formed Dearne and Dove Canal Company built a reservoir on the river to supply the canal with water. At the same time, arrangements had to be made to allow water down to the old mill. A complex system was agreed to ensure the mill wheel kept turning. A weir and head race were constructed and the water came into the mill through a pipe to fill a header tank above the overshot wheel. The mill itself was extended, and provides an excellent example of the way in which milling remained, in its essentials, much as it had been in medieval times yet had to adapt to changing circumstances in a changing world. That was not the end of the story for in the 1840s the mill was again enlarged. The two-storey old mill was joined by the three-storey 'New Mill', and power was no longer supplied by water wheel, but by steam engine. Today, the mill has been restored as a working museum, and all the different stages of development can still be clearly seen.

There are as many variations in mill design as there are mills and one important difference lies between the mills of Scotland and those of England. In many parts of Scotland, the grain to be treated was not corn for flour, but oats for oatmeal, and an important part of the process was the drying of the grain. The typical meal mill complex thus

includes a drying kiln. This is beautifully exemplified, in every sense
of the word, at Preston Mill in Lothian (NTS). The complex may
date back to the sixteenth century and it is the oldest working water-
powered meal mill in Scotland. It is splendidly picturesque, a single-
storey stone building with pantile roof, power being supplied by a
wood and iron low breastshot wheel. The kiln is conical, with a fire-
place at the bottom from which the hot gases rose to the grain spread
out on the iron floor above. The gases eventually escaped through a
ventilator at the top of the cone.

A further variation in basic mill design can be seen in the tide mill,
though the variations only really affect the water supply, for the
construction of a tide mill involves no special alterations to the actual
mill machinery. The most imposing feature of the tide mill is often
not so much the mill itself as the amount of work put in to control the
tidal waters. At Eling Mill at Totton in Hampshire a dam was
constructed on the landward side of the mill. The rising tide passed
through sluices which were then closed off at high tide to form a
millpond, from which water could be released to the mill. The disadvantage of the tide mill lies in the fact that the use of the mill is

strictly governed by the state of the tides, and the working day had to shift accordingly. The obvious advantage is that you can be sure your water supply will never dry up, no matter how hot the summer. A further advantage can be seen at Eling, where the dam built to control the water was so substantial that it could be used as a causeway, with tolls being paid by the road users.

In more recent times other ways of using water have been developed, notably the Pelton wheel, named after its inventor, Lesley Pelton, and its successor the turbine. The turbine is an enclosed wheel. Water is forced in through a nozzle to strike blades or cups, so that the whole turbine will rotate at high speed. This has proved a very useful device, especially in hydroelectric schemes, and the turbine principle has also been adapted for transport. But the ordinary water wheel still remains a remarkably versatile and valuable tool for man. If we look back at the mill machinery we can begin to see why this should be so. The introduction of gearing meant that the slow-moving water wheel could be made to turn fast-moving machinery, and even in the simplest of grain mills power was never limited merely to turning the grindstones. Auxiliary machines, such as sack hoists, form an integral part of all mill operations. Indeed, if you think of the wheel as simply providing rotary motion, it soon becomes evident that, with suitable gears, all manner of machines could be powered by water. And indeed they were, and the importance of the old water-powered grain mill to the whole history of industrial development can be seen in the use of the word 'mill', which could mean anything from a cotton mill to a strip rolling mill. This is in fact where the true importance of water power lies, and the most magnificent example of its use in Britain is not to be found in the rural grain mill but in the world of deep mining. The Lady Isabella Wheel is a 72-foot diameter wheel, built in 1854 to power pumps to lift water from the mines of the Great Laxey Mining Company on the Isle of Man. It stopped working in 1929 and is preserved as an industrial monument – and as a monument to the importance and durability of water power. We shall see a good deal more evidence of the versatility of water power as we move on to look at other industries.

The other great natural force harnessed over the centuries was the force of the wind. The origins of the windmill are somewhat uncertain, but the first appearance in western Europe came some time after the appearance of the water mill, several centuries later in fact. It has been suggested that the windmill was introduced from the Near and Far East, but if so there was very little influence on western European designs. The Eastern mills were of the horizontal type, with sails attached to a vertical axle, very different from the windmills with which we are familiar today which have sails moving in a vertical plane. Turning to written records, the earliest mention of a windmill in Britain seems to be that of a mill working at Weedley in Yorkshire in 1185. That mill has long gone, but we know from medieval illustrations what such mills were like, and although no mill of quite that antiquity survives, mills of the basic medieval pattern can still be seen.

The development of the mill is closely tied to the development of the sails. Typically, the mill had four sails, suitably angled to provide continuous motion, a task that is not as simple as it might appear to be. The design of sails must have owed something, other than just the name, to the work of shipwrights, and the early sails were, like their marine counterparts, made of canvas. And, like a ship's sails, they could be reefed, the actual area of sail reduced in high winds, by pulling the cloth diagonally across the frames. Later, this type of sail, known as the common sail, was joined by a new type which was shuttered, rather like a Venetian blind, the most sophisticated version of which came to be known as the patent sail. But whatever the type of sail, it would never work unless it could be turned into the wind and in the earliest type of mill, the post mill, this was achieved by moving the building as a whole.

A mill which shows almost all the features of the medieval post mill is Bourn Mill in Cambridgeshire, built in the early seventeenth century, but somewhat altered over the years. In its appearance and method of working, however, it is very close to the mill of the Middle Ages. The grinding machinery is housed in a wooden structure, the buck, which is covered by a pitched roof. The buck, with its attached sails, is balanced on a central post, which gives this type of mill its name. If the wind direction changed, the ladder leading up to the buck was raised to clear the ground, and the miller would grasp the long wooden pole, the tail pole, that came down from the buck at an angle. Then, with a good deal of effort, he could move the buck by levering it with the tail pole and thus reposition the sails.

There are many variations on the basic pattern. Bourn is a good starting place, simply because the underframe has been left open. A

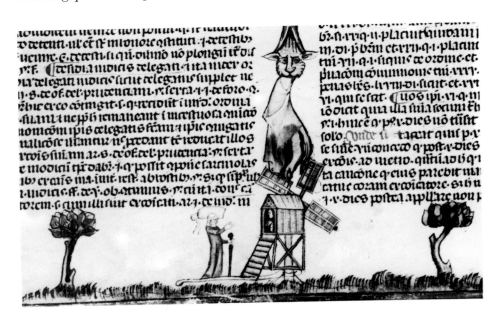

The medieval post mill shown in the thirteenth-century Decretals *of Gregory. The crude tail pole is shown sticking out under the ladder.*

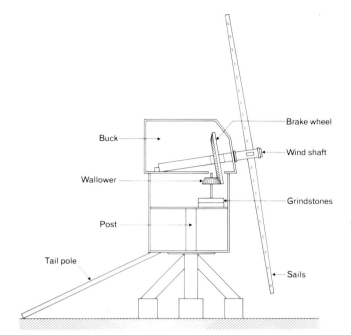

ABOVE *A fine post mill in which the post is protected by a roundhouse: Pitstone Mill, Buckinghamshire (NT). Note the wheel at the end of the tail pole.*

ABOVE RIGHT *The mechanism of a typical post mill.*

mill of equal if not greater antiquity, Pitstone Mill (NT) in Buckinghamshire, which carries a date of 1627 carved on one of its timbers, has the underframe protected by a brick roundhouse, which also provides a useful storage space. Various devices were introduced over the years to help the miller with his task, particularly with the strenuous job of moving the buck. In some mills, the tail pole ends in a small wheel running on a smooth track, and further help might be supplied in the form of a winch, as at the post mill preserved at the Avoncroft Museum of Buildings at Bromsgrove, Hereford and Worcester. A more sophisticated device can be seen at Saxtead Green Mill in Suffolk. This is a late eighteenth-century mill, with a three-storey buck mounted above a two-storey roundhouse. This very large mill uses the wind itself to move the buck, for here not only does the tail pole end in a wheel running round a track, but above that is mounted a fan tail. This is, in effect, a miniature set of sails: as the wind direction changes, so the fan tail begins to turn and in turning it acts rather like the sails of a ship and moves the whole mill.

It eventually became apparent to millwrights that in the case of a large mill a great deal of effort would be expended in turning the whole structure to face the wind. It would clearly be far simpler to mount the sails on a rotating cap at the top of the building, where a fan-tail device of the type just described could turn the comparatively small cap. This idea was developed and resulted in two closely allied types of mill, the all wooden smock mill and the tower mill, where the movable cap was mounted on a brick or stone tower.

Perhaps the finest and one of the largest surviving smock mills in Britain is Shipley Mill in West Sussex. Built in 1879, the mill had a working life of only half a century, yet it remains one of the most attractive of all mills. There is an added attraction for visitors with literary tastes in that she – and sailing mills like sailing ships are always ladies – was once owned by Hilaire Belloc. Vying with Shipley Mill is Union Mill, Cranbrook, Kent, a magnificent structure built in 1814, standing over seventy feet high and completely dominating the small town. Size is perhaps the one factor that distinguishes such mills from the earlier post mills, for once the necessity to move the entire mill was removed, the building could be greatly increased in size. Not that an increase in scale necessarily meant that the new mills were in some way less attractive than the old. Look, for example, at Stembridge Mill (NT) at High Ham in Somerset. A tower mill, it has an undeniably romantic appearance, stemming in good measure from its thatched cap. Early tower mills were, however, often plain and unadorned and their attractiveness to modern eyes reflects more the general appeal of windmills rather than any particular merits in individual designs. Bembridge Mill (NT), on the Isle of Wight, is a perfectly straightforward, undecorated mill but none the less delightful for that.

Even within the broad categories of post, smock and tower mill there are, it seems, an almost infinite number of variations. A tradition grew up in East Anglia, for example, of building large tower mills with more than the customary four sails. Heckington Mill, in Lincolnshire, is the last survivor of the most extravagant of such devices, having no fewer than eight sails.

As with the water mill, the internal arrangement of machinery in the windmill reflects both functional necessities and the individual preferences of miller and millwright. In its essentials, however, the layout of machinery tends to follow a fixed pattern. The same basic problem faced the designer of windmills as faced the water mill planner – how to convey rotation in one plane into rotation in a

Shipley Mill in West Sussex: the fan tail of this elegant smock mill is attached to the movable cap and positions the sails in the wind.

LEFT *Tacumshane Windmill, Wexford, a simple small tower mill which is very unusual in having a thatched cap.*

different plane – and a similar solution was found. Here, the pit wheel of the water mill has its equivalent in the brake wheel of the windmill.

The windmill never found the wide range of uses of the water mill, mainly because of the unpredictability of the wind. Water could be controlled by building weirs and millponds: there was, alas, no method of storing wind, so that when the industrialists of the seventeenth and eighteenth centuries cast around for a source of power it was largely to water that they turned. There was, however, one significant exception – the reliance on wind in the draining and improvement of the water-logged lands of East Anglia. This is not, perhaps, too surprising since much of the original expertise for land reclamation came from the Netherlands across the North Sea. There, where there was a lack of suitable water sources to provide the power for machinery, but where the wind blew regularly and strongly across the flat landscape, a sophisticated technology of wind power was developed. Perhaps the most spectacular embodiment of that power is to be seen at Kinderdijk, where fourteen windmills stand in a row, each contributing its portion to the reclamation of the land.

Britain can offer nothing comparable to Kinderdijk, but a number of drainage mills have survived. A most interesting example is the Herringfleet Mill in Suffolk, an octagonal smock mill, somewhat dour in unrelieved black. Built in 1823, it has canvas or common sails, and it provides power to turn a scoop wheel which, as its name suggests, scoops water up in buckets on the wheel's rim. It is worth noting that wind power for land drainage continued to be used well into modern times. Indeed, two of our best preserved drainage mills – at Horsey in Norfolk and Wicken Fen in Cambridgeshire (both NT) – were built in this century. So the windmill, like the water mill, has served the people of Britain for many centuries, and there are many who believe that, as fossil fuel reserves dwindle, they will serve us again. If so, then we should perhaps be grateful that so many examples of the millwright's art remain for us to study, for these old mills represent a remarkably high degree of craftsmanship, perfected over centuries of trial and experimentation. Even if a new generation of mills does not materialize, we will continue to derive pleasure from the beauty of the old and to be astonished at the ingenuity displayed by their builders. Mills also represent an important step in the evolution of the technological world. Millwrights were the first mechanical engineers, and the lessons learned in mill construction found many applications. But long before the day of the naturally-powered mills was ended, a new power appeared to move the wheels of industry – steam. This new power developed in a world far removed from the treatment of grain from the fields; it developed in the darkness beneath those fields, the world of the deep mines. To understand how that power developed, it is necessary to understand something of that sunless world.

2 Wealth from Underground

Britain was particularly rich in mineral wealth, much of it easily accessible, a factor which was of major importance in the country's development as an industrial power. Coal was widely available in England, Scotland, Wales and also Ireland, with the notable exception of southern England, East Anglia and the far south-west counties of Devon and Cornwall. There was, too, a great variety of mineral ores to be found, from the exotic gold and silver of Wales to the copper of south-west England, and the lead of Derbyshire, Somerset, Wales and Scotland. Iron ore was spread almost as widely as coal but iron mining became concentrated on the major coal fields when technical developments resulted in iron production being closely tied to coal. The metal ores all require treatment before they can be used by man and this aspect of the subject is covered in Chapter 4. Here we shall be wholly concerned with the task of burrowing down to these riches and the problems encountered in working underground.

Mining could be described as man's first truly industrial activity, in that from the beginning it involved groups of workers collaborating to produce something not just for themselves, but for a wider community. The first mines date from the Neolithic or Stone Age, which is defined in terms of man's use of stone for arrowheads and for tools such as axes and knives. Where he found a suitable stone, as at Great Langdale (NT) in the Lake District, he set up 'axe factories'. High above the valley stands Pike o' Stickle, a hill of tuff, a volcanic rock suitable for tool-making, and still today flakes knocked off in shaping axe heads and even partially shaped axes can be found in the scree of the hillside. There is a similar site at the mound fort of Doonmore on Rathlin Island, Antrim. Best of all the hard, stoney materials, however, is flint. The great advantage of flint is the ease with which it can be knapped. When a piece of flint is struck by a heavy stone or an improvised hammer made out of a deer antler, then it flakes rather than crumbles. The skilled knapper can produce a variety of shapes from his flint and can then polish the implements to a smooth, fine finish. But flint is not universally available, nor is it always of good quality. Early man soon discovered where the best flint was to be found, and he set out to exploit it. Evidence of his work can be seen in many places, but the most dramatic and the most revealing site is Grimes Graves in Norfolk.

The flint found here was of first-rate quality, but the very best lay at a depth of thirty to forty feet below the surface. Nearly four hundred mines were dug to reach this flint and excavation has revealed the extent and complexity of these individual pits. The shafts themselves were remarkably wide, but the width did greatly reduce the risk of collapse. The flint lies embedded in soft chalk, which can easily be removed with simple picks made out of antlers. Narrow, low tunnels radiate out from the bottom of each shaft, ending in wide, low caves where the flint was worked. The miners could not work economically at any very great distance from the shaft. Flint and spoil had to be passed down the narrow passageways by a chain of men, and a point was reached when there were simply too many men in the chain to make it worth continuing with that particular part of the workings. A new tunnel was then begun from the bottom of the shaft, and the process continued. Eventually there was no space left for extra tunnels and that shaft was abandoned and a new shaft was sunk. Occasionally tunnellers found themselves breaking through into old workings, and today it is possible to look from an excavated pit into part of the workings as yet untouched by modern man. This provides a glimpse into the working life of the mine, for the old, simple antler picks can be

BELOW LEFT *The Neolithic flint mine, Grimes Graves, in Norfolk. The antler picks remain just where they were left when work stopped 4000 years ago.*

seen precisely where the Neolithic miners left them four thousand years ago.

The most striking feature of Grimes Graves, apart from the discomfort involved in crawling and wriggling through the narrow tunnels, is the standard of mining expertise. These early miners were very much masters of their underground domain so that, as the world moved on from the Stone Age to the metal ages of Bronze and Iron, there was already a considerable store of knowledge about mining to aid the hunt for minerals and ores. In Britain, the second great age of mining came with the exploitation of metal mines and in some areas the history of metal mining goes back a very long way indeed. The Phoenicians, for example, traded with the Cornish for tin and later explored up the River Severn to the Forest of Dean where the local population offered to sell them iron bars. But perhaps the greatest increase in mining activity – as with so many other activities – came with the invasion from Rome. The mineral wealth of Britain was one of the lures that drew in the Roman settlers, and they were soon at work extracting iron, lead, silver and gold. Unfortunately, it is often difficult to gauge just how extensive Roman workings were, for many areas where they mined were worked again by later generations of miners.

Two great lead-mining areas were the Mendips and Derbyshire. The area around Charterhouse in Somerset still shows evidence of considerable activity, but the problem remains of deciding what could be attributed to Roman efforts. Within the Blackmoor Educational Nature Reserve, for example, there are many traces of mining work. A deep shaft, crudely formed, might be Roman, but might equally have been sunk many centuries later. Whatever evidence there might have been was largely destroyed in the nineteenth century when the slag and spoil left by earlier generations was substantially worked over.

More direct evidence of early activity can be found to the north in Derbyshire where the rakes are almost certainly the earliest form of workings. These are deep slits in the ground, where the miners have attacked vertical bands of ore, digging down from the surface and then following the band across country, sometimes for miles. The depth to which a rake could be worked depended on the water-level below ground – but there was no limit to how far across country it could be pursued. A particularly spectacular example is Dirtlow Rake, near Castleton, now a long, deep fissure left in the rock. But putting a precise date to such workings is almost impossible, and really positive evidence for Roman activity is not to be found in the ground, but in the lead 'pigs' cast in the second and third centuries, of Derbyshire origin and carrying Latin inscriptions.

One undisputed site of Roman activity does, however, remain – the Dolaucothi gold mine (NT) near Pumpsaint in Dyfed. The Dolaucothi site, like those of the lead mines, has been extensively worked over in more recent years, but here at least sufficient remains to show Roman methods of working. In order to reach the ore-bearing rock, the miners had first to remove the overburden, the soil and vegetation that overlay the rock, and here the Romans used a technique known as 'hushing'. Water was collected in reservoirs on the hilltop above the site and then released in a great flood down the hill, producing a man-made landslide. Here, however, the Romans faced a problem. They needed water at the top of the hill, and the only available sources, the rivers Cothi and Annell, were down below in the valley. But if there was one area where the Romans could claim special expertise then it was in civil engineering and the construction of aqueducts. They followed the rivers upstream until they reached a point a little above the proposed reservoirs and then cut their aqueducts as ditches following a contour line round the hills. The Cothi aqueduct was seven miles long and can still be traced from the river to the point where it ends in a series of depressions that mark the site of the reservoirs.

Having stripped the hillside bare, the miners then followed the veins of ore into the hillside. The mine passages are far roomier than the narrow crawl-ways of Grimes Graves, and they had to be forced through far more difficult material – hard rock, instead of soft chalk. Here, however, the miners had the advantage of tools made of metal. They also used a technique known as 'fire setting'. A fire was lit up against the rock face and then, when the rock began to glow with heat, cold water was dashed against it. The sudden contraction caused the rock to split, and also filled the narrow passageway with thick smoke and steam. Working conditions were far from ideal, but as that sort of work was left to the primitive natives – that is, the British – the Romans would not have been unduly concerned. The miners also faced another problem in the workings – water. The Neolithic mines of Norfolk never penetrated below the water-table, but generally speaking as soon as a mine reaches any great depth below the surface it becomes liable to flooding. If work is to continue, then the water has to be removed. At Dolaucothi a scoop wheel was used (parts of which were found on site and are now preserved, together with a model showing how the system worked, in the National Museum of Wales, Cardiff). The wheel had a series of buckets on the rim, which scooped up the water and carried it to a higher level. The power came from human feet, so this wheel was essentially like the treadmills already described. Such devices could be used in relays, each wheel lifting the water a little higher. The Romans also used an alternative method of removing water, the adit. This is simply a tunnel constructed below the level of the mine passage to carry water away from the workings. At Dolaucothi adits still run with water as they have done for centuries.

Dolaucothi is both fascinating and historically important, not just because of its antiquity but because it provides a demonstration of so many different techniques that were to remain in use for many hundreds of years. The treadmill scoop wheel is of minor importance, but its close cousin the water-powered pump found extensive use in medieval mines. The water wheel could be used to power an endless chain of buckets or alternatively to work suction pumps in which a piston moving in a cylinder drew up the water. Such pumps were often arranged in a series of three. These methods, and others, are all described in the great source book of medieval mining practice, Agricola's *De Re Metallica* published in 1556.

Draining by adit can still be seen in many places, but most spectacularly in the lead-mining district of Derbyshire. There are records showing that the construction of adits, or soughs as they are known locally, was an important part of the mining industry in the seventeenth and eighteenth centuries, and probably much earlier as well. Some represent major engineering achievements. Their exploration is no job for the casual amateur, but those who have ventured underground along these watery passageways have found an amazingly complex system. In Hillcar Wood, beside the Derwent in Darley Dale, water can be seen flowing out from under a low stone arch. This marks the end of Hill Carr Sough, which stretches back for miles to a point 700 foot below the surface of Stanton Moor. This immense work took the miners over twenty years to complete, starting in 1766, and finally

A simple drainage pump from Agricola's De Re Metallica *(1556). The pump is worked by the men in the treadmill on the left.*

cost the owners of the mine £50,000 in the days when miners' wages were considerably less than one pound a week. The scale of the work is itself a measure of its importance – and of the magnitude of the problem represented by mine drainage.

It is only rarely that the opportunity arises to explore the underground world of the older mines, but in recent years a few have been opened to visitors. The Clearwell Caves in the Forest of Dean, Gloucestershire, are very old ironstone mines, heavily worked in the Middle Ages, but as in so many cases they have been much altered by later workings. They form a labyrinthine complex of man-made caverns linked by narrow passages that continue down for many hundreds of feet. It is in the upper levels, however, that the oldest workings are to be found, including direct evidence of the use of fire-setting in soot-blackened roofs.

Derbyshire offers an example of a different method of working, the drift mine. This is, essentially, a mine dug more or less horizontally into the hillside, much in the way the Romans worked at Dolaucothi. The Good Luck Lead Mine at Via Gellia is a drift mine, but the underground workings are far more extensive than those of the Romans. The entrance, first dug in 1830, is low and narrow, for the ground was poor and the risk of collapse considerable. As the miners reached the firmer limestone the passageway was opened out, using hand picks and by driving wedges into cracks and seams. Then, as the rock became harder, the miners had to use black powder and blast through it. Holes were drilled using hand drills that were laboriously hammered home. The hole was then packed with powder, stopped up with clay and lit by a straw fuse. Conditions in the mine at this time must have been horrific. The only light was a candle stuck in the miner's cap. He frequently worked on all fours, kneeling in cold water, breathing in air heavy with smoke and dust from the workings. It was cold, uncomfortable and dangerous work. Today's visitors get little more than a hint of this, but they can penetrate a quarter of a mile along the old mine workings, and from their final vantage point they can see the three-dimensional labyrinth that stretches out into the hillside as the miners followed the line of the ore. Historically, however, the next major development in mining technology came not from the metal mines but from the extraction of coal, which began at least as far back as Norman times.

Early coal mines were either drift mines, very similar to the Good Luck Mine, or bell pits. In the latter a shaft was dug down to the coal level, at which point the miners began working outwards from the foot of the shaft, forming a cavern shaped like the bell which gives this type of working its name. In time, as the miners got ever further from the shaft, the whole cave would begin to collapse inwards, at which point it was simply abandoned and a fresh pit sunk. The similarities to the methods used at Grimes Graves are obvious. The physical remains appear now as a series of craters with high rims. The centre of the

Brancepeth Colliery, Co. Durham, in the 1930s. The photograph gives some idea of the difficulties of working in a 2 foot 10 inch seam.

crater represents the collapsed pit and the raised rim the spoil that was heaped all round the shaft. Such remains can be seen in many parts of the country, for example near Wakefield in West Yorkshire and at Muirkirk in Strathclyde.

The bell pits were shallow, and deeper workings required different methods: the expense of sinking a multitude of shafts each of them several hundred feet deep would clearly be insupportable. So, instead of hacking out all the coal from round the shaft bottom, the miners worked out on headings, leaving huge, thick pillars of coal to support the roof. When they had reached the furthest extent to which they intended to push the workings, they began to work back towards the shaft 'robbing the pillars'. The roof was supported by wooden props while the pillar was hacked away, after which the props were removed and the section allowed to cave in. This method of working, pillar and stall, continued in use well into the twentieth century. A second method, longwall working, came into widespread use in the nineteenth century and, as the name suggests, involves removing the coal as a continuous wall, advancing outwards from headings. This method is particularly well suited to modern mining techniques and modern machine cutters. The face is pushed forward with the roof supported by movable props in the working area. Then, as the props are advanced, the roof is simply allowed to fall in behind the miners, leaving the headings as passageways.

While drift mines are comparatively easy to explore, the world of deep mines has, until recently, been closed to all but the men who worked in the pits. Now two museums have opened based on recently closed mine complexes: Big Pit Colliery at Blaenafon in Gwent and Chatterley Whitfield Colliery at Tunstall in Staffordshire. The Big Pit, opened as a museum in 1982, is unusual in that the pillar and stall method of working was retained right to the end, and can be seen by visitors on their underground tours. Chatterley Whitfield, slightly the senior of the two museums, now has extensive underground workings showing the different mining methods and the variety of tools and machines, from the simple pick to the modern cutter-loader. The confined space gives some notion of the conditions under which the miners worked, though these are comparatively wide seams of coal. In the narrowest seams men would hack out the coal in spaces so narrow that they were forced to lie on their sides to work. Although visitors see only a small part of the workings which stretch out literally for miles from the shafts, yet even a little exploration makes two points very clear: apart from digging out the coal, two of the biggest problems miners face are concerned with ventilation and getting the coal from the face to the shaft.

The solutions to the problem of shifting the coal have been many and various. The cruellest conditions of all were those which prevailed in Scotland in the eighteenth century. Robert Bald, who wrote *A General View of the Coal Trade in Scotland* in 1812, described the work in

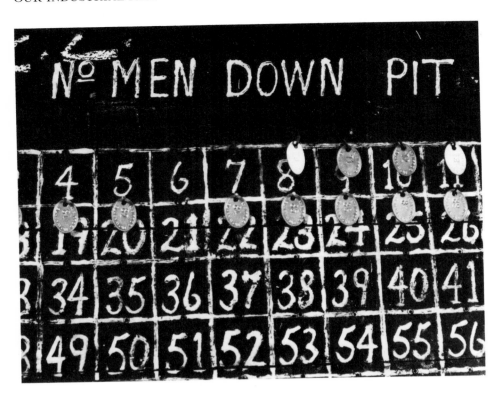

detail. Coal was loaded at the face into a wicker basket which Bald himself weighed fully loaded at 170 pounds. This heavy load was then carried on the bearer's back to the foot of the shaft and the rest of the journey was up near-vertical ladders to the surface. And this work went not to the men of the pit but to the women, who in the course of a day would carry on their backs two tons of coal, covering a distance underground of some two miles and a total climb of 3000 feet. For this they received the handsome wages of eightpence per day. The cruel system was eventually banned by law.

The eighteenth century saw a great improvement in underground transport with the introduction of waggons running on rails – wooden rails at first, later metal. This considerably eased the task of moving coal, yet until well into the nineteenth century the task of hauling the trucks went to children, both boys and girls, harnessed like animals. Later, after repeated legislation, pit ponies took over the work. These often spent their lives underground and a range of underground stables can be seen at Big Pit. There still remained, however, the problem of raising the coal to the surface. The simplest method was the use of the jack roller, a simple hand operated windlass set above the shaft, a device that can be seen at many an old well. Horse power was also used, offering a far more efficient system for heavy loads. The horse whim or gin consisted of a stout frame holding a vertical rotating post, topped by a winding drum. The horse walked round a circular track, turning the drum, around which rope was wrapped. The rope was led off over a pulley and down the shaft. A fine preserved whim can be seen at Wollaton Hall, Nottingham. The use of such simple, mechanical devices at least took some of the load off human backs.

Ventilation problems were not so easy to solve and the problem is not easy to see, in the literal sense, but the solution to the problem can be felt in any colliery in the movement of air. Where there is a complex pattern of underground galleries, the air has first to be made to move and then kept moving through the whole length by means of a series of air-tight doors which close off any short cuts and ensure that the air takes the longest possible route through the workings. Responsibility for operating such doors fell, until the middle of the nineteenth century, to the youngest of the children in the mines – the trapper boys who spent their solitary days in total darkness, opening and closing the doors. In modern mines, movement of the air is caused by a fan set at the top of one shaft, the upcast, which sucks the air down a second shaft, the downcast. The same basic system of air coming down one shaft and up another has been in use for centuries. What has changed is the method of providing the impetus to move the air. The typical method in use in the eighteenth century was to set a furnace at the bottom of the upcast, the rising hot air dragging cold air in to replace it. At that time, the dangers of mining were only dimly understood, though today the idea of lighting a fire at the foot of a mine shaft seems quite incredible. Fires in the mine were all too common, for the naked candle remained the main source of illumination for a very long time – even the men of Grimes Graves used a form of candle, with a wick floated in animal fat or oil set in a simple bowl fashioned out of chalk. Coal miners were, inevitably, aware of the hazards from what they knew as fire damp, and the main defence used was to ignite the gas in what was supposed to be a controlled manner before a major

A pit head scene of the 1780s showing a horse gin, an early form of winding machine. Landscape with a Mine *by Paul Sandby.*

explosion could occur. That hazardous job went to a man known as 'the penitent', so called from the pointed hood he wore, reminiscent of the Catholic penitent's costume. Covered in wet sackcloth, the penitent would crawl forwards towards a pocket of gas which he ignited with a light on the end of a long pole – the theory being that the resulting blast would pass over his head, leaving him unscathed. It was scarcely a very satisfactory method, and there still remained the danger of explosion from the naked candles used by the workers. It took a major disaster at Felling Colliery on Tyneside in 1812, when 92 men and boys were killed, to set in motion the search for a better and safer method of lighting the mines. The answer came with the safety lamp, which, in its essentials, kept the flame away from the atmosphere. Of the two versions of the lamp, the best known is that of Sir Humphry Davy; the second was the effort of a young colliery worker, George Stephenson, later to go on to win fame as a railway engineer. The safety lamp was of immense importance and its development can be seen at the National Mining Museum, next to the Bevercotes Colliery in Nottinghamshire. It did not, however, mark an end to the story of mining disasters.

Difficulties of ventilation and transport plagued miners for centuries, but as shallow seams became exhausted, and ever deeper pits were sunk, these problems were overshadowed by the need to find ways to drain mines satisfactorily. It was in response to this problem that engineers produced a device which was to be of vital importance far beyond the world of mines. In 1698, Captain Thomas Savery designed a machine which, in his patent application, he referred to as 'The Miner's Friend'. It was an engine with two cylinders. These were alternately filled with steam, which was then condensed to form a vacuum. When the vacuum was formed, water was sucked into the cylinder, and then pushed upwards towards the surface by high pressure steam. It worked, but required a vast amount of fuel, and the engine had to be set at the foot of the shaft. The sight of a large furnace and a primitive boiler at the bottom of the mine must have caused the miners to view their new friend with something less than wholehearted enthusiasm.

Savery's machine might not have been the answer to a miner's prayers, but it did introduce a new and vital force to mine engineering – steam power. This theme was very soon taken up and developed by a second engineer, Thomas Newcomen. He, too, used the idea of condensing steam in a cylinder. In his engine, the steam was led into the cylinder and then condensed by spraying cold water into the cylinder. The top of the cylinder was a movable piston, so, as the vacuum was formed by condensation, air pressure forced the piston downwards. Newcomen suspended this piston from one end of a beam which was pivoted at its centre. From the other end were hung pump rods descending into the mine shaft. When the piston was forced down into the cylinder, that end of the beam dropped down, while the opposite end of the beam tipped up, raising the pump rods. When pressure in the cylinder was equalized, the weight of the rods dragged that end of the beam down again, raising the piston ready for the start of a new cycle. So the beam rocked and the pump rods rose and fell in the shaft. Here was a highly satisfactory way of pumping water, and the first engine was installed in 1712 in a pit near Dudley Castle in Staffordshire. Dudley is now home to the Black Country Museum where, at the time of writing, a working replica of Newcomen's first engine is under construction.

Original Newcomen engines have survived, and can be seen at the Science Museum in London and at Dartmouth, in Devon, Newcomen's home town. The latter engine was brought from the Coventry region, and was last used at Hawkesbury Junction to provide water for the Coventry Canal. Today, the engine is turned over by hydraulic power and has a new engine house, though its old engine house still stands beside the canal. But to get a view of a Newcomen type of engine in situ, the best place to visit is Elsecar Colliery in South Yorkshire. The engine here was built in 1795 and worked very steadily right through to 1923. It is very large with a four-foot diameter cylinder and a piston stroke that is also four foot. Engines such as this require their own engine houses which need to be strongly built, for they have

A model Newcomen engine. It was whilst working on this model (1765) that James Watt devised his separate condenser.

to do rather more than simply give protection from the elements: the engine house is itself providing the frame to support the heavy, rocking beam. At Elsecar the main supporting wall – the bob wall – is immensely thick, and engine houses such as this were to become a dominant feature of the mining landscape. The engines they were to contain were destined, however, to change and develop in the second half of the eighteenth century.

The Newcomen engine represented a great advance over the Savery engine, but it still used large quantities of fuel. This was no great problem in the coalfields where fuel was available as a matter of course, but was a major disadvantage in metal mines, such as the tin and copper mines of the south-west, where coal had to be imported from other regions. The basic problem lay in the necessity to heat and cool the cylinder alternately, a problem that was first resolved by James Watt in the eighteenth century. Popular romance would have us believe that James Watt was a simple lad who, seeing a kettle singing on the hob, was at once struck by the power of steam and promptly invented the steam engine. Reality is, alas, somewhat duller. Watt was employed at Glasgow University and whilst there he was sent a model Newcomen engine to repair. He recognized the flaw in the design, and devised an answer. Instead of condensing steam in the cylinder, he led it away to a separate condenser, which meant that the cylinder no longer needed to be alternately heated and cooled. It could also be insulated to reduce heat loss. Having taken this basic design decision, it was at once obvious that it would not be possible to conserve heat energy if the top of the cylinder was left open to the atmosphere. So Watt enclosed the top of the cylinder, and instead of using air pressure to force the piston down, he used steam pressure. This had important implications for engine design, for the cycle could now be extended by admitting steam on either side of the piston. The engine was no longer a one-sided affair with the piston only being powered in one direction, for now steam power could move the piston both up and down. The way was open for the steam engine to provide continuous motion and a famous association ensured that the new idea would be adopted. Many an invention has been lost simply because the inventor was adept at solving a particular problem, but had no idea how to present his invention in the market place. James Watt was lucky, for he met his entrepreneur, Matthew Boulton of Birmingham, and together they formed one of the most successful partnerships in industrial history.

Boulton and Watt began manufacturing steam engines at their Soho works in Birmingham, the remaining parts of which are now occupied by the Avery Company. They worked under the protection of a patent which gave them a virtual monopoly of steam engine construction until the end of the eighteenth century. This was a boon as far as Boulton and Watt were concerned, but effectively stifled innovation from all other engineers, who had to wait until the stroke

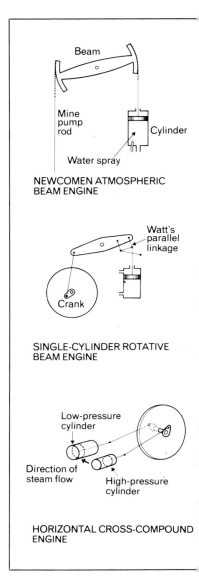

NEWCOMEN ATMOSPHERIC BEAM ENGINE

SINGLE-CYLINDER ROTATIVE BEAM ENGINE

HORIZONTAL CROSS-COMPOUND ENGINE

Types of steam engine. (Courtesy, Neil Cossons/Peter Stoddart)

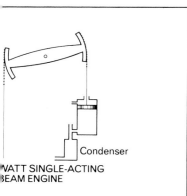

Condenser

WATT SINGLE-ACTING
BEAM ENGINE

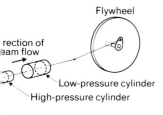

Flywheel

rection of
eam flow

Low-pressure cylinder
High-pressure cylinder

HORIZONTAL TANDEM-COMPOUND
ENGINE

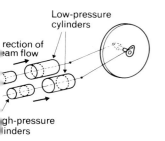

Low-pressure
cylinders

rection of
eam flow

gh-pressure
linders

IZONTAL TWIN TANDEM-COMPOUND
NE

of midnight on the last day of the century before they could bring their new ideas to fruition. However, when the time came, when the bottle was at last uncorked, those new ideas flowed freely and in profusion, and nowhere was the flow greater than in the coal-starved West Country, the land of tin and copper mines. The absolute dominance of Cornish technology in the early nineteenth century was born of necessity. The West Country miners needed economies far more than any other region and bitterly resented the Boulton and Watt patent and the royalties paid to Birmingham. Having said that, however, the debt owed by all those later innovators to the Birmingham pioneers must be acknowledged. They built well and they built to last, and it is no coincidence that the oldest steam engine in the world, still able to work at the job it was built to do, is a Boulton and Watt engine. It is not, in fact, to be found in the mining region at all, but it performs precisely the same function as any other pumping engine, raising water from one level to another. In this case, the lower level is a lake and the upper level the Kennet and Avon Canal. The engine supplies water to the canal summit level at Crofton, and it works today precisely as it did when first set in motion in 1812.

We shall be looking at other, similar, uses of beam pumping engines in Chapter 8. Where mining is concerned later developments in steam engines can best be traced in the tin and copper mines of Devon and Cornwall. Travel in that region and you will see on every hand the remains of the engine houses that once held the old nodding monsters.

The engine house of Wheal Prosper (NT), a copper mine opened in 1832, stands above Rinsey Cove on the south Cornish coast.

Even the empty shells tell us a good deal. For a start, their sheer number is an indication of both the extent and importance of mining in this part of the country. In the area around Redruth and Camborne there is an absolute profusion of engine houses. They were none too cheap to build, and that too is an indication of the mineral wealth that justified such a heavy expenditure. A further measure of the importance of the steam engine is that engine houses are to be found in somewhat remote and seemingly unlikely locations – high up on the moorland in some cases or on lonely clifftop sites. Most remarkable of all are the engine houses of Botallack at the very tip of Cornwall. Here there are two houses perched on ledges half way down the cliff, in a situation where building of any sort must have presented the most appalling difficulties.

In other places, a site may represent a continuity of use that goes back over generations. Wheal Busy – Wheal is the Cornish name for

A royal visit to Botallack Mine in north Cornwall in 1865 by the Prince and Princess of Wales. The remains of the engine house can still be seen.

mine – near Chacewater is just such a site. Ten engines have been installed here, starting with a Newcomen engine of 1725 and including an engine built by James Watt. The last of the line was finally broken up for scrap in 1946 – and still the engine house endures. The site shows all the characteristics of the Cornish engine house. The main building is stone, stoutly built with a hugely thick wall on one side. This is the bob wall on which the massive beam pivoted, and it is still stained with grease from the bearings. Alongside is the less robust boiler house. These buildings, which had to endure none of the stresses of the engine house, were comparatively flimsy and consequently few survive. Adjoining the engine house is the chimney or stack, built in stone as high as the engine house roof, and then completed in brick. The height was needed to ensure a good strong draught to the boiler. This is very much a standard pattern for engine house construction and the style which developed to house the big Cornish engines can be seen repeated with minor variations throughout the south-west, and indeed wherever the men of the south-west travelled taking their experience and expertise with them.

The surface remains of mining form a fascinating area of exploration, and one of the fascinations lies in tracing the spread of West Country influences. In the lead-mining district of Derbyshire, for example, there are extensive remains, the best preserved being those of the Magpie Mine at Sheldon. Here the most striking feature is the un-mistakable silhouette of a Cornish-style engine house. In fact, there are two engine houses, the larger originally housing a pumping engine, and a smaller house for a winding engine. There are other buildings and structures, including a circular gunpowder store and a jigging machine for sieving out the crushed ore. The mining landscape seen here is replicated in many other parts of Britain, wherever Cornish mine engineers plied their trade. Evidence of the work of Cornish miners can also be seen elsewhere in the world, but the furthest point they reached in the British Isles must be the south-west corner of Ireland. Copper was discovered here, and the Cornish duly arrived and founded the village of Allihies. High on the hill above the village, the engine houses still stand above the deep, open cleft of the mine shaft.

Not all engine houses are, however, empty shells and the preserved engines of Cornwall tell us a good deal about what happened when the Boulton and Watt patent expired in 1800. The moment the restrictions were removed, engineers set to work to try and improve the efficiency of the beam engine. Efficiency was measured as 'duty', and a 'duty war' began, with rival engineers contesting to see who could produce the most efficient engine. Great engine building firms grew up, such as Holman of Redruth and Harveys of Hayle, and Cornwall became the testing ground for such famous engineers as Richard Trevithick. Engines not only became more efficient, they also became larger. At Pool, to the east of Camborne, stands the pumping engine (NT) that worked the Taylor Shaft of Agar Mine. It was built by Harveys in 1892 and was moved to the present site in the 1920s. The first glimpse shows at once why the engine houses were so sturdily built for the enormous beam can be seen poking out through the bob wall. Inside, it is the scale of the machinery which again is so impressive. The cylinder is vast (90-inch diameter) and everything about the engine is on the same gigantic scale. The beam weighs over 50 tons and the engine could lift 400 gallons of water in a minute from a depth of more than 1500 feet, even though it only worked at a ponderous five strokes a minute. And although this is a big engine, it is by no means the only engine of such a size that worked in the local mines. Nor was it, by any means, the largest engine built in the Duchy. In the 1840s

Cornwall supplied three engines to drain the Haarlem Meer in Holland, and one of these has been preserved at Cruquis. These engines had 144-inch diameter cylinders, powering pumps with eleven-foot strokes. In the first twenty-five hours of working, the three giants shifted a million tons of water.

The steam engine, however, soon became something more than just a device for pumping water. Engineers realized that a double acting engine could be adapted to provide a circular motion by means of a crank. New engine houses were built alongside the pumping engine houses. Instead of pump rods descending from one end of the beam, the new engine had a sweep arm ending in a crank and driving a drum. Now the engine could be used for winding men and materials up and down the shaft. Across the main road from the Taylor engine is just such a rotative or whim engine, the East Pool engine (NT) of 1887. Whim engines are usually smaller than the pumping engines, and the cylinder here is a third the diameter of the Taylor engine. In time, a third type of engine appeared at the pithead, powering the stamps that were used to crush the ore. A set of Cornish stamps, powered not by steam but by water, can be seen at the Tolgus Tin Company, Redruth, while the site of the old Wheal Peevor, near the A30 east of Redruth, still has the houses for the three engines – pumping, winding and stamping.

Although new developments were particularly prominent in the south-west, elsewhere in Britain engineers came up with their own individual designs too. Over in the coalfields of north-east England, Phineas Crowther was another who, the moment the Boulton and Watt patent expired, rushed forward with a new engine, one that was to become very popular in that region. This was a winding engine, but one that entirely did away with the rocking beam by placing the winding drum directly above the piston. A vertical engine of this type was built for the Beamish Colliery (Co. Durham) in 1855 and has now been restored and moved a few hundred yards down the road from its original site to stand in the North of England Open Air Museum. Here a complete pithead installation has been established. Cable from the engine house passes via the headstock, the system of pulleys above the shaft, to the shaft itself where coal tubs, or kibbles, are hauled up and down. The area is covered in and as the kibbles reach the top they are wheeled across a metal-plated floor to a tip which upends the kibbles, allowing the coal to drop to the screens below. These are adjustable metal bars which hold the good coal, but allow dirt and small pieces to fall through. From here, the coal drops into trucks running on rails. These would originally have been pulled by horse, though steam locomotives were later introduced.

The idea of using direct drive from the piston to the winding drum was adapted by other engineers in different ways. Some, instead of using the vertical engine of Crowther, went for a horizontal engine as can be seen today at Washington F Pit in Tyne and Wear. Washington

Steam engines and horse gins mark the mining landscape of Wolverhampton, West Midlands, in the 1860s. It is not difficult to see why this area became known as the Black Country.

was once a typical mining town, and F Pit was first sunk in 1777. Now work has stopped, but the nineteenth-century steam winder in its twentieth-century engine house has been preserved. The engine has two 30-inch cylinders working parallel to each other, and they were used to turn the drum that brought up coal from a thousand feet below ground.

Coal mining may be finished at Washington, but elsewhere it remains one of the country's vital industries, providing a present-day link with some of our earliest industrial remains. The history of mining stretches right back into the time before written records, and so much remains that we can piece together a remarkable story of what was, literally, an underground occupation. In a brief survey it is not

The pit head of Chatterley Whitfield Colliery, Staffordshire. Work at the colliery has now ceased and it has reopened as a mining museum. The headstock gear still stands over the shaft and is still in use taking visitors underground.

possible to do more than indicate a few of the main lines of development, but it would be wrong to stop at this point without at least a glance at some of the implications of man's hunt for mineral wealth. Mining was, and is, an activity that involved more than just the workers who went to the pits – it involved the whole community, so that the mining village is as much a part of mining history as the steam engine or the horse gin. Mines can only exist where the raw material, coal, metal ore or whatever, is to be found. There the mine would be established, and there the mining community would grow. There has always been something special about such communities, drawn together partly by shared work but more particularly by the shared

Parys Mountain, Anglesey, at the end of the eighteenth century when half the mountain was hacked away to get at the rich copper ore; by Frank Louis Thomas Francia.

dangers which are an ever-present feature of underground work. In the eighteenth and nineteenth centuries, the ties were even stronger than they are today, for then mining involved whole families, men, women and children. Within the community, the mine was paramount, often providing the sole source of employment. Other early industrial communities were also dependent on a single industry, but lacked those other elements of remoteness from the rest of the world and the danger of catastrophic accidents. The oldest villages have often disappeared, either absorbed into larger towns or simply abandoned as the mineral supplies were exhausted. It is the latter which provide the most poignant reminders of what has gone, as at Talywain, near Abersychan in Gwent, where the terraces of cottages stand remote and crumbling beside the few visible remains of a once active pit.

There has always been, too, another dark side to the mining story. There have been the atrocious accidents, where hundreds of lives have been lost, and there has been a long history of bitter struggle between masters and men. There has also been a lasting effect on the land itself. Go to Anglesey and walk up Parys Mountain and you will find an area as barren and desolate as any in the land. The mountain was once a pleasant, green hill, until it was discovered to be rich in copper. In the eighteenth century the miners moved in to strip it bare, leaving only heaps of rubble and artificial lakes stained in brilliant and amazing colours by the ore. Here, too, there is evidence of the power used by the miners to help with the work. At the top of the hill stands a windmill stump, a monument to an early source of power, while lower down the slopes is an empty engine house. Once the miners had removed the ore, the site was simply abandoned, a barren wilderness that remains barren to this day. It can be taken as a monument to man's ingenuity in finding and removing what he needs from the earth beneath his feet, or it can be read as a condemnation of his unthinking greed. But in that one building, the ruined engine house, is a reminder that it was in just such places as this that man developed a new power source that was to affect not just the world of the miner, but the whole of the industrial scene.

3 Warp and Weft

Historians have traditionally allocated a date somewhere around 1760 as the starting point for the Industrial Revolution. This has had the somewhat unfortunate result of suggesting that industry as a whole began at that time. As we have just seen, that is far from being the case, though the invention of the Boulton and Watt engine marked a distinct quickening in the pace of change. The textile industry was certainly in existence long before the eighteenth century, but it provides the clearest evidence of just why the 1760s seem, in retrospect, to be of such importance. For this period marked more than just an acceleration in the rate of change; the industry developed in a quite new direction and took on a quite different form. The magnitude of the changes, however, can only be understood in the context of earlier developments.

The traditional textile industry of Britain was based on wool. It became so important to the economy that entire villages were removed by landowners to provide grazing for sheep. In East Anglia, for example, one can still find churches, such as that of Egmere in Norfolk, standing alone among fields where only a few bumps and ridges remain to show that there was once a human settlement. It was estimated that, by 1500, the sheep population of Britain outnumbered the human by three to one. The fleece from the sheep's back was turned into cloth, known either as woollen, using a short or mixed wool fibre, or as staple or worsted, using a long fibre. This involved a number of different processes.

Once the shearing was complete, the wool had to be washed, after which it was carded to separate out the fibres. The cards themselves were originally boards studded with wire. The wool was laid on one card and the second card was dragged over the top of it. If worsted was to be made, the wool then had to be combed to separate the long staple or fibre from the short. The next stage was spinning, which twisted the fibres together to form a yarn and which involved the simple mechanical device known as the distaff and spindle. The wool was wound round a stick, the distaff, which was held under the spinner's arm. The end of the wool was then attached to the spindle, a small weighted rod which was spun and dropped, stretching out and twisting the fibres. Traditionally this was woman's work, giving us the words spinster and distaff (the female line). This somewhat crude device was replaced by the spinning wheel, which changed and developed over the years. Essentially, the turning spindle was retained but it was no longer powered by gravity but by a simple mechanism such as a foot treadle, and regularity of motion was ensured by the use of a flywheel. There are many examples of the different types of wheel in museums, and it has achieved a new popularity with the growing craft movement.

After spinning the thread is either woven into cloth or knitted. We shall be concentrating on weaving where a network of threads is constructed on the loom. Essentially, a series of parallel threads, the warp, is laid down. The second thread, the weft, attached to a shuttle, is passed over and under alternate warp threads to form the cloth. The loom is a bulky device set in a solid wooden frame. First the warp threads are set in place and passed through reeds. These were at first precisely that, split reeds, but were later wires with loops in the centre to take the threads. The reeds could be moved up and down by means of a foot treadle, so that alternate reeds rose and fell, leaving a gap through which the shuttle with its trailing weft thread could be thrown. Once the shuttle had passed through the gap, known as the shed, the trailing thread was banged firmly into place by a heavy wooden batten. The shuttle itself was originally thrown by hand and, in the case of the broad cloth loom, two workers were needed as the loom was too wide for one man to span.

Up to this stage, the work was generally carried out in the homes of spinners and weavers. Women and children looked after carding and spinning while the men wove the cloth. The spinning wheel was portable and could be set down by the window for light or even taken out of doors in summer. In contrast the loom was massive and fixed and required good light so from these requirements a special form of house developed, the weaver's cottage. The small, portable spinning wheel was kept downstairs in the family living area while the loom was kept upstairs in a special workshop. Light was provided by long windows, generally running the length of the room but broken up into narrow openings by mullions, the narrowness of the opening being largely a security precaution. Such cottages were common in England and continued to be built right into the nineteenth century. In the Yorkshire village of Golcar, a terrace of such cottages has been restored and demonstrations of both spinning and weaving are given. Similar cottages can also be seen in the other great woollen area, the west of England, in towns such as Bradford-on-Avon. The prosperity of the trade in the seventeenth and early eighteenth centuries attracted many workers, who built up their own squatters' villages on common land. Such a village is Dilton Marsh in Wiltshire, where a straggle of weavers' cottages can still be seen. Here, however, it was common to build a separate, small loom shed next to the house. Scottish weavers' cottages have a quite different character. These tend to be single storey, with a central doorway separating off the weaving area from the living quarters. A typical eighteenth-century cottage (NTS) can be seen at Kilbarchan, just south of Glasgow. It has been refurbished in the style of the period and equipped with a loom.

The cloth from the loom was rather loosely woven, and covered in dirt and grease from the machinery. It needed to be cleaned and the fibres had to be matted closely together. Originally, this was done by treating the cloth with a detergent after which men would stamp up and down on it – the origin of the common family name, Walker. As early as medieval times, however, the task was mechanized in the fulling mill. Such mills were water powered, and the feet of the walkers were replaced by heavy wooden hammers, the stocks. The cloth was folded into a trough of water with a suitable detergent, such as Fuller's Earth. The water wheel turned, and projections on the turning shaft connected with the ends of the stocks. The stocks were lifted and then, as the projection cleared, fell back down on to the cloth. There were many such mills, and many mill buildings have survived. It is often, however, quite difficult to identify them as many were converted later into grain mills – water power was always too useful to be wasted and many a mill served a variety of functions during a long working life. Fulling stocks can still be seen at the Higher Mill Textile Museum at Helmshore in Lancashire and at the Welsh Folk Museum at St Fagans in South Glamorgan.

The cloth was taken from the mill and dried by being hung out in an area known as the tenter field – suspended by the tenter hooks which

Fulling stocks at Helmshore Higher Mill, Lancashire. These were used to felt woollen cloth from the loom.

became synonymous with another form of suspense. At some stage the wool might be dyed, either as yarn or in the piece, and certain areas were famous for particular colours. The Stroud region in Gloucestershire, for example, was well known for its scarlet. Then there was the finishing of the cloth. The nap was raised by brushing the surface with a card studded with spikey teazle heads and then cropped smooth with shears. The teazles themselves were dried and stored in special buildings. A teazle house can be seen, recognized by its perforated brick wall, at Studley Mill beside the Town Bridge in Trowbridge in Wiltshire.

Finally, the cloth was taken away either on the weaver's own back or on the back of a pack horse to be sold at market. The Piece Hall in Halifax, West Yorkshire, built in 1775, shows how prosperous this trade once was. It is quite magnificent, with two storeys of merchants' offices round a big courtyard. The whole has a sense of style and perhaps just a touch of self importance, but then the local merchants had something to be proud of. Woollens were the country's most important trade not only because of the work they gave to those directly involved, but also because there were a whole succession of other trades dependent on the textile industry such as builders, millwrights, machine makers and the various trades concerned with transport. And there were others involved in particular aspects of the processing of wool. Dyes, for example, had to be made fast so that the colours would not wash out, and this required a special agent known as a 'mordant'. The principal mordant in use was alum, a mineral found in large quantities in shales which outcrop on the cliffs of North Yorkshire. Alum mines and quarries were established there at the beginning of the seventeenth century and processing was also carried out on site. The shale was piled high in the quarry and then heated or calcined to remove some of the impurities, the long slow burning of the heaps lasting sometimes for weeks. The calcined shale was then leached (placed in tanks through which water was slowly run), and the resulting liquor was finally evaporated to produce the alum crystals. A typical alum mine (NT) can be seen at Ravenscar, near Robin Hood's Bay, where apart from the obvious signs of extensive quarrying there are also remains of surface buildings, including stone-flagged leaching tanks.

Wool was not, however, the only branch of the textile industry to flourish, and in other parts of Britain other cloths were dominant. In Ireland and Scotland, linen was the main product, manufactured not from wool but from flax. The flax fibres were loosened and freed by a process known as retting. This involved soaking the plant for weeks, during which time it would ferment producing both the loose fibres and an absolutely atrocious smell. As with wool, the fibres were separated into short (taw) and long (line), and it was from the line that the linen was produced. Spinning and weaving were essentially the same as for woollens, but finishing was somewhat different. Linen

These handsome eighteenth-century houses in Spitalfields, London, were used by silk weavers, who worked in garrets at the top of the buildings.

48

was given a surface sheen either by beating or by pressing under heavy weights. The beating process is similar to that of fulling, and again the water wheel was called into service in special mills. The stocks were known here as beetles, and the mills as beetling mills. A fine beetling mill, Wellbrook Beetling Mill (NT), has been preserved at Cookstown in Tyrone. It was built in 1765 and contains seven beetling engines, while the mill manager's house has also been preserved alongside. Linen is a somewhat grubby looking material as it comes from the loom, and always had to be beetled to make it acceptable.

The first tentative moves toward a new and revolutionarily different approach to production in these industries came in a branch which was really of rather minor importance in Britain – the throwing (to separate out the fine threads) and weaving of silk. Silk weaving was brought to Britain by Huguenot refugees who established themselves in the Spitalfields area of London at the end of the seventeenth century. Their houses with workshop garrets, marked as with so many textile workshops by long windows, can still be seen. More importantly, however, the idea of using water-powered machinery to throw the silk thread had become established in Italy, and the same notion was taken up and made into a commercial success in Britain. The foundations for the industry were laid by Thomas Cotchett and George Sorocold, who established Britain's first water-powered throwing mill. Had their endeavours succeeded, their names would have appeared in every history book, but they failed and have been relegated to footnotes attached to the names of the brothers Thomas and John Lombe. In 1724, the Lombes established a silk-throwing mill on the Derwent at Derby. That mill, although much changed since its establishment, still survives and now houses Derby Industrial Museum. It was a pioneering effort, but produced few imitators, for silk was far too expensive for large-scale mass production.

The story of the Derby silk mill has, therefore, comparatively minor importance in the overall story of the Industrial Revolution. It did, however, give rise to some splendidly romantic and bizarre tales of a different sort. It was claimed that the Italians, infuriated by the English stealing their secrets, sent a beautiful spy to Derby. She succeeded, in best beautiful spy tradition, in seducing John Lombe and then began systematically to poison him with all the cunning of the land of the Borgias. John Lombe died three years after the mill was established. True or not, the story says rather more about the importance of silk to Italy than of its importance to Britain. Silk mills continued to be built, however, in spite of the threats of seductive Italians, and a small but thriving industry was established in the Macclesfield area of Cheshire. A particularly handsome silk mill has survived at Whitchurch in Hampshire.

Shortly after the establishment of the Derby mill, there were new developments in the traditional textile industry that were to mark the start of a period of great change. In 1733, a Bury man, John Kay, who

had already been working at ways to improve the old hand loom, came up with his most important invention. He began to look at the broad loom, and realized that quite a simple change in the mechanism would make it possible for one man to do the work that had previously needed two. The problem lay with the width, too great for a pair of human hands to reach across. John Kay saw that this problem could be solved if those human hands could be replaced by artificial hands. The first step was to ease the movement of the shuttle itself by putting it on wheels and setting it running along the top of the batten that was used to push the weft thread home. Then, at either end of the batten, he placed boxes in which were his artificial hands, or pickers. The weaver could now send the shuttle flying across the loom simply by using a handle suspended centrally in front of him which jerked the pickers by means of a cord strung across the frame. So Kay's flying shuttle was introduced, a machine that not only used one man instead of two, but was faster as well.

The implications of the new loom were considerable, and the way in which you viewed its introduction depended very much on your status. The ordinary weaver saw only a road to unemployment, while his employer saw that same road stretching off towards a glorious and prosperous future. Neither, however, felt very much sympathy for John Kay. The weavers smashed the new machines, while their employers built a multitude of replacements but quite neglected to pay the royalties due to Kay, who eventually left the country and died, a poor man, in France.

The flying shuttle upset the balance of production in the textile industry. Now one vital process had achieved a vastly improved productivity.– but there was little hope of an all round increase in output unless more yarn could be supplied to the improved looms. Even then, there was no great incentive to increase production unless there was a market for the extra goods. In the middle of the eighteenth century, all the elements came together. A sudden demand for a new fabric provided the initial impetus, and that impetus came from across the world in India. When the British began empire building in Asia they did so with no real sense of direction. Indeed, they only arrived in India at all because the Dutch had secured a monopoly of the East Indies and the rich spice trade. Casting around for trade goods, the East India Company found bright, cheap cotton cloths. These proved immensely popular back in Britain and no amount of restrictive regulations, designed to protect the domestic woollen trade, could diminish the enthusiasm for cottons. They combined the lightness and bright colours of silk with low cost, an irresistible combination. British manufacturers, working on the well-known 'if you can't beat 'em, join 'em' principle, began to explore ways of manufacturing cottons for themselves. The search was on for a cheap and efficient method of spinning the yarn.

The first successful cotton-spinning machine, patented in 1738, was

Hargreaves' spinning jenny. The first jenny was made about 1764. This is an improved version; originally the wheel was set horizontally which made it awkward to turn.

the work of two men, Lewis Paul and John Wyatt. It was successful in the sense that it worked but it was not a commercial success. This was followed by a second invention, the work of James Hargreaves in the 1760s, which was known as the spinning jenny. Essentially, this was little more than the old spinning wheel turned on its side and now used to turn several spindles instead of just the one. This represented a major increase in productivity, but Hargreaves found like Kay that the success of the invention was no guarantee that the inventor would prosper. He suffered what was coming to seem an all too common fate: his machines were broken by traditionalists and pirated by the unscrupulous. The jenny did, in time, find acceptance among the spinners and was used either in the home or in small workshops. But the lessons were not lost when the next invention appeared on the scene. Its inventor, a forceful, quarrelsome man, had every intention of making his invention pay and he succeeded. His name was Richard Arkwright.

Arkwright began his working life as a barber, and his invention of a spinning machine was surrounded by controversy. Two other inventors claimed it as their own and the machine was, in fact, very similar in many ways to that of Wyatt and Paul. The threads were pulled out by being passed through rollers moving at different speeds, and were then twisted together. What set this machine apart from its forerunners was the way in which it was put into use. Arkwright began working on his invention in Lancashire, but mindful of the likely local reaction he moved off to the safer ground of Nottingham. There he received financial backing from two local industrialists, Samuel Need of Derby and Jebediah Strutt of Belper. A small mill was established

Arkwright's water frame, the first type of cotton spinning machinery to be powered by water, preserved at Helmshore Higher Mill, Lancashire.

as a trial, using horses as a source of power. The system worked, so Arkwright set about looking for a permanent site to establish a spinning works, deciding at once to change from horse power to that universal power source of the age – the water wheel. It was the use of the water wheel that was to give the new machine a name – the water frame.

Arkwright needed a site that was both suitable for a water mill, and well clear of potential wreckers and pirates. In 1771 he moved to Cromford, a tiny hamlet on the River Derwent in Derbyshire. There, under conditions of great secrecy, he began building what was to become the world's first successful cotton mill. At the same time, he had to build a whole new village to house the workforce. The mill and the village are still there today and a new museum is being developed in the original mill buildings, which are now little more than empty shells. Nevertheless, certain features that typified the early mills can still be seen. The buildings are tall and narrow, a shape dictated by the nature of the machinery. The frames, with their rollers and spindles, stood in rows across the mill. A shaft above them carried the drive from the water wheel, which was transmitted to the machines via belts. There were other machines, too, in the mill, notably carding engines, which replaced the old hand cards. Here, instead of spiked cards being drawn across each other, spiked rollers turned to produce the same effect.

The mill represents more than a change in scale from the old methods. Traditionally, women and children had worked at carding and spinning, and they did so again in Arkwright's mill; but, in the past, they had worked in their own homes and at their own pace. Now the mill imposed regularity. Once the water wheel began to turn the machines demanded attention, and they needed that attention until the wheel stopped. It was claimed that conditions were good in the mill, though Arkwright's son, Richard, giving evidence to a Parliamentary Committee in 1816, stated that most of the employees were children aged from seven to thirteen who worked a thirteen-hour day, and he admitted that, because of the particular design of the machine, many suffered permanent deformity. The initiative taken by Arkwright unquestionably led the way towards the Factory Age, with its promise of increased production and a new prosperity. At the same time, those forced to make the change from domestic work to factory work loathed the new ways, and there was much suffering.

It is tempting to write the Cromford story in terms of heroes and villains, either wicked capitalist exploiting labour, or brilliant entrepreneur hampered by worn-out attitudes. The reality was far more complex. The old style of work represented no idyllically happy pastoral scene: spinning and weaving were dully repetitive work, with long hours and poor pay. The new methods would eventually lead to a more prosperous future, but in the short term they represented riches for a few and misery for many. Richard Arkwright was very much one of the few. On the hillside overlooking the town and the mill stands Willersley Castle, the grand house he built for his own use. In the village can be seen the houses he constructed for his workers, including the terraces in North Street. These are sturdy, well-designed stone cottages. Downstairs is a small living-room-cum-kitchen with a bedroom immediately above that. The top floor has the traditional weavers' window marking the workshop where men worked either at the loom or at the stocking frame, knitting hosiery, for there was little

Houses built for Arkwright's workers in North Street, Cromford, Derbyshire. The long 'weavers' windows' on the upper floors mark the workshops.

Arkwright's mill at Matlock Bath, Derbyshire. The original, central section was later extended.

work for men in the new mill. Much of the rest of Cromford also dates back to Arkwright's time, including the Greyhound Hotel in the main square.

Arkwright did not stop at Cromford. He took out patents, and under their protection went on to establish other mills in the region, such as Masson Mill, Matlock Bath, which, although enlarged at a later date, still displays a very handsome eighteenth-century frontage to the world. He also licensed others to build mills using his machines, and they soon spread out from Derbyshire into other textile regions, such as Lancashire. Here the new mills met with violent opposition, and in 1779 the mill at Chorley was burned to the ground. Josiah Wedgwood, the famous potter, was in the area at the time and described in a letter how he saw the marching men and heard their threats 'to take Bolton, Manchester, and Stockport on their way to Cromford, and to destroy all the engines, not only in these places, but throughout all England'. The threat was taken seriously in Derbyshire. Jebediah Strutt, Arkwright's partner, had established his own works at Belper and he set about fortifying them against the expected attack. He had built mills on either side of the main road and joined them by a bridge. That bridge still stands, and the gun embrasures that were cut for defence can still be seen. But the attack never came. The riots died away, and Arkwright was able to return to the serious matter of making his fortune. Mills were built in many areas, including Scotland, and it is one of those Scottish mills that was to become famous not as an industrial development but as the starting point for a unique social experiment.

In the 1780s, David Dale built a mill beside the Corra Linn falls on the Clyde. Just as Arkwright had done at Cromford, he was forced to build an entire mill village to house the workforce, largely imported from the Poor Houses of the district. He called his village New Lanark. Dale was, by all accounts, a kindly man. He built a comfortable house for the apprentices, and tried to limit the intake to older children. The local authorities, however, insisted on sending younger children so that, in the event, the work force was very similar to that at Cromford. Then, in 1798, a new man arrived to run the mill complex, Robert Owen, a man with revolutionary ideas. Children under the age of ten were taken out of the mill and put into school. Hours in the factory were actually reduced, and adults as well as children were encouraged to receive education in the New Institution Owen had built for them. The productivity of the mill increased. Owen showed conclusively that people forced to work thirteen hours a day were incapable of giving of their best: he proved the point, but no one, it seemed, was prepared to accept his proof. His evidence before the 1816 Committee was met with total incredulity, and he found no followers. New Lanark, however, remains much as it was in his day, with its tall tenements standing in ranks high above the mill and the New Institution.

In 1783, Arkwright's patents were challenged in the courts and overthrown. The way was then open for a huge expansion in mill building. The process was helped by the invention of a second type of spinning machine, the mule, so called because like the animal it was a hybrid, containing elements of both Arkwright's water frame and the Hargreaves' jenny. In this machine, the yarn was again passed through rollers, but was then wound on to spindles mounted on a movable

A typical nineteenth-century mill with spinning mules. The carriages move backwards and forwards along the rails, alternately drawing out and winding in the thread.

carriage. The carriage moved one way to extend the yarn, then back the other to wind on to the bobbins. It was a highly efficient device, but its inventor, Samuel Crompton, was no entrepreneur and followed the downward path of Kay and others rather than the road to prosperity taken by Arkwright. The addition of the new machine gave added impetus to the cotton trade, which was already expanding rapidly to meet new demands. The result was a great flurry of mill building, exemplified by what is perhaps the most complete mill and village complex in Britain: Styal in Cheshire (NT).

The mill at Styal was first established by Samuel Greg of Belfast in 1784. In general layout it is similar to the early Arkwright mills, but it was built on a very grand scale. The main building is four storeys high, and was originally powered by two water wheels, later replaced by a single wheel, 33 foot in diameter. It was a big mill for its time and, within ten years of its foundation, was employing around 300 workers. It would, today, be just one of many mill buildings had it not been built in an area to the south of Manchester which was not to see much subsequent development. So Styal has become, as it were, fossilized, providing a vivid physical record of the industrial past. The story Styal has to tell is as much social as technical, for the arrangements Greg made to house his workforce are at least as important as the work place itself.

Visiting Styal today, the elements of the original complex can be clearly seen. Next to the mill is an elegant private house, the home built by Greg for his own use. Follow the path up the hill, and you come to another large, red-brick house. This, however, had a quite different place in the story, for it was here that the mill apprentices had their home, over a hundred of them, young boys and girls who worked in the mill. One of the great attractions of the Styal complex lies in the fact that a great deal of documentation has survived to add flesh to the bare, architectural bones of the place. The life of the apprentices is particularly well recorded. We know, for example, that the children came to Styal from all parts of the region, some from the poor houses, others from pauper families. We know a good deal about the hardships of their working lives, and of the dangers of working with unguarded machines. A 13-year-old apprentice, Thomas Priestley, had one of his fingers torn off in the mill, and this was his description of life at Styal, recorded when he ran away and was brought back and hauled up in front of the magistrates:

'Our working hours were from 6 o'clock morning Summer and Winter till 7 in the evening. There were no nights worked. We had

Quarry Bank Mill at Styal (NT): originally water-powered, later adapted for steam. The factory bell summoned the workers at the start of the day.

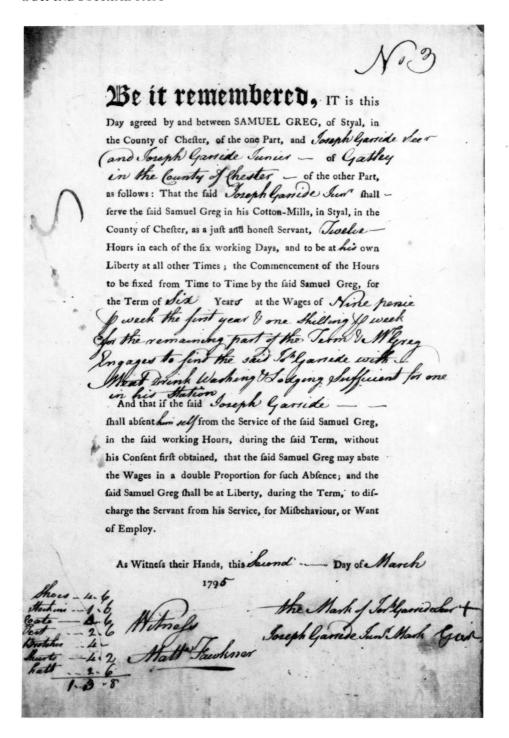

Apprentice's indenture from Styal – an agreement to work twelve hours a day, six days a week for six years. It is interesting to note that the clothes supplied (listed bottom left) were equivalent to 32 weeks pay.

only 10 minutes allowed us for our breakfasts which were always brought to the Mill to us and we worked that up at night again – 2 days in the week we had an hour allowed us for dinner, while the machines were oiled, for doing this I was paid $\frac{1}{2}$d a time, on other days we were allowed half an hour for dinner.'

Yet when reading the accounts of the apprentices it must be remembered that they were considered fortunate in comparison with many of their contemporaries, who worked in worse conditions and laboured for such long hours that they were only kept awake by constant beatings.

Across the fields from the apprentice house is the village itself. The houses now wear a picture postcard air which can be somewhat misleading, particularly as the buildings we admire today were generally home to not one but two families. Nevertheless, with their gardens and surroundings of green fields, the Styal cottages offer a pleasant contrast to what was happening elsewhere in the world of textiles, where rapid developments were taking place in many areas, not just in the manufacture of cotton.

Woollen textile manufacturers were comparatively slow to change from the old methods to the new, but once change had got under way it proceeded just as rapidly as it did elsewhere. It was particularly marked in the traditional West Country woollen areas where the drive to modernity is epitomized by Stanley Mill at King's Stanley in Gloucestershire. Built in about 1813, modern notions and modern methods were utilized throughout the structure. Where older mills had been built of brick or stone on a wooden frame – and thus represented a considerable fire hazard – the new mill was built on an iron frame. The earliest mill of this type had been constructed in 1796 for spinning flax at Ditherington, near Shrewsbury, Shropshire, and was later adapted for use as a maltings. This is a plain, unadorned, functional building; the same could never be said of Stanley Mill. Here the builders have made full use of the decorative possibilities of iron work. The columns which support the floor beams are classically styled and end in elaborately worked arches. Even the iron window frames show a splendid richness, varying from an elegant Venetian window to a circular rose window that would not look out of place in a cathedral. The mill is still in use, but is a somewhat lonely survivor of a once important industry, for the centre of the wool trade shifted away from the West of England towards Yorkshire. This was not, however, a sudden and dramatic change, nor was it a complete movement towards that area. Throughout the late eighteenth and early nineteenth centuries, a number of mills were also established in Wales, taking advantage of abundant water supplies for power. And precisely because the region failed to develop subsequently as a textile manufacturing district, many of those mills have remained virtually unchanged since the nineteenth century, and they work now much as they did at the height of the Industrial Revolution.

One major difference can be seen that marks off the Welsh mills from those of the eighteenth century. By the nineteenth century, mechanization had extended beyond the spinning phase of manufacture to weaving. The first power loom was invented as early as 1786 by a clergyman, Dr Edmund Cartwright. It was a cumbersome and unwieldy device, but was soon improved to a point where the power loom began to supplant the old hand loom. These were troubled times

The village of Styal (NT): the houses were often home to more than one family, and the cellars were used for weaving.

in many regions, as the hand workers battled to retain the old ways, but there is little hint of that struggle in the small Welsh mills. At Maesllyn woollen mill, Dyfed, for example, the full range of processes employed in turning raw wool into cloth can still be seen, much as they must have been done a century and a half ago. One of the few concessions to modernity is the replacement of the old overshot wheel by the more efficient Pelton wheel. What cannot be seen is the machine that divides off the first phase of the Industrial Revolution from the second, the steam engine.

The steam engine provided greater power and greater reliability than the water wheel, and it also provided the millbuilder with something else – freedom of movement. The water-powered mill was necessarily located where a sufficient water supply could be maintained: the steam mill suffered from no such restrictions. Now mills could be built according to quite different criteria. They could be set down next to the best available transport system, they could be clustered together in the centres of towns and they could be located near the coalfields. Furthermore, they could be built bigger than ever before. A new style of mill building developed, consisting of a squat, often featureless block that housed the spinning machinery, alongside which was a single-storey building with multiple pitched roofs containing north-facing lights which provided regular illumination to the power looms beneath. And towering over them all was the mill chimney, marking the presence of steam. And it was not just the mill that changed; the mill community began to change as well. The old village gave way to the mill town. The mill owner no longer needed to build his own village to attract the workers to some remote river valley, for now he could build in established settlements and let the workers sort out their own housing problems. The new industrial workers had to turn to the speculative builder, whose cheap back-to-back terraces became synonymous with the mill town.

The coming of the power loom and the steam engine marked the virtual end of the old way of working. Soon every aspect of textile manufacture had been taken away from the domestic worker and passed across to the new machines in their custom-built factories. It was not a painless transition. The old workers resisted fiercely, faced as they were by a steady loss of jobs and by unprincipled employers who used the excuse of unemployment to hack wages ever lower. There were riots and outbreaks of machine breaking, though when the new machines were smashed, the breakers left the older generation of machines strictly alone. It was a battle that could, however, have only one outcome. The new ways were more productive and more profitable, and they could not be kept at bay for ever. The tragedy lay less in the nature of the new methods than in the way in which change, in all too many cases, was introduced. Few of the new towns could boast the sort of solid standard of building craftsmanship that marked the first mill villages, such as Cromford. The new was shoddy,

Moorside Mill, West Yorkshire, a nineteenth-century woollen mill now home to Bradford's Industrial Museum.

gimcrack and insanitary: no one should be too surprised at the struggle put up by those who wanted to keep the old way of life intact.

Many of the nineteenth-century developments have been swept away in slum clearance schemes and in recent years with the collapse of the traditional textile regions, but enough remains in Bradford and Paisley, Blackburn and Rochdale for us to have at least some notion of what such towns must have been like a hundred years ago. And there is also a reminder in some regions that not all industrialists took the same narrow, profit-counting view. Sir Titus Salt was a Bradford manufacturer who was horrified by what he saw in his native town, and he set out in the 1850s to build a factory and a model town to go with it. The result was Saltaire, West Yorkshire, built on the banks of the Aire, with an elegantly imposing mill straddling the river and the Leeds and Liverpool Canal and a no less imposing town to go with it. The houses are handsome, and there is a full range of civic amenities – church, almshouses, library and hospital. It was a splendid model but found few imitators. Look around the region and you will find no shortage of grand, imposing mills – Moorside Mill, which now houses the Bradford Industrial Museum, being a fine example. There is, however, no equivalent wealth of good housing and fine amenities.

The steam engines that once powered the great mills are now very rare, but a few have been preserved, one of the finest of which is the splendid Dee engine at Shaw, near Manchester. This is a comparatively modern engine, built in 1907. It is of the type known as twin tandem compound, which is to say that it looks at first like two identical engines, so arranged that they work together, though it is in fact a single machine. Early in the nineteenth century it was realized that with improved boilers capable of producing steam at ever higher pressures there was a great waste of energy every time the steam, still under pressure, left the cylinder. The answer was to feed the exhaust steam from the high-pressure cylinder into a larger low-pressure cylinder. At Dee, the cylinders are arranged as the name 'tandem' suggests, one behind the other. There are two such sets, each consisting of a 21-inch high-pressure cylinder and a 44-inch low-pressure cylinder, with an 84-ton flywheel in between. The wheel is grooved to take ropes which transfer the drive to shafts throughout the mill, just as shafts took the drive from the water wheel in earlier buildings.

It took a long time to move from human power to water power, and from water power to steam power, but the effects of that series of changes were widespread. They were seen at their most dramatic in the textile industry, where the factory age was born and for which the first industrial towns were developed. But the effects of change did not stop there: the demand for new machines meant an increased demand for the metals from which they were constructed.

4 The Metals

Iron must take pride of place in any discussion of metals, for none has found wider or more extensive use, from nails and chains to bridges and ships. It occurs naturally as an oxide, so to produce the metal itself a way has to be found to remove the oxygen. This can be done comparatively easily by heating the ore with some form of carbon. As the basic technology is so simple, it might be expected that iron would have come into use at much the same time as other metals, yet copper was extracted around 3000 BC, and 2000 years were to go by before the Bronze Age gave way to the Iron Age. The explanation lies in the fact that, with early technology, iron production was a two-stage process. Heat copper ore and liquid metal is produced which can be run off into moulds. Heat iron ore in the same way and you end up with a spongy lump of no apparent significance. The first experimenters to heat metal ores must have been quite delighted with the results they got with copper, but simply abandoned the other useless lump as being of no further interest. They could have achieved a similar result with iron ore to that obtained with copper, had they been able to raise the furnace to a high enough temperature. But that was quite beyond the scope of early technology.

There are no written records to tell us when man first began to take an interest in that unengaging lump, known as a bloom, but at some stage someone tried the experiment of hitting the bloom with heavy hammers. The hammering, or forging, of the bloom removed the impurities and for the first time man had a usable form of iron, wrought iron. Heating the ore with some form of carbon in a hearth and beating out the resulting bloom represented the basic technology of the iron age until around the fifteenth century when the charcoal blast furnace was first used. Charcoal is an ideal fuel for, being a very pure form of carbon, no impurities are introduced into the resulting iron. The furnace itself differed from the early bloomeries in that it worked at a higher temperature, caused by a steady blast of air from huge bellows powered by a water wheel. The blast raised the temperature to such a high point that the metal now appeared in molten form, rather than as bloom. This meant that the iron could be run straight off into moulds and cast in whatever shape was needed. The simplest mould comprised a central channel with small channels leading off it, a shape that suggested a sow and her feeding piglets to the more imaginative iron workers. Thus iron bars produced by this process came to be known as pig iron. More elaborate shapes could produce more elaborate ironwork.

The siting of these charcoal furnaces depended on the availability of the natural ingredients – iron ore, wood for charcoal making and water for power. All occurred together in south-east England, in Kent and Sussex, and the area known as the Weald still carries many traces of the industry. The first process, the production of charcoal by the carefully controlled, very slow burning of wood, was carried out in temporary camps set up in the heart of the woodland. Such a camp, with its simple burners' huts and the charcoal heaps, has been re-constructed at the Weald and Downland Open Air Museum, West Sussex. But to find actual iron-making sites can involve a little detective work. Look at any large-scale map of the area and you will find many of the small streams strung with lakes carrying names such as Hammer Pond, Furnace Pond or New Pond. The ponds are in fact artificial, built to store water for the water wheels of the foundries. At some of these sites quite substantial remains can still be seen. In East Sussex the Ashburnham furnace near Ninfield (TQ 685 170) has an almost complete wheel pit where the water wheel once turned and at the Pippingford furnace near Wych Cross (TQ 450 316) the pit where cannon were cast can still be seen.

Iron making has long since vanished from the Weald, so that today it requires something of an act of imagination to comprehend that this was ever an industrial area at all. Other areas, remote from any current industrial use, present even more startling challenges to the imagination. The Wye valley at Tintern, Gwent, is one of Britain's most popular tourist spots, and very few either know or care that they are also visiting an important industrial site. In Tudor times this was a very busy and bustling place, following the arrival of German crafts-men who came to make iron wire. Originally they had planned to make their wire of brass not iron, but they soon turned to iron to meet the growing demand for iron for cards for the textile industry. New furnaces were built and have survived in various stages of decay, the best preserved being the Coed Ithel furnace in the woods near Llandogo, Gwent (SO 527 027). The outer shell of the furnace has crumbled, leaving the furnace itself exposed, so that its form and arrangement can be clearly seen. Internally, it is roughly cylindrical, the barrel gently widening from top to bottom as far as an area known as the boshes where there is a pronounced reduction in diameter above the hearth. Charcoal and ore were fed in at the top, and some volatile impurities were driven off. The charcoal and ore charge settled in the boshes, the metal melted and further impurities, the slag, floated on top. The slag was tapped off before the metal was run out at the bottom of the furnace. The blast from the bellows came in through a pipe, the tuyere.

The best preserved of all charcoal furnaces is to be found in an even more remote location, at Bonawe on the shore of Loch Etive on the

RIGHT *The overshot water wheel at Cotehele Mill, Cornwall. The Cotehele Estate (NT) is a fine example of a self-contained medieval community; the mill was the manorial water mill.*

RIGHT *The engine house of Wheal Betsy lead mine (NT) on the west edge of Dartmoor, Devon.*

LEFT *Preston Mill, Lothian (NTS): a water-powered meal mill and drying kiln. In 1948 the mill was flooded to the height of the roof line on the mill building.*

LEFT *The landscape of early mining at Grassington, North Yorkshire. The mounds represent the spoil from bell pits, the hollow centres showing where the pits have collapsed inwards.*

ABOVE *The steam engine of 1918, built to wind men and materials up and down the Hesketh pit at Chatterley Whitfield Colliery, Staffordshire.*

A detail of the Chatterley Whitfield engine showing the superb quality of craftsmanship involved.

west coast of Scotland (Strathclyde). It was established here in 1762, worked for just over a century and had the reputation of producing iron of exceptionally fine quality. Here the whole structure, including the outer cladding, is more or less complete. It is built up against the hillside for ease of operation. The charge was wheeled from the store rooms to the charge house which was built level with the top of the furnace. From there the charge was taken across a short bridge to the furnace itself. At the bottom of the furnace is the hearth where the molten metal was tapped, and the wheel pit can also be clearly seen. The Bonawe furnace is, however, something of an anomaly, for by the time it was built the charcoal furnace was already obsolescent.

The problem with this type of furnace was the fuel. Charcoal making required great quantities of timber, and there were other users making demands on the woodland, especially the Royal Navy. A single warship could use up to 2000 tons of timber, and it has been estimated that during the seventeenth and eighteenth centuries the navy cut down two-thirds of the New Forest for shipbuilding. The other obvious source of carbon was coal, available in vast quantities, sufficient to meet all foreseeable furnace needs. Unfortunately, coal was found to contain too many impurities which contaminated the iron. The solution to the whole problem came from one individual, but from a mixture of circumstances. A Bristol Quaker, Abraham Darby, served an apprenticeship in the brewing industry before going on to work in the most important local industry, brass founding. In the course of his work, he went to Holland where he saw local craftsmen casting large cooking pots. He felt that the same technique could be used for making iron pots and, with the help of an apprentice, John Thomas, he succeeded. In 1707, he took out a patent for his 'new way of casting iron-bellied pots, and other iron-bellied ware in sand only'. Local merchants, however, showed little interest, and Darby decided to start his own iron works to put the process to use. At the same time he gave a good deal of consideration to the fuel for the furnaces and remembered his early days in the brewery maltings where the fuel used was coke. In the manufacture of coke from coal (see p. 166), the elements which cause contamination are removed, and this was the vital factor in the new process.

Darby looked northwards for his new works, to Coalbrookdale, high up the Severn valley in Shropshire. Here there was excellent coal for coking, and a well-established charcoal furnace should the new system fail. It did not fail, and in 1709 the first iron smelted by coke began to flow. That old furnace still stands at Coalbrookdale, the different stages of its history marked on the lintels above the hearth. The original furnace had a small hearth, dated 1638, but this was later extended and the new date, 1777, inscribed – a date of no little significance in the Coalbrookdale story. Not that Coalbrookdale suffers from any shortage of important dates and achievements for, under successive members of the Darby family and their associates, the works

The old furnace at Coalbrookdale, Shropshire. It was in this furnace that coke was first used for iron smelting. The furnace was enlarged by Darby in 1777 in order to cast the parts for the iron bridge over the Severn.

played a prominent part in the development of industry. It was here that many of the early steam engines were built and the first iron rails were cast and it was on those rails, at Coalbrookdale itself, that Trevithick ran what would appear to be his first successful locomotive, parts of which were also cast at Coalbrookdale. But the 1777 date marks what is perhaps the best known of the Darby achievements, for it was then that the furnace was enlarged to allow the casting of the parts for the world's first iron road bridge, completed in 1779 and still to be seen crossing the Severn at nearby Ironbridge.

The importance of this whole region led to the establishment of a major industrial museum complex, the Ironbridge Gorge Museum, based on existing remains. These include three impressive blast furnaces, and a new source of power to supply the blast. Instead of a water wheel being used to work giant bellows, air was blown into the furnace by a steam engine. The first successful experiments in this field were made by John Wilkinson; remains of the Willey Iron Works where he made the first trials in 1776 can be seen at Broseley in Shropshire (SO 674 006), though the engine and engine house have long gone. It was an important development, not just for the iron industry, but in that it was the first use of steam power for anything other than pumping. For Wilkinson its importance lay in the great improvement in the efficiency of the furnace. If there is little trace to be seen of this pioneering work at Broseley, there is a good deal at Blists Hill Open Air Museum (part of the Ironbridge complex) to show how steam power developed in the iron industry. One of the old engine houses has been restored and a large vertical blowing engine installed. Equally impressive are a pair of beam engines of 1851 which drove a common crank and flywheel. They are known as David and Sampson, though whether the latter name reflects the importance of a local dignitary or inaccurate Biblical spelling is uncertain. What is certain, however, is that they are a fine example of Victorian engineering and make a fitting introduction to the Blists Hill complex.

It is tempting to see the establishment of the Coalbrookdale works as offering an instant answer to the major problems of iron making in Britain. Like the man who invented the more successful mouse trap, Abraham Darby might have expected to find the world beating a path to his door. This did not happen, or at least not very rapidly. One reason was that Darby had only solved part of the major problem. His furnaces could produce iron for casting and, indeed, Coalbrookdale was to become famous for the exceptionally high quality of the castings made there, examples of which are shown in the Coalbrookdale section of the Ironbridge Gorge Museum. Other iron masters found, however, that not all coal was as good for coking as Shropshire coal, nor was all the ore free from impurities, so that much coke-smelted iron was of rather poor quality. The answer to that problem was found at the end of the eighteenth century, and again the innovator was John Wilkinson. He remelted the iron in a second, coke-fired furnace, where the remaining impurities were burned off. Such furnaces, known as cupolas, were simple structures, little more than metal tubes lined with firebrick, a very good example of which can be seen at the Welsh Slate Museum at Llanberis in Gwynedd.

This museum is based on the maintenance workshops of the famous Dinorwic quarry, and here everything needed at the quarry was maintained, repaired and even, if necessary, replaced. There is a

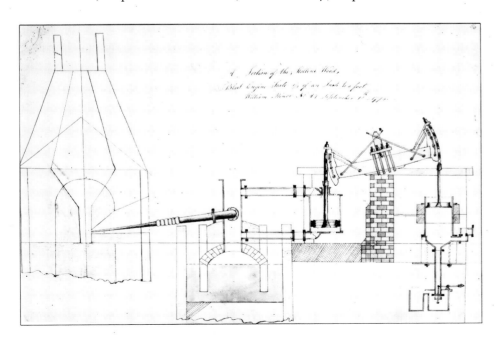

William Reynolds' sketch of a steam-powered blowing engine, 1798. The beam engine on the right provides the blast of air which passes through the tapered blast pipe to the furnace on the left.

complete range of workshops, power for the different departments coming originally from a 50-foot diameter water wheel, which worked until 1925. It was kept in situ, but work was transferred to a smaller, more efficient, Pelton wheel. Many of the machine parts needed at the quarry were cast in the foundry here. The first step was to make a wooden version of the required part in the pattern makers' shop. The pattern was then taken on to the foundry itself. At one end stands the tall tower of the cupola furnace, with a loading platform at the top from which the charge, coke and pig iron or scrap iron, could be fed in. The patterns were set out in front of the cupola on the casting floor, and sand was packed around them. Then the wooden patterns were carefully removed leaving an exact impression behind. The pure molten metal was tapped from the furnace into ladles and then poured into the moulds.

However, there still remained one basic problem to be solved. The iron from such furnaces, cast iron, was very brittle; other older processes had produced a malleable metal, known as wrought iron. The differences between the two were chemical, depending on carbon content, but were not then understood. There were numerous attempts to convert coke-smelted cast iron into wrought iron. Abraham Darby II devised a method, of which few details are known, and in 1783 a new furnace for converting pig iron into wrought iron was patented by Peter Onions. Here the methods used are clear, but the furnace was not a commercial success. That had to wait a further year until Henry Cort of Funtley in Hampshire patented his puddling furnace, together with a system of grooved rollers for making iron bars. Cort, like Onions, used a reverbatory furnace: that is, one in which the fuel and the iron never come into direct contact, the heat being supplied by the hot gases from the furnace. The molten metal was stirred – puddled – with iron rods passing through the brickwork of the furnace. It formed into lumps which could be removed and passed to the rolling mill, to be squeezed out into long bars. The process was successful but represented immensely hard physical labour for the puddlers working the heavy metal in the intense heat. It is not perhaps surprising to find that the puddlers had the reputation of being heavy drinkers. Cort was no great innovator: the furnace was similar to Onions' and a rolling mill had been built in Sweden as early as 1745. He did, however, bring the two vital elements of reverbatory furnace and rolling mill together and in doing so brought a new impetus to iron making in Britain. The old centres began to decay while new ones developed.

Coke blast furnaces can be seen in many parts of Britain. Sometimes they have been left behind as strange, isolated structures in a landscape where all other traces of industry seem to have disappeared. Perhaps the most striking examples are the furnaces of the Morley Park Iron Works at Heage in Derbyshire. Built between 1780 and 1818, the furnaces stand, huge truncated pyramids, lonely, but rather splendid, amidst an expanse of green fields. Elsewhere the iron industry was more firmly established. In Scotland, the great Carron works were founded at Falkirk in 1759 and continued working until 1982, but much of the old has vanished in the continuing process of renewal and modernization. The past has not been altogether ignored, however: embedded in the outer wall of the factory is the name plate from James Watt's first steam engine, while outside the entrance is a carronade, a highly efficient wide-barrelled cannon, which played its part in the Napoleonic Wars. Today, we find it hard to appreciate the sense of wonder that such sites evoked in the early years. A French visitor to Carron, Faujas St Fond, wrote of the scene in 1799 that 'one doubts whether he is at the foot of a volcano in actual eruption, or whether he has been transported by some magical effect to the brink of the cavern, where Vulcan and his Cyclops are occupied in preparing thunderbolts.' One region where, although the great furnaces are dead, something of the awe felt by the eighteenth-century traveller can still be experienced is South Wales, an area where the arrival of the new works of the second iron age was to have a dramatic effect on the face of the land.

There are many sites in this part of Britain where the results of the new technology on what had been a peaceful thinly populated rural area can be seen, but quite the most dramatic and important site is Blaenafon in Gwent. The story here begins in 1789, when a group of Staffordshire iron workers took out a lease from the Earl of Abergavenny. There was no great tradition of iron working in the area, so a core of skilled workers was brought in from England, and they built both the

The Blaenafon furnaces at work in 1800.

works and the houses for the first of the newcomers. An open square of houses was constructed literally in the shadow of the furnaces, and their style is very much that of the English Midlands, not that of rural Wales. They proved quite inadequate, and as the works grew so some quite extraordinary measures were resorted to in order to house the workers at the minimum possible cost. Transport to and from the works was by tramway, an early form of railway on which waggons were pulled by horses. This tramway crossed the valley on a viaduct, the ten arches of which were blocked in to provide homes for the workforce. No records survive to show what life was like underneath the arches, but contemporary accounts suggest that it must have been desperately noisy for they speak of the trucks that 'continually pass and repass' on the tramway. We can, however, still see the more conventional houses and life there cannot have been especially pleasant, surrounded by the noise and dirt of a busy foundry. At the end of one terrace is a reminder of another burden on the life of the iron-worker – the Truck Shop. Men were paid in notes exchangeable only in the company shop, giving the shopkeepers carte blanche to charge what they would. The system was only eradicated after a long struggle, in which the men of Blaenafon played their part. The iron masters and the iron trade dominated the town, and their influence can be seen everywhere – from the ironwork in the church to the old school, the first industrial school in Wales.

Today, the furnaces are silent, but how eloquent they are in their silence. They loom up from the hillside like medieval towers; some form bold square towers of stone; in others the outer case has crumbled away to reveal the inner furnace. This was the new age of iron making, and it gave rise to industrial building on the grand scale. Here, too, is the evidence of new technology in the form of steam-powered blast replacing the old water-powered bellows. Yet even the furnaces seem comparatively insignificant in comparison with another tower, constructed of huge stone blocks and topped by almost incongruously elegant classical pillars. This is the water balance tower, in effect a simple form of lift using counterbalanced boxes. In order to carry material to the top of the furnace bank, the lower box would be filled with the goods – ore, coal or whatever – and the upper box filled with water. When the weight of the upper box was greater than that of the lower, then it would start to descend and the other would rise.

Blaenafon was never one of the really great works, which is why so much has survived from the early period. Elsewhere the old vanished as the new came in to replace it. Whole towns grew up around the twin industries of iron making and coal mining, towns such as Merthyr Tydfil, Mid Glamorgan, home of the Dowlais Iron Company. The area was to become synonymous with a particularly strict form of paternalism, where the masters were all-powerful, seeming to believe that their authority was divine. One master sent a pamphlet to his workforce pointing out that wage demands were sinful: 'you are not to

Restoration work in progress on the furnace bank at Blaenafon, Gwent. The outer stone cladding has been replaced on the nearer furnace, while the far furnace shows the circular inner core.

infringe on the providential order of God . . . by attempting to force upon those whom God has set over you, the adoption of such regulations and the payment of such wages as would be beneficial to yourselves.' The tracts would seem to have had little effect, for the valleys of South Wales were to see scenes of bitter and sometimes violent conflict between masters and men. But the area was blessed with natural resources, and the towns continued to grow and industry to spread.

And traces of that past can still be found, even amid the concrete and glass of new developments. At Merthyr Tydfil, in the heart of the town, stands the magnificent stone engine house of the Ynysfach Iron Works.

So far, we have only looked at two forms of iron, cast iron and wrought iron. A third variety, steel, was, however, known from an early age. The difference again lay in the amount of carbon it contained. Long before the metallurgy was understood, it was well known that steel could take a hard cutting edge making it ideal for tools such as scythes and sickles, while the very best quality steel was much sought after by swordsmiths. The city of Sheffield became particularly known for the quality of its steel and happily there is still a great deal to see

The crucible steel furnaces at Abbeydale Industrial Hamlet, South Yorkshire; a crucible stands beside the row of open furnaces. The loaded crucibles were lowered through the holes to the heart of the fire.

there. But to look at one of the earliest forms of steel production it is necessary to make an excursion into the woods near Hamsterley, Durham (NZ 131 565). Here can be found the remains of a furnace in which very pure wrought iron was heated with carefully measured quantities of charcoal. These furnaces, known as cementation furnaces, were found in the north-east of England because the best wrought iron was made in Sweden and imported through Newcastle. The Hamsterley furnace is a conical structure, with hearths on either side where the earthenware containers filled with iron and charcoal were set. It is very dilapidated, for it has long been out of use. The 'blister steel' it produced was of poor quality and other methods were introduced which resulted in a much higher grade of steel.

An alternative method of making steel was invented by Benjamin Huntsman in the 1740s, and it came into widespread use, especially in the Sheffield region. Many of the historical aspects of the City of Steel can still be traced through preserved sites in the area. The Abbeydale Industrial Hamlet is, as its name suggests, more than just an old works and represents a complete community. Here steel was made and worked to produce scythes; and here, too, are the homes of those who did the work. As with so many sites, the story begins with the source of power. A site was selected close to the River Sheaf, which was dammed to create a reservoir in 1772. The dam was enlarged in 1777, and the works developed quite rapidly until the 1830s when the new steel furnace was installed and the works attained very much the form that we can see today. Scythe-making begins with the manufacture of the steel, by Huntsman's crucible process. In essence, this involves heating either pure wrought iron or blister steel with charcoal in a special crucible – and the first stage was the making of those crucibles. They were made from a mixture of fireclay, china clay and coke dust which was kneaded together on the treading floor by the pot maker stamping up and down on it with his bare feet. This process was, according to one retired worker, amazingly therapeutic, and no pot maker ever suffered corns or bunions. When thoroughly mixed, the material was shaped in moulds and the crucibles were allowed to dry out before use.

The furnace room is topped by a very distinctive oblong chimney, the distinguishing mark of the crucible furnace. The furnace itself is in the basement and the crucibles, after being filled in the charge room, were lowered down through holes in the floor above into the very heart of the fire. The tall chimney ensured a good draught to the fire, which reached a temperature of around 2700°F. After three to four hours, the reaction was complete and the crucibles were lifted out, using special tongs, and the molten metal poured into ingots. This was a skilled job, a heavy job and a desperately hot job, so hot in fact that the men wore sackcloth aprons soaked in water from a trough by the door to keep themselves from being burned. It could even be dangerous. One former worker recounted how, on one occasion, a pot was dropped and shattered. As the molten metal hit the wet floor it solidified and shot around the room like a hail of bullets. He still carries the scars from that day.

The next stage was the forging of the blades which was done by employing a manufacturing technique that has been fundamental to the use of iron from the earliest days: shaping metal on an anvil by using a hammer. Here, however, the hammers were not wielded by the strong arms of blacksmiths, but were worked by water wheel. The mechanism itself was very similar to that already described for fulling stocks. The scythe blade was made out of a sandwich of iron on the outside with steel in the middle, and before the blade could be given shape that sandwich had to be welded together. It was first heated in a hearth brought to a high temperature by air from a blowing engine. This is a splendid device, again powered by a water wheel. Rotating cams (projections) on the shaft work two pistons in cylinders which expel the air with a good deal of asthmatic wheezing. The actual welding of the hot metal was done under one of the hammers, powered by the water wheel and known as tilt hammers, which delivered 126 blows per minute when the wheel was working at its customary speed of two revolutions per minute. Once welding was complete, the sandwich could then be shaped under a second hammer with the steel

Scythe grinders at work in Sheffield, 1866. The wheels turned in water, which helped to keep down the lethal metal dust.

filling being squeezed out between the iron slices as it flattened. This protruding steel could then be given a sharp edge. But first, the blade was given its final shaping and tempering in one of the small hand forges, very like the traditional blacksmith's shop.

The blades were given their cutting edge in the grinding shed or hull, where they were sharpened on water-powered grindstones. This is the darkest side of the story for grinding could be, and all too often was, a fatal occupation. The Abbeydale workmen were at least wet grinders, that is the wheels turned in water, which saved the men from the worst effects of dry metal dust blowing into their faces. Nevertheless, all grinders suffered to some extent from lung disease. In the very worst cases, those of the fork grinders, nearly fifty per cent of the workers died before they reached their thirtieth birthdays. The Abbeydale men were spared those horrors.

Continuing on a tour of Abbeydale, one finds the workshops where handles were fitted to the blades and a warehouse with pillars actually constructed out of used grindstones. They are canny folk up in Yorkshire, and not much given to waste. Completing the buildings are the offices and the houses, manager and men living close together. The houses are sound, sturdy dwellings, and they needed to be. On working days the ground around the works shook with the beat of the giant hammers, and no Abbeydale housewife could ever keep ornaments on her mantelshelf. Nevertheless, the overall effect today is of a pleasant spot where harmony rules. It was not always so. The middle of the nineteenth century came to be known as the time of the Sheffield Outrages. It was a period of violent confrontation between masters and Trade Unions, and Abbeydale was not immune. In 1842, the management began to import low-paid non-Union labour, and the Union made sure they never started work. The grinding hull was blown up. As time went on, the struggle became more vicious, with attacks on people as well as buildings. One Abbeydale manager, Joshua Tyzack, was shot at five times.

Today, Abbeydale is peaceful again and the hammers are still. However, a similar forge making edge tools can be seen at Sticklepath, down in Devon. These works, misleadingly known as Finch's Foundry, are, like Abbeydale, water powered through a series of overshot wheels. But here the hammers still work and metal heated in the hearth can still be pounded into shape. The water-powered grinding stone gives a new perspective to the common saying 'nose to the grindstone', for the grinder lies on a platform with his head above the turning wheel. Back in Sheffield, it was common for grinding hulls to be set up as quite separate establishments. One such place, Shepherd Wheel, has rows of grindstones each worked by belt drive from a line-shaft turned by an overshot water wheel. Here the workers spent their days in an atmosphere thick with metal dust, putting edges on cutlery. There was another local tradition that remained strong throughout the nineteenth century, that of individual cutlery grinders working in their own

OVERLEAF *Finch Foundry Museum, Devon, showing the water-powered tilt hammers (RIGHT), used for forging agricultural tools.*

workshops – the 'little mesters'. A new industrial museum at Kelham Island, Sheffield, has recreated the world of the little mesters, with a series of small workshops where knife blades are forged and ground.

Until the middle of the nineteenth century, steel production remained a small-scale affair. Then in 1856 Henry Bessemer developed a new and larger type of furnace, which became known as the Bessemer Converter. The furnace itself was mounted on trunnions, so that it could be tipped backwards and forwards. It was first tipped horizontally and loaded with molten pig iron. It was then returned to the vertical when air was blown in at the base. This was a very dramatic operation for it caused flames to shoot out of the top of the furnace and it was from the colour of the flames that the steel maker could judge what stage the process had reached. At the right moment, the blast of air was turned off and the molten steel poured out. The whole process was greatly improved by two cousins, Sidney Thomas and Percy Gilchrist who, in 1879, changed the furnace lining to get rid of troublesome impurities. The entrance to the Sheffield Industrial Museum at Kelham Island is quite dominated by a Bessemer Converter, standing more than thirty foot high. This increase in furnace size made a greater scale of production possible.

So far, we have been concentrating on the actual production of iron and steel, and have looked at just a few ways in which the metals

The dramatic sight of a Bessemer Converter at work. Air blown through the bottom of the furnace sends the flames shooting out of the top.

were then used in casting and forging. There are, of course, many varied uses of iron and preserved sites are listed in the gazetteer. A few are of special importance, in that they show features which helped to give identity to whole regions. Although we think of iron making in the Sheffield area primarily in terms of the city itself, the work spread far out into the countryside: indeed, at the time it was founded Abbeydale was very much a rural site. One other local forge is of particular interest, not just because it is still in the countryside and has not been swallowed up by the creeping suburbs, but because it shows remarkable continuity of use. Wortley Top Forge was begun in 1640 and extensively modernized in 1713. The tilt hammers are basically similar to those of Abbeydale, but here we also have a site where Cort's puddling furnace and grooved rollers were introduced. The rollers remain as do the grooved anvils where railway truck axles were forged in the nineteenth century.

Another great iron-working region was the Midlands, especially the Black Country, with a long history of making nails and chains. Nail making was very much a domestic industry, with nailers working in small workshops in the yards behind their homes. The nails were shaped out of metal rod using an oliver, a small hammer, worked by a foot treadle. A typical house and workshop complex can be seen at the Black Country Museum at Dudley, West Midlands. Chain making was

Wortley Top Forge, South Yorkshire. At the end of its working life, axles for the railways were forged here. An axle can be seen in place on the grooved anvil.

also a job that went to the smaller workshops in the region. Here metal rod was heated, bent into a U shape and then, after reheating, the two ends of the U were flattened and bent round to lie one on top of the other and welded together. Again the hammer was worked by a treadle, but this was larger than the oliver and was known as a tommy. A complete Black Country chain works can be seen re-erected at the Avoncroft Museum of Buildings, Hereford and Worcester.

Not far from Avoncroft is Redditch, the centre for the needle-making industry. The Forge Mill at Redditch is a typical, small, water-powered needle factory, and very charming it looks too with its old water wheels and millpond. Inside, the effect is somewhat different. The starting point for manufacture was steel wire, which first had to be cleaned of its heavy scale. The wire was packed into wooden boxes filled with stones, which were then rocked backwards and forwards by gearing from the wheel shaft. The wire was given a fine polish in rotating wooden barrels packed with pebbles. Then the needles were pointed on grindstones, and even the Sheffield grinders fared better than the men of Redditch. Lung disease was inseparable from the job. The rooms were cramped and unventilated and Dr G. Calvert Holland who wrote a book on the disease in 1843 reported that the casual visitor found breathing all but impossible in the Redditch works.

Iron was by no means the only metal to find considerable use in British industry. In Chapter 2 we looked at some of the other metals mined in Britain, and all found wide and varied applications. Lead, for example, which has been mined in Britain for at least two thousand years, was widely employed in the building industry and its processing has left us with some spectacular monuments. As with many ores, the raw material has to be crushed before treatment, and at the Killhope Lead Mine in Weardale, Co. Durham, this was done by rollers. The rollers have long gone, but the building with its impressive 34-foot diameter water wheel remains, solitary but splendid, in its moorland setting. Such settings are, indeed, common in the lead industry, where it was generally felt to be better to take the processing plant to the ore rather than incur the high transport costs of carrying the ore for large distances. So we find the smelters spread out along the long spine of the Pennines, the major source of lead, and many of the remains are as spectacular as those of Killhope.

In the smelting process, lead was sublimed. Ore was heated in a furnace, the vapours from which passed through long flues, where the lead would condense. In the early furnaces, much of the valuable metal was simply deposited all round the smelting works and was lost. It was a particularly dangerous form of industrial pollution for all plant life died where the vapours settled. Early industrialists were not especially noted for their commitment to conservationist causes, but they were decidedly cost conscious and spreading good, expensive lead around the country-side was not only unsafe but unprofitable as well. Flues were built ever

RIGHT *The magnificent Piece Hall, Halifax, West Yorkshire. The Hall was built in 1775 as a cloth market and is a clear reflection of the prosperity that was brought to the north by the textile industry.*

BELOW RIGHT *Cotton workers' tenements, New Lanark, Strathclyde, part of the village that David Dale built in the 1780s for the workers at his mill.*

Nineteenth-century woollen mills: Sowerby Bridge, West Yorkshire. These are typical of the multi-storey textile mills which were the first of many types of building resulting from the Industrial Revolution to make an impact on the British landscape.

A vertical steam-blowing engine which supplied the blast of air to the iron furnaces at Blists Hill Open Air Museum, Shropshire.

RIGHT *Nineteenth-century lead flues at Grassington in North Yorkshire: the lead was scraped off the flue walls by hand.*

The foundry of the Welsh Slate Museum, Gwynedd: note the wooden patterns on the right from which machine parts were cast.

longer, as much as two miles long, and they ended in tall chimneys, which often survive in lonely grandeur among the bracken and gorse of the high moorland. The most spectacular of such sites is at Grassington in North Yorkshire, where flues lead away from the smelters for almost a mile to a sixty-foot high chimney. Although the surroundings were no longer polluted, this was little comfort to the men who had the task of scraping the lead off the inside of the flues.

Ore smelters are generally situated where both ore and fuel are

The smelt mill chimney of a lead mine high on the Grassington Moors, North Yorkshire. It would have been connected to the smelter by long flues (as shown in the previous illustration) in which the lead was recovered.

readily available. The tin and copper mines of Cornwall were, therefore, at something of a disadvantage: they had the ore, but no fuel. In an age when water transport was far cheaper than overland transport, West Country industrialists looked across the sea to South Wales, with its rich coalfields. There were a few attempts to establish smelters in the south-west, but on the whole it proved more economical to take the ore to the fuel rather than the fuel to the ore. The remains of the earliest smelters are rare, but by the picturesque Aberdulais Falls (NT) in West Glamorgan the foundations of a copper smelter can still be seen. It was established here in the 1580s, when a German expert arrived to set up the works, his fare having been paid by Queen Elizabeth I. Before that date ore had been exported for smelting, but now a new industry was developed which spread rapidly through the region. It grew into a major industry, but with the decline of copper mining in Cornwall during the twentieth century the smelting industry declined as well, and there are few reminders of an industrial past that once dominated areas such as Swansea. Even Aberdulais has little to show for three centuries of work.

The other important raw material to be imported from the south-west into Wales was tin and this, too, led to the foundation of a new industrial complex, devoted to tin plating. The idea of tin plating is an old one, but it was during the nineteenth century that the tin can, using tin and steel together, came into its own. The technique was devised to get the best of two worlds, combining the strength of steel with the corrosion-resisting properties of tin. Coat a thin sheet of steel with tin and you have a material which can be roughly handled with little fear of damage, material absolutely ideal for making into containers for food. It was, and is, used extensively for just that purpose. Remains of the tinplate industry are few, usually incorporated into later developments. The techniques used involved the production of even, thin sheets of iron or steel, followed by immersion in molten tin to provide the plating. This bare description makes the process sound very simple, but it was in reality far more complex, involving repeated cleaning and treatment of the metal surfaces. One important site has been preserved – the Melingriffith Tinplate Works, north of Cardiff, in South Glamorgan. Here also is a water-powered pump, installed both to supply water for the works and for the adjoining Glamorgan Canal.

Copper, too, was used in combination with other metals, notably with zinc in the manufacture of brass. Brass and copper works were established in Bristol and the Avon valley to take advantage of West of England copper and local deposits of calamine, a zinc carbonate. Any journey up the Avon from Bristol brings many reminders of this once important industry. At Swineford there are substantial remains of the old copper works, complete with two undershot water wheels, while at Kelston there are two prominent annealing ovens, tall pyramids where the copper and zinc were heated. The water courses also survive here, and tracing them reveals that there were once as many as six water wheels on the site, powering a variety of machines for cutting, slitting and shaping the brass. As with iron, brass can be worked in this way or melted and run into moulds for castings.

Further up the Avon at Bath were the works of J.B. Bowler, brass founder, general engineer and mineral water manufacturer. The works were established in 1872 and continued operating until 1969. The entire contents of the workshops and offices were then removed and reinstated, precisely as they had been left, in a new museum, the Museum of Bath at Work, housed in a building originally used as a real tennis court. It is a fascinating spot, not only for what it tells us about the work of the brass founder, but for what it says about engineering and working with metals as a whole. The general engineering department has a wealth of old machines – often of uncertain age since Bowler always bought second hand. It contains drills, lathes, milling machines and shapers, all driven by belts from line-shafting. Originally power came from a gas engine. The brass foundry is also a complete workshop complex, similar in many ways to a small iron foundry. Here there is a pattern-making shop, where the object to be cast was first made in wood. The furnace itself is a pit furnace, in which brass was melted in crucibles, rather as at Abbeydale, before being poured into the moulding boxes. After casting, the moulds were allowed to cool overnight, ready for the fettler who came in at four o'clock the next morning to trim the castings by hand. He was also required to collect up all the trimmings after he had finished so that they could be melted down ready for the next job. Not the least of the appeals of Bowler's works is that it carries the visitor back to a former age of engineering craftsmanship that depended on individual skills and labour.

One other important site in the Avon valley is Saltford Mill, currently undergoing restoration. It has a single annealing oven and a surrounding workshop complex. There is substantial evidence to suggest that the original appeal of the site was the availability of river transport, for there is a considerable and well developed wharf area. At first, raw materials all came in by water and finished goods went out the same way, but in time this method of transport proved inadequate. A crudely carved inscription on a wall records that in 1836 they began 'Diggin' The Rail Road Juncn', a reference to the extension of the Avon and Gloucestershire Railway to the Keynsham wharf. It is a reminder that, ultimately, all industrial development is dependent on accessibility. Transport facilities were, and are, vital. Industrial expansion could never have occurred unless goods could be moved easily and, just as importantly, cheaply. In a very real sense, the story of increased industrial efficiency is also the story of increased transport efficiency.

5 On the Road

The story of road transport is concerned with both the construction of the way itself, the civil engineering aspect, and also the vehicles that use the road, the mechanical engineering. The former presents particular problems, for while an old vehicle may be preserved much as it was when first used, the roads are changing all the time. A new road may follow the route of an old in a general way, but might be greatly altered in detail: the surface will be altogether different, curves might have been smoothed out and old structures might have been replaced by new. Moreover, unlike waterways and railways, there is no road conservation movement in the sense of preserving a stretch of road as being of special importance. And, indeed, with a very few exceptions, there is no reason why such a movement should exist. Equally, it is very rare to find roads being given any great prominence in museum projects, a noteworthy exception being the Chalk Pits Museum at Amberley in West Sussex, where different types of road surface have been reconstructed and where there are extensive plans for showing different aspects of road engineering. But anyone wanting to trace the history of roads on the ground, in a literal sense, faces many problems. Some structures, notably bridges, survive for a very long time, but elsewhere the evidence is scant.

The tracing of ancient trackways presents a special challenge since no satisfactory way of dating the great majority of such tracks has yet been found. It used to be thought that the existence of many of these tracks could be deduced from the presence of prehistoric remains and settlements along the route. But now new archaeological evidence is indicating the existence of far more settlements – and far more widely scattered settlements – than at one time seemed possible. With comparatively dense settlement, the old, simple lines can no longer be drawn. Nevertheless, in many cases there is a strong tradition supporting the existence of long-distance tracks, such as the Jurassic Way, running from the Bristol Avon to the Humber. But what is meant by describing something as 'an ancient trackway'? Was it in fact anything more than a well-used route? Were any attempts made to provide a surface or markings? Was it a road as we understand it today or a route followed by animals, spread out as a broad, perhaps indistinct, trodden way? There is no immediate answer available. There is, however, one part of the country where early man has left direct evidence of genuine road making.

An excavated track of brushwood hurdles constructed across the boggy ground of Walton Heath, Somerset, c. 3000 BC.

The area immediately to the north of the Polden Hills in Somerset is a region of mainly peat marsh, dotted with small islands of firm ground. This was an area of Neolithic settlement, and in order to cross the marshy land special causeways were built here as early as 3000 BC. There are two types of track. In one, brushwood hurdles were constructed and laid down on the boggy ground, after which they were pegged securely into place. In the second and later type, a firm surface of split logs was provided, these planks again being held in place by long wooden pegs. Many miles of such wooden trackway were produced and represented an immense labour, since each mile of track required many miles of timber.

Not much other evidence exists of ancient road making, and what there is suggests that road building as such could scarcely be said to have existed at all, except in such difficult areas as that described in Somerset where special circumstances demanded special measures. The one other area where direct evidence might be expected is in bridge building, but here the evidence, if evidence it be, is difficult to interpret. The simplest form of bridge to survive is the clapper bridge, which consists of nothing more than piles of stones with stone slabs laid on top of them. A particularly fine example can be seen on Exmoor in Somerset, where the River Barle is crossed by a 180-foot long bridge, built in just this way, with the stone slabs each measuring about 7 foot by 4 foot. Because the techniques are so simple and even crude, it is tempting to think of this as a very ancient bridge, but there is absolutely no evidence to support that assumption. Indeed, such little evidence as does exist suggests a medieval or possibly even later date. But if the very distant past presents us with more questions than answers, then we do at least have a great body of evidence to inform us on the work of the first great period of civil engineering in Britain, the years of the Roman occupation.

Ask anyone to name one thing they know about Roman roads and the chances are that they will tell you that they were straight. And they would be quite correct, for the main roads can still be traced

The simple clapper bridge: Tarr Steps across the River Barle on Exmoor, Somerset. The primitive construction suggests an early date, but there is no evidence to say precisely when it was built.

heading directly across country from point to point, regardless of
what lay between. The names have survived – Akeman Street,
Watling Street and the rest – and so, too, have the lines of the roads,
showing an incredible continuity of use stretching back almost two
thousand years. Sometimes, if you look at a modern road atlas, the
line seems to falter or even vanish, but turn to the 1:50,000 OS map
and it soon re-emerges. Akeman Street, for example, runs a little to the
north of the Oxfordshire village where I live, and in the course of a few
miles its modern character changes quite dramatically. Approaching
Bicester from the east it is the modern A41, but then it meets the old
Roman town of Alchester and the new road swings north. The Roman

*The unmistakable straight
lines of the Roman road: Fosse
Way, a major road that
traversed Britain from south-
west to north-east. This
section is west of Castle Cary
in Somerset.*

Wade's Causeway, a Roman military road across the North Yorkshire moors. The 'agger', the raised bank that typified Roman road construction, can be clearly seen.

road continues on, however, first as a minor road and then, when it seems to peter out, as footpaths and bridleways, until it again re-emerges as a recognizable road.

Walking the road tells us something, but not a great deal, about Roman engineering techniques. In other parts of the country we are more fortunate. Because most Roman roads formed links between major centres of population, their importance remained through the centuries and they have been repeatedly modernized, but the Romans also built roads connecting frontier posts in wild, remote country where all traces of the original road have not been obliterated. Here there is a great deal to be seen, including evidence that the Romans were not limited to those famous straight lines. At Hardknott Pass in the Lake District the road can be traced snaking down in a series of hairpin bends from the ruins of the old fort. But perhaps the most exciting spots are those where something of the road itself has been preserved, and the finest example of all is the road known as Wade's Causeway on the moors above Goathland in North Yorkshire.

The road was almost certainly built for military purposes as part of the campaign to subdue the Brigantes. It was not, therefore, part of one of the great arterial routes, but had considerable importance in its day – in modern terms, an A road rather than a motorway. It linked the more isolated Roman outposts to the main camp at Derventis, modern Malton. It was probably built around AD 80, but once its military role had ended its entire importance disappeared as well, for there could be no other reason to maintain an expensive road across the North Yorkshire moors. This has proved fortunate, for the road was well constructed and with no one to disturb it a good deal has survived the centuries.

The road itself follows a high-level route, keeping well clear of the boggy land in the valleys. It keeps to the true Roman line in spite of the very hilly landscape. This makes for some steep gradients, but as it was intended for use by soldiers, carrying their equipment themselves or on pack animals, this was no great problem. Other characteristics become evident as soon as the road is examined in more detail. The first essential for a military road is that it must be usable under all conditions, if the army was not to become literally bogged down. So it needed a good surface and adequate drainage. Wade's Causeway was built on the same principle as the major roads, using the agger, an embankment built to raise the road surface above the surrounding land. Aggers varied both in height and width, and here the agger can be seen as a bank some twenty foot in width. The hill streams running down the moor are still carried through beautifully constructed stone-lined culverts that pierce the agger.

A typically narrow and high-arched pack-horse bridge at Allerford in Somerset (NT).

The top of the agger was covered by paving slabs (setts), up to five inches thick, and this metalled surface may have had a further covering of gravel, though this has long since disappeared. The sides of the roadway were marked with vertical kerb stones, many of which still remain in place. Anyone walking the length of the causeway today is inevitably impressed by the quality of construction, and can hardly help wondering what the main roads must have been like when a comparatively minor military road was built to such a standard. What is perhaps most remarkable of all is that this represented a standard of road building which was not to be reached again for the best part of two millennia. Of the other major activity, bridge building, few traces remain. But we know from elsewhere in Europe that the Romans were competent, constructing their bridges on simple, semicircular arches.

As the Romans withdrew, so decay set in and the old road system began to decline. If we pick up the story again in medieval times, we find a quite different pattern of road transport. The metalled roads used by the Roman armies and the chariots of their leaders had gone, and in general the age of the tracks had returned. Bulk transport on the road depended more and more on the pack horse. Long trains of animals would set off, goods carried in panniers slung over their backs. As with the Roman pack animals, steep gradients were no great obstacle, so the roads frequently followed the dry, high-level routes, dipping down sharply for a river crossing. It is in these dips downwards that the characteristics of these routes can now be most clearly seen. The narrow road sweeps down the hill to cross river or stream on a narrow, high-arched bridge, which either had a very low parapet to provide clearance for the panniers or no parapet at all. Many pack-horse bridges can still be seen today, a particularly fine example being Holme Bridge near the A6 at Bakewell, one of the longest in the country.

The other major feature of medieval life was the driving of animals to market – cattle, sheep, poultry and fowl were all driven in vast herds and flocks. The drove roads that they used were similar in many ways to the prehistoric tracks, routes worn by regular usage which today are scarcely recognizable. Sometimes the only indication of a former track is a pub on a lonely hillside, with a sign announcing it as the 'Drover's Arms'. The droves continued right into the present century, ended not by road improvement but by the railways. The distances travelled were often immense, and the beasts had to be shod for the journey – even the geese were given protection, their feet being dipped into tar and then pressed on to fine gravel to provide stony shoes for the long march. As the animals moved so they trampled out a broad path, no road works were necessary along the way and rivers were crossed at fords, not by bridges. True road improvement had to wait for a time when carts and carriages became more widespread. Even in medieval times, however, there were vehicles out on the highway, and that meant that bridges needed to be built to carry them across the rivers.

Britain has a remarkably large number of medieval bridges, mainly because the peculiar organization of society made them necessary. William the Conqueror rewarded his supporters with land grants, but was very well aware that noblemen with large land holdings were potential rivals. So, being a canny politician, when he handed over the land he gave it not as one huge chunk, but parcelled it out over a large area. As a result, the new landlords were forced to provide connecting links between the different parts of their holdings and this frequently involved the construction of bridges. Typically, these had high, pointed arches with narrow spans between the piers, a structure in which the stresses were comparatively slight – one reason why so many have lasted so long. The narrow spans made life simple for the bridge builder, but were a confounded nuisance to river users. The old London Bridge was a notorious obstacle to boatmen on the Thames. That bridge has long since disappeared, and no early bridge of quite that type, with shops and houses crowded on top of the structure, has survived. There are a number of long bridges such as that at Bideford in Devon which has no fewer than twenty-four arches in its 667-foot length. Other early bridges of note include the fourteenth-century Trinity Bridge, which was built on a triangulated plan to cross three streams at Crowland in Lincolnshire, and the fortified bridge at Monmouth in Gwent, which acted as both a river crossing and a fortified entrance to the town.

The craftsmanship of early bridges is often of a very high order, establishing many of the techniques and features which were to be

The fourteenth-century Trinity Bridge at Crowland, Lincolnshire, which once crossed three streams but now stands high and dry.

used by bridge builders for many centuries. At water level, you can see the piers pointed to face the current. These are known as cutwaters and ease the flow of water round the piers, minimizing damage to the stonework. The shape of the arches owed a good deal to the design of wooden bridges. It seems likely that these once outnumbered stone and brick bridges but, being less durable, the old wooden bridges have long since decayed. Nevertheless, wood would have played an important part in the construction of bridges that have survived for the arches would have been built over a wooden framework which was later removed.

Fine as they are, medieval and renaissance bridges show little technical improvement over Roman structures, and the study of the roadways themselves suggests a very definite deterioration in standards. The grandly rolling phrase 'The King's Highway' too often meant in practice an ill-defined trackway of cloying mud and clay. Everyone, it seems, grumbled about the state of the roads, but no one did very much about them. The problem was not so much technical as legislative. Responsibility for the roads rested with local parishes, a system that sounded fine in theory. A surveyor of roads was appointed and empowered to call up every able-bodied male parishioner to put in six days work a year. The rich quite simply bought their way out of the system, while the poorer parishioners regarded the six days as a bit of a holiday, when half an hour's stone breaking was considered a good enough excuse for several hours drinking.

So the roads deteriorated and the highways spread, in a quite literal sense. As the middle of a road became boggy, so travellers simply moved to the dry bit on the edge, and as that was churned up so they moved further out again. This was all very well as long as transport was mainly on foot and horseback, with the occasional broad-wheeled cart or simple sledge, but became increasingly less suitable as vehicles became more sophisticated. What had proved adequate for a horse-drawn sledge was totally inadequate for a narrow-wheeled carriage. Until the sixteenth century the rich had been carried around in litters, either borne by servants or slung between horses. In 1555, however, the Duke of Rutland was reported as riding in a wheeled carriage; thirty years later, Queen Elizabeth I gave the royal seal of approval to the newfangled machines. By the middle of the seventeenth century, comfort was greatly increased by the introduction of springs. But all these improvements meant very little without decent roads, roads that would not disintegrate with regular use.

At first, the answer was thought to lie with more legislation. Laws were passed limiting the loads that could be carried, and a whole series of Acts appeared stipulating the use of broad wheels rather than narrow, to limit the damage to road surfaces. Such laws were treated with scant regard, and roads continued to deteriorate, largely because no one in authority had any very pressing need to do much about them. That all changed with the Jacobite rising of 1715. As the

English army trudged slowly up to Scotland, the English officers found they were spending an uncomfortably long time marching alongside the men while their carriages were dug out of the mud. The generals learned the lesson well known to the Romans: an army is only as good as its lines of communication. The first modern road-building programme in Britain was put in hand by General Wade, whose military roads still thread the Highlands. Between 1726 and 1737, troops under Wade's command built some 250 miles of road and numerous bridges. Whatever the Scots' view of the invading English, they could at least take some comfort from the fact that what Wade built he built well. The finest example of his work is undoubtedly the four-arched bridge at Aberfeldy in Tayside, completed in 1733. Not content with the plain, simple structure that might be expected from a military man, Wade brought in the architect William Adam, and the results of his artistry are there for all to see. Perhaps Wade was aware that as long as the bridge stood the name of General Wade would not be forgotten.

Wade's roads were a response to a particular set of conditions, but as the eighteenth century advanced, so new circumstances began to appear demanding more general measures. The increased trade generated by the Industrial Revolution put ever greater stress on the

Road builders at work, from William Pyne, The Microcosm, 1806. Piles of stone setts which would eventually form the road surface can be seen.

old road system, while at the same time a burgeoning commercial life demanded better and faster communications. Improvement proceeded on two fronts: better roads were constructed, and better vehicles were built to use them. It was something of a chicken and egg situation: why build better roads if the traffic was not there to use them, but then, why bother to build improved vehicles that had no decent roads to travel on? Progress was, therefore, decidedly slow, though it would seem that the greatest barrier to progress, literally and metaphorically, was the state of the roads.

Until well into the eighteenth century, road repair was still organized on the old basis of six statutory days of labour, and road construction was non-existent, apart from the military roads. Horrific tales were recounted of the state of the roads, with carts sinking up to their axles in mud and pot holes so deep that deaths by drowning were reported in the middle of the King's Highway! Many of the more outrageous tales were no doubt put about by those with a vested interest in road improvement, but there must have been a basis of truth. Government attempts at legislating good roads into existence by limiting vehicle specifications continued to appear, and continued to be either ignored or circumvented. Waggons were built with wide wheels as required, but with a pronounced curve to the rim so that only a small area came into contact with the ground. Judging by the number of pamphlets issued during the early years of the century, there was a steadily growing public demand for improved roads with better surfaces.

The main obstacle to road improvement was money – who was to pay for the work involved? One solution was to make the road users pay. This was no new notion. The earliest records, for example, date back to the thirteenth century, when Edward I granted rights of pontage, empowering locals at Huntingdon to collect tolls from users of the new bridge, while physical evidence of this system can be seen in the toll house on the medieval bridge at Baslow in Derbyshire. Similarly, pavage rights were granted for toll collection for road upkeep, but it was in the eighteenth century that the idea was developed and adapted with the establishment of a whole new road system through Turnpike Trusts. Local bodies were formed to raise money for road construction, after which they would petition Parliament for an Act that would empower them to go ahead and build the road and recoup their investment by charging tolls. The first Turnpike Act was passed in the seventeenth century and covered part of the Great North Road, but here it was the local justices who were empowered to collect the tolls and it was not until the beginning of the eighteenth century that the first Turnpike Trusts proper came into being. At last Britain was to enter a period of real road improvement, thanks largely to finance being made available by the Trusts and to the work of three brilliant engineers, Metcalf, Telford and McAdam.

The first of the three was the most remarkable, for John Metcalf was blind. Yet, in spite of his handicap, 'Blind Jack' was responsible for building up a new, improved road system throughout the West Riding of Yorkshire in the 1750s and 1760s. He placed the highest priority on good surveying techniques to establish the line for the road, and on providing adequate drainage. The lack of good drainage had been the curse of British roads for centuries; Metcalf built up his roads on a solid foundation, giving them a smooth, convex surface with deep drainage ditches on either side. The surveying instruments used by this remarkable man can be seen in the Castle Museum in his native Knaresborough.

Thomas Telford's influence stretched far beyond that of Metcalf. He built roads throughout the country, many of which are still in use today, and he built some exceptionally fine bridges. His road-building career began when he was appointed county surveyor to Shropshire in 1786, though his finest achievements are to be seen in Wales and his native Scotland. In 1801, he was asked by the government to investigate the state of communications in Scotland, and as a result of his findings work began on a major road-building programme under Telford's supervision. Between 1803 and 1820 he was responsible for the construction of over 900 miles of road and more than a thousand bridges. The bridges, such as Craigellachie Bridge over the Spey, are the most spectacular features, but the importance and difficulty of road construction alone in the bleak and desolate regions of the Highlands should not be minimized.

In the 1820s, Telford was given a major assignment – to improve the main road from London to Holyhead. He was not content, as earlier road builders had often been, merely to improve the surface of existing routes. He set out bold new routes, many of which remain in use today. The most striking section passes through the mountains of Snowdonia where, by careful surveying, Telford negotiated the mountain passes without ever imposing a gradient greater than 1 in 22.

One of Telford's toll houses and Holyhead road milestone re-erected at the Blists Hill Open Air Museum, Shropshire. The individuality of milestones is a reminder that roads were not always the responsibility of the State.

The road surface he supplied for the new roads was intended to last. He used carefully graded stones to build up a solid foundation, which was then topped with gravel. A Telford-type road has been reconstructed at the Blists Hill Open Air Museum at Ironbridge in Shropshire together with one of the toll houses that originally stood on the Holyhead road and its toll gate. The toll gates or turnpikes marked the different staging points along the way, and to pass through the traveller had to pay the toll keeper. The house has a distinctive bay, jutting out towards the road and providing a view in both directions, and it carried a board setting out the charges for different types of traveller. The arrival of the turnpike was not universally popular, and there were many who resented having to pay to go where they had travelled free before. The new roads might be of great advantage to the gentleman in his carriage, but were not so obviously an improvement for the labourer and his cart. There were sporadic outbreaks of rioting in different parts of the country in which toll houses were attacked and gates and turnpikes destroyed.

The Telford road was undoubtedly very fine, but was extremely expensive to build. A cheaper and perfectly adequate alternative was provided by John Loudon McAdam who demonstrated that Telford's stone foundation was unnecessary. He followed Telford's lead in using graded stones for the road itself – none were to exceed six ounces in weight – but he argued that the stones would compact together with use to form a solid, impervious surface. He put down a six-inch layer of stones and then, when that had settled into place, laid another six inches on top. Eventually the road compacted to a thickness of around ten inches. This was the McAdam road, not to be confused with the familiar tarmacadam road of later years. The combination of durability and cheapness was recommendation enough for the Turnpike Trusts, and the McAdam system came into very general use. McAdam himself was in constant demand. Writing in 1814, he calculated that he had travelled thirty thousand miles, inspecting and advising on road works.

Together with this improvement in road construction, the eighteenth century also saw a revolution in bridge-building techniques. By this date, stone bridges were built mainly on semicircular arches or, less frequently, on segmented arches, that is arches which take the shape of a segment of a circle. Arches were still built comparatively narrow and, although there had been improvements in the construction of foundations over the centuries, notably in dredging the river bed, there had been few major advances in bridge design since medieval times. One notable bridge could be said to have inaugurated a new age. It was built at Pontypridd, Mid Glamorgan, and opened in 1756. Its designer, William Edwards, had little or no previous experience, his normal occupation being that of farming to which he added the role of minister of religion. This lack of experience no doubt goes some way towards explaining the complete failure of his first three attempts

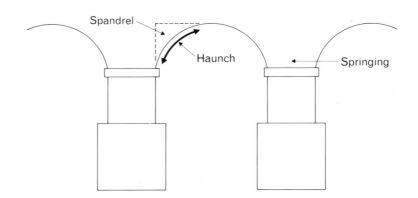

The parts of a bridge.

at Pontypridd. His fourth bridge had a single span of 140 foot, and by then he had tracked down the problems which had beset the earlier versions and come up with a solution. The difficulty had been that the haunches at the side of the arch had been too massive and had collapsed inwards under their own weight, so he lightened the load by piercing the spandrels with cylindrical holes. These reduced the weight of the arch and it was discovered, paradoxically it seemed, that the holes ringed by masonry keyed into the main structure actually increased its firmness. That fourth bridge stands to this day, though it is no longer, as it was for many years, the longest span in the world.

Some twenty years after the opening of the Pontypridd bridge, another structure was completed of far more revolutionary design. The 1770s saw work going forward on the world's first iron bridge, the parts for which were cast at the Darby works in Coalbrookdale, Shropshire. It is now rightly regarded as not just one of Britain's but as one of the world's most important industrial monuments, for it marked the beginning of a new age of construction in iron and steel. Yet, in itself, it presents something of a paradox. It is a bold enough structure, crossing the Severn in a single arch, but in its details it looks backwards all the way to medieval practices. The iron members of the bridge were treated as though they were baulks of timber, and were fitted together using mortice and dovetail joints, made firm by wedges. There is, however, a passing stylistic reference to Pontypridd in the iron rings simulating Edwards' pierced spandrels. Other engineers soon went on to develop iron bridge-building techniques that were rather more appropriate for the material, and among the early masters was Thomas Telford, who learned his craft among the iron makers of Shropshire. Two bridges, in particular, might be selected to demonstrate his skills, the Waterloo Bridge at Betws-y-Coed, built as its inscription announces in the year the battle was fought, and the Craigellachie Bridge over the Spey, completed in 1814.

Bridges are among the more obvious survivors of the turnpike age, but by no means the only ones. Toll houses are still common, and a few still retain their old boards with their lists of tolls payable. There are reminders, too, that the Trusts were established under Acts of

Parliament, and that those Acts laid down a number of rules, including the requirement that milestones and signposts should be erected along the way. The signposts have mostly gone, but milestones survive in happy profusion, for each Trust had its own notions of design. There are stones and iron posts, plain markers and elaborately carved wayside monuments. They still provide firm evidence that roads which now seem to be no more than extensions, one of the other, were once individually owned and individually marked.

The improved roads brought more traffic, and more traffic created a demand for yet more road improvements: a state of affairs which continues to the present day. Demands for improvement, coupled with increasing constraints on navigable rivers, stimulated new ideas in bridge construction. The need became apparent for something other than the arch to carry the roadway for there was a limit to the width of the single arch beyond which it simply collapsed under its own weight. The answer was found in the suspension bridge. This solution was possible thanks to improved methods of chain making, originally initiated in the navy by Captain Samuel Brown. He realized that the new chains made suspension bridges possible, and built his first such bridge across the Tweed at Kelso in Scotland. That no longer exists, but his second bridge across the river at Berwick, Northumberland, does. The Union Chain Bridge, completed in 1820, is the oldest such bridge to survive, and very impressive it is too, with a span of 361 foot. Brown's lead was soon followed by other engineers, with Telford again proving an enthusiast for new ideas.

Telford was faced with precisely the sort of problem for which the suspension bridge was well suited. He had to carry his Holyhead road across the Menai Straits, with the extra difficulty that the Admiralty demanded that the Straits be kept clear for navigation. His answer was the suspension bridge that is still in use today. The 580-foot long deck is a full 100 feet above the water, to allow tall ships to pass underneath. It was originally suspended from sixteen massive chains, but these were replaced by the present steel chains in the 1940s. Telford built a second fine suspension bridge at Conwy (NT) and the two together can be counted among his greatest works. But most people would argue that the best of all Britain's suspension bridges is that across the Avon gorge at Clifton.

The story of the Clifton Bridge is quite remarkable but, alas, too long to recount in detail in these pages. In brief, there was a competition for the best design and no one who saw the entries had any doubt that the most elegant solution was that proposed by a young engineer, Isambard Kingdom Brunel. The Committee, understandably nervous at giving a major project to a very young man, passed the designs over to the Grand Old Man, Telford. Telford, in his turn, declared the design impractical and produced his own version which, it must be said, was both hideously ugly and quite unnecessarily complex. The Committee bowed down before the old engineer's reputation and

Brunel's great Clifton suspension bridge, Avon, under construction. Although work began in 1836, it was not opened until 1864.

handed him the job. Public opinion would have none of it, and the Committee were forced to do another smart about face and give the work back to Brunel. Telford's design had consisted of two Gothic towers rising up from the foot of the gorge, while Brunel's was, by comparison, a masterpiece of lightness and grace, with the platform hung from towers on the rim of the gorge. Unhappily, money ran out during construction and Brunel never lived to see his great design realized. It was finished in 1864, almost thirty years after the piers were completed. It still seems in its dramatic setting as impressive as it must have done a century ago.

The suspension bridge served admirably to lift roadways clear of shipping on the river beneath. An alternative to building such a huge structure was to make a bridge that moved. Small-scale wooden bridges, which could be moved by hand, were common enough across Britain's rivers and canals, but to make a movable bridge across a major river was rather more of a problem. Some form of mechanism would be needed to supply the power, and the most popular development was the hydraulic bridge. One of the great pioneers of hydraulic power was Sir William Armstrong, who designed his first hydraulic crane in 1846. He established a factory at Elswick, Tyne and Wear, in 1847, which was to grow over the years and is now the home of the famous engineering firm of Vickers Armstrong. In 1868, work began on a new road bridge across the Tyne, which would pivot on a central island so as to provide a clear lane for shipping. The essence of Armstrong's machinery was the use of steam power continuously to pump water upwards, thus producing a column of water which could be allowed to fall when needed to power the plant, in this case the engine that actually moved the bridge. The bridge is still there, and although the steam engine has been replaced by electric pumps, the original Armstrong hydraulic engine is in full working order.

But the most famous of all applications of the hydraulic engine to moving the road platform of a bridge must be the lifting bridge across the Thames, Tower Bridge. The bascules weigh a thousand tons, and are moved by Armstrong engines. It was completed in 1894, but is perhaps less famous for its engineering, the work of Sir John Wolfe-Barry, than for its appearance, the responsibility for which lies with the architect, Horace Jones. Whether one likes this massive exercise in mock medievalry or not, it has become such a well-known part of the London scene that we should all be sad to see it go. It is an amazing sight – and an amazing example of Victorian engineering.

The great expansion of road and bridge building at the end of the eighteenth and the beginning of the nineteenth centuries had an immense impact on road travel. The smoother surfaces meant smoother rides and faster times, and one very important effect was a general improvement in the speed of communication brought about by the introduction of the mail-coach service. The first coach commissioned for the carriage of the Royal Mails ran in 1784, covering the 117 miles from London to Bristol in seventeen hours. By the end of the century there were eighty coaches leaving London daily for different parts of the country. The journeys were made in stages, with stops at the different coaching inns for a change of horses, for when out on the road the coaches never slackened pace. Where other road users were forced to pay tolls, the mail coaches passed straight through and, indeed, any toll keeper who failed to have the gate open and ready for the mails would have been liable for a hefty fine.

An aura of romanticism surrounds the mail coaches, but reality had little enough romance in it. A lucky few passengers had seats inside, but as many as fifteen rode on top and in winter they would stuff their clothing with straw to keep out the cold. Even that precaution was not always enough, and a case was recorded in 1812 when two passengers literally froze to death on the journey from Bath to Chippenham. That was a rare event, but spills and overthrows were common. The end of that era came in the 1850s, when mail-carrying finally passed from the coaches to the railways. It might have seemed the end of a glorious era to some, but was probably greeted with a sigh of relief by as many more. A few of these old coaches have survived in transport museums, together with their close relations, the private coaches and carriages.

Even in the heyday of the horsedrawn vehicle, other ideas were being tried out. Nicholas Cugnot, a French artillery officer, built a steam engine which he originally intended should be used for hauling cannon. It had a successful trial in 1769 in that it did actually work, but as there was no mechanism for refilling the boiler with water, it had a decidedly short range. Experiments with steam road vehicles soon followed in Britain, starting with William Murdock's steam carriage

Nineteenth-century carriages in the setting of a stable yard at Dodington House. In the foreground is a Park Drag, a four-in-hand driving coach; behind it is a smaller trap.

of 1784 and carried on enthusiastically by several engineers, including Richard Trevithick. Their ideas were not destined to find any immediate application on the highroads, for steam traction went instead to the new railways, effectively pushed off the roads by high toll charges. So the horsedrawn vehicle continued to dominate road travel until the end of the nineteenth century when steam returned through steam waggons, traction engines and agricultural engines. The traction engine is still with us, and is to be seen at many a steam fair throughout Britain, but they are comparatively rare. When development was finally permitted on the roads, the alternative form of power, the internal combustion engine, appeared at the same time and has dominated twentieth-century road travel.

The horsedrawn vehicle had a long life, but even as early as the eighteenth century it was generally recognized that it was unsuitable for moving bulky goods over long distances. The best that could be expected of a single horse pulling a stage waggon along one of the best of the new McAdamized roads was that it would shift a load of two tons. But that same horse set down on a towpath could haul a river barge carrying 30 tons, and on the still waters of a canal the possible load was even greater. The improvement in road transport in the years of the Industrial Revolution was of immense importance in speeding up the movement of people – and the movement of ideas. But when industrialists wanted to shift large quantities of basic raw materials such as coal, they turned not to the roads but to the waterways.

6 Goods by Water

The rivers of Britain have been used for navigation since prehistoric times – at least since the construction of Stonehenge, when the blue stones from the Prescelly Mountains were brought from South Wales. Rivers were used as trade routes and as routes of invasion, but they did not become a true part of the industrial scene until man began to tamper with the natural flow of water. The earliest controlled use of water was described in Chapter 1, when mill owners diverted rivers to provide water for the wheels of their mills. But the weir which permitted the build up of a good head of water was also an obstacle to navigation. To overcome that obstacle devices enabling the water-level to be adjusted were built, known variously as stanches, staunches, flash locks and navigation weirs. Whatever the name, the principle remained the same. A stout timber was laid horizontally in a gap in the weir and fixed to the river bed. Above this was a second movable timber, set above water-level, and joined to the lower by vertical planks or rimers. The rimers could be lifted out to allow water through and once the pressure of water was sufficiently reduced the whole structure could be swung open to allow boats to pass. Vessels travelling downstream shot through on the flood; those going upstream had to be winched through against the current. As mill owners were loath to lose their water supply, even temporarily, there was great reluctance to allow boats through and long delays resulted. There was also a certain danger in riding down on the flood, and sixty-four passengers were drowned when a boat overturned at Goring lock in 1634.

Remains of these old flash locks are scarce, but similar techniques were in use elsewhere. The system of using hand winches to haul boats against the current can be seen at West Stockwith, Nottinghamshire, where the Chesterfield Canal joins the fast-flowing Trent. Here they hauled big barges out of the river and into the canal. A device very similar to a flash lock can be seen at Thames lock at Weybridge, Surrey, on the Wey Navigation (NT). Downstream of the lock, a single gate stretches across the river, and can be used to raise the water-level in order to help deep-drafted vessels clear the bottom of the lock. The Wey Navigation itself is of considerable interest as it was built in the 1650s and was one of the first river navigation schemes.

Great improvements were made to navigation with the introduction, from Europe, of the mitre-gated pound lock in the 1560s. The first lock of this type was designed by Leonardo da Vinci for the Naviglio

A flash lock at Eynsham, Oxfordshire, on the River Thames; it remained in use until the 1930s.

Interno in 1497. This is, in essence, the familiar lock to be seen on Britain's rivers and canals today. It consists of a chamber which can be filled and emptied to enable vessels to pass between the higher river level and the lower. The chamber is closed by gates which meet at an angle, as in a mitre joint, the pressure of water against the gates helping to ensure a good, watertight fit. Water can be let in and out through sluices covered by movable paddles set either in the gate (gate paddles) or in the side of the lock (ground paddles). These new locks first appeared in Britain on the Exeter Canal in Devon, built in 1564–7, the forerunner of many similar navigations. In order to overcome the shoals and shallows of the River Exe, a parallel channel was cut and river water was diverted into it by the construction of weirs, just as water was diverted to fill the mill leat. The locks allowed the new canal to fall in a series of controlled steps, instead of in the haphazard manner of the natural river. The old locks have long since been

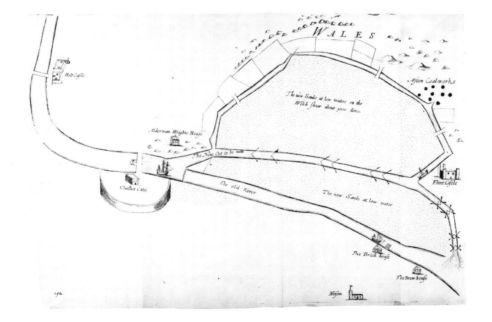

Plan of a scheme for improving the navigation of the River Dee; the new cutting with locks is clearly shown. From Andrew Yarranton, England's Improvements by Land and by Sea, *1677.*

replaced, but the effect of the canal in allowing ships to reach the heart of Exeter can be seen in the canal basin and the riverside quays, surrounded by warehouses and with a handsome Customs House, built in 1681. The area is now home to the Exeter Maritime Museum, which contains a splendid variety of vessels from all over the world.

River improvement continued throughout the seventeenth and on into the eighteenth century, and in some schemes it seemed that the natural river almost disappeared from sight, such was the extent of the artificial cuttings and locks. Some of the most impressive schemes took place in the north-east of England. In 1699, an Act was passed authorizing the construction of a waterway to join the rivers Aire and Calder. The Aire and Calder Navigation, as it was called, would link the industrial centres of Leeds and Wakefield to the Ouse and thus to the sea. Ten locks were built on the Aire and four on the Calder, each fifty-eight foot long and fifteen foot wide. The navigation is still very much in use, though the locks have been more than doubled in size to take a new generation of big, motorized barges. Their original size was determined by the size of the largest vessels most likely to use the new waterway, the sailing keels of the Humber. These were single masted, square rigged ships with a big mainsail and small topsail above that. One of these vessels, *Comrade*, has been restored and is regularly sailed by the Humber Keel and Sloop Preservation

The canal basin of the Exeter Canal, the first in Britain to be built with pound locks. The basin is now home to Exeter Maritime Museum.

Society. She is berthed among the more modern barges and lighters in the dock at Hull.

The success of the Aire and Calder scheme led to its extension by a second waterway, the Calder and Hebble, linking Wakefield to Sowerby Bridge, near Halifax. This was work on an immense scale. It was begun in the 1750s under the direction of John Smeaton, who took time off from his work on the Eddystone lighthouse. Twenty-six locks were built in twenty-four miles of navigation, but the unhappy Smeaton was to see virtually all his work destroyed in the great flood of October 1758. It was not until 1769 that work was restarted and the scheme pushed through to a satisfactory conclusion. Like the Aire and Calder, the Calder and Hebble is still in use, but in a somewhat different way, for it is now mostly given over to pleasure boating and the impressive warehouse complex at Sowerby Bridge no longer provides shelter for a busy cargo trade.

The Aire and Calder presents a quite different picture and, at its eastern terminus, the port of Goole shows ample evidence that the waterway continued to grow in importance throughout the nineteenth century. Great impetus was provided by the work of the Aire and

'Tom Puddings' being un-loaded at Goole, Humberside, on the Aire and Calder Navigation. The containers full of coal are lifted from the water and tipped into the ship's hold.

Calder engineer, W.H. Bartholomew, who, in 1862, introduced his 'Tom Puddings' to the waterway. They are more properly known as compartment boats and are in effect steel boxes, each capable of holding thirty-five tons of coal, which can be fastened together to form a train. The train is hauled by a tug, much as a locomotive would haul a train of freight waggons on the railway. Bartholomew also designed two hydraulic hoists at Goole which picked up individual compartments and emptied them into sea-going ships. The trains of Tom Puddings still run and the hoists still work a century later. They are not merely a link with the past but a reminder that the waterways still have a part to play in the commercial life of the nation. However, even before the Calder and Hebble was begun, engineers had begun work on a quite different type of waterway.

Early in the eighteenth century, numerous proposals were put forward in the hope of providing a new impetus for economic development in Ireland, and prominent among those schemes were suggestions for improved navigation. A few small-scale works were undertaken, but in 1729 Parliament approved an Act for a waterway to be built on a quite different principle from anything seen in the British Isles before. It was already clear that there was a limit to how far navigation could be extended by works on the upper reaches of rivers. Further extension would however be possible if a completely artificial channel could be cut across the watershed between two river systems, a summit level canal. And this is precisely what the Newry Canal was to be, linking the navigable river at Newry to Lough Neagh, and providing a route to the sea for the coal from the mines of Tyrone. It was opened in 1742 when a cargo of coal was sent from the lough, down the canal and on into Dublin. The canal is no longer in use but, as with the Exeter Canal, some measure of its former significance can be gauged from the eighteenth-century warehouses that line Merchants' Quay and Buttercrane Quay in Newry.

There are two important elements in the Newry story: the construction of a completely artificial waterway and the dependence on coal as a major cargo. Both were to prove important to new developments in mainland Britain. The chief engineer on the Newry Canal was Thomas Steers, and his assistant Henry Berry came across to England to work on another new waterway. In 1755 an Act was passed authorizing work to make the Sankey Brook navigable from St Helens, Merseyside, to the Mersey near Widnes, Cheshire. In effect this meant the construction of an entirely artificial canal, for the brook itself could scarcely take a rowing boat. It was, however, in the river navigation tradition insofar as it paralleled the brook and used it for water supply. In terms of engineering, it offered nothing new other than the introduction of the canal concept to that part of England. The idea was soon picked up and another scheme begun which contained some new technical features and, just as importantly, caught the public imagination.

In 1759, the young Duke of Bridgewater obtained an Act of Parliament authorizing him to construct a canal from his coal mines at Worsley into Manchester. He had originally considered a short cutting down to the River Irwell, but the Irwell Navigation Company set such outrageous terms for the use of the river that the plan had to be abandoned. So the Duke put up his own money for the new scheme, which involved building a broad, lock-free canal which would cross the Irwell on a stone aqueduct at Barton. It was a daring scheme, the planning for which was left to the Duke's agent, John Gilbert, and a Derbyshire millwright, James Brindley, who had shown his skill as a hydraulic engineer in a complex drainage scheme at the Wet Earth Colliery. The canal was duly built, and the Barton aqueduct carried the new venture across the Irwell. The sight of boats moving easily on the still waters of the canal set high above the labouring crews dragging barges against the river current had an immense impact on contemporary observers. Quite suddenly, it seemed, everyone was talking about canals. At a period of industrial expansion in general, the need for improved transport existed and here was a way to supply it. Moreover, the Duke of Bridgewater's canal had provided one particularly impressive argument in favour of the new mode of transport: thanks to his canal, the Duke was able to halve the price of coal in Manchester.

Looking at the Bridgewater Canal today, it is difficult to appreciate its importance. It emerges from the underground workings at Worsley, stained tomato soup red from the ore in the mines. It then proceeds to meander across country to Barton where it crosses the Irwell. But the old aqueduct has long gone. At the end of the nineteenth century the river was absorbed into the new Manchester Ship Canal and the stone aqueduct was destroyed to make way for a new marvel, the Barton swing aqueduct. The height of the old aqueduct was not great enough to allow passage of the big ships down the ship canal, so the engineer for the latter, Leader Williams, devised the present structure. The whole aqueduct, complete with trough full of water, pivots on a pillar set on a central island. But the old has not entirely vanished, for the abutments of the original aqueduct can still be seen beside the new.

Following the success of the Bridgewater Canal a number of new schemes were initiated, and James Brindley found himself in constant demand to act as consulting engineer. These canals, begun in the 1760s, all show the marks of his thinking. He favoured a method of construction known as contour cutting which involved designing canals to follow the natural contours of the land as far as possible, thus avoiding the necessity for large numbers of locks or extensive earthworks. This method can be seen at its most elaborate on the southern section of the Oxford Canal, particularly on the long summit length between Napton and Fenny Compton, Warwickshire. The canal sidles across the landscape in a series of extravagant twists and turns

until, at Wormleighton Hill, it seems determined to complete a circuit and turn itself into a moat. This meandering line meant frustrating delays for boatmen, and on one section there was a much repeated complaint that you could travel all day and still hear the same church clock strike the hours. This, though, was of less importance than another of Brindley's decisions: the decision that led him to set the size for the canal locks.

Brindley's first locks were constructed when the Bridgewater Canal was extended to the Mersey at Runcorn. Just as the Aire and Calder locks had been designed to accommodate the Humber keels, so these were built to take the trading vessels of the Mersey, the Mersey flats, and were constructed seventy-two foot long by fifteen foot wide. Brindley, who was not much given to listening to advice from others, wanted to build them of unbonded masonry, blocks held together by their own weight, even though Smeaton had already demonstrated the virtues of using hydraulic lime mortar, which held firm even under water, in his own work on the Calder and Hebble. In this instance Brindley gave way, and one suspects that John Gilbert had much to do with the settling of the argument. But Gilbert was not to be wooed away from the Bridgewater estate, and in his later schemes Brindley was very much his own master.

Far and away the most important of the new schemes to start up after the success of the Bridgewater Canal was that for a major waterway to link the rivers Trent and Mersey. The moving spirit during the anxious months when the plan was promoted was the celebrated potter Josiah Wedgwood, a man acutely aware of the need for bringing water transport to the land-locked Midlands. In surveying the line of the canal, Brindley found himself confronted with the high ridge of Harecastle Hill to the north of Stoke. It was too large even for one of Brindley's more extravagant circumnavigations, so he was faced with two alternatives: the first was to build locks to take the canal up one side of the hill and down the other, but water supply problems made this impractical; the second alternative was to burrow straight through the middle. This was the option Brindley selected, but it was by no means an easy option. Nothing of the sort had been attempted in Britain before, and once the decision to tunnel had been taken, other decisions followed from it.

The size of boats that can use a canal is determined by the physical limitations of the canal itself. If the locks were to be constructed to the same dimensions as those at Runcorn, then the tunnel would have needed to be of the same width or the wide boats would never have got through. This was a daunting prospect, and Brindley was already worried about the problems of ensuring there was sufficient water to fill the big locks. Which of these considerations was decisive there is now no means of knowing, but we do know that Brindley took the decision to build his locks to half the width of those at Runcorn and built his tunnel to the same dimensions. This meant that the largest

The two Harecastle tunnels on the Trent and Mersey Canal, Staffordshire. Telford's new tunnel, with a towpath on one side, is on the left; Brindley's original on the right.

boats using his canals would be slightly over seventy foot long and just over seven foot wide. And because Brindley was engaged in a series of interconnecting canal schemes in the English Midlands – the Oxford, the Staffordshire and Worcestershire, the Coventry and the Birmingham Canals – the same lock dimensions were used throughout this system. There was, after all, little point in building an integrated system unless the same boats could travel throughout the network. Once that decision had been taken and the standard set, the characteristic vessel of the English canals came into being – the narrow boat.

The narrow boat, approximately seventy foot long by seven foot beam, remains very much with us, not just preserved in museums such as the boat museum at Ellesmere Port, Cheshire, but still to be seen out on the water. Today, it is most likely to be powered by motor, but horsedrawn narrow boats can still be found. Preserved craft frequently have the 'traditional' decoration of the canals, roses and castles, painted on them. This form of decoration is of uncertain origin, and seems to have arrived quite late in the canal age, probably at some time in the latter part of the nineteenth century. This was a period which brought great changes to the canal world, for railway competition began to have a serious effect on trade. Before that date, the canal boatman had lived a conventional life, comparable to that of any other sailor – working his boat and then returning to his cottage on land. Competition produced economies, and one of the first economies was the house on the land. The boat families moved aboard. Now the narrow boat had to be a floating home as well as a cargo vessel. Space was desperately short, with the back cabin generally only some ten foot in length, and the width limited by the width of the boat. Here the whole family lived, and the back cabin was a masterpiece of organization, living room by day and bedroom by night. Until the Canal Boat Acts of 1877 and 1884 there were no regulations covering such matters as overcrowding, and some idea of what conditions must have been like before the legislature stepped in can be gauged by the fact that the Acts limited that tiny cabin to two adults and three children.

The boats were sometimes owned by the canal companies, more often by independent carrying companies, such as Pickfords or Fellows, Morton and Clayton, and just occasionally by 'Number Ones', boatmen who owned their own boats. But whoever owned the boats, the work was hard. Tunnels represented a major obstacle and, in the days when boats were all pulled by horses, the boat had to be legged through tunnels without towpaths. This involved the boatman lying on his back and pushing against the tunnel wall or roof with his feet. Perhaps the hardest part of the work was loading and unloading, which was generally also part of the boatman's job. In time the boat people came to form a community within the general community, isolated by their nomadic life from the rest of society. They had their own way of life and their own customs. They were regarded by the rest

Narrow boats at the Ellesmere Port Boat Museum, Cheshire. The site was originally the northern terminus of the Shropshire Union Canal.

of the world as argumentative, dirty and dishonest. In fact, they were somewhat well known for enjoying a good fight, and most boatmen in the nineteenth century regarded poaching, for example, as a natural right rather than a crime. But the charge of dirtiness seems quite unfounded. Indeed, many commentators remarked on how the cabins were kept absolutely spotless in the most difficult circumstances. Most unprejudiced observers who took the trouble to get to know the boat people found them to be at least as honest as the rest of humanity – and, in some respects, more so. When boat families gathered at some of their favourite meeting places such as Hawkesbury Junction, where the Coventry and Oxford Canals meet, boat cabins were never locked. They trusted each other – if not the rest of the world.

The canals of the Brindley age form a remarkably coherent group, and travelling along them by boat both Brindley's genius and his shortcomings can be appreciated. He was an immensely industrious man, but cautious and somewhat conservative in his thinking – a difficult colleague, as many a canal official soon discovered. What cannot fail to impress is the sheer magnitude of the work he undertook and its essential importance. The Trent and Mersey Canal makes a splendid example. At its heart lie the Potteries, and along its banks a myriad of pot works were established, including the new works at Etruria, built by Josiah Wedgwood. Most of those works have now vanished, apart from a scattering of decayed buildings and a few of the houses Wedgwood built for his work force. Wedgwood's own home, Etruria Hall, looks down on the canal, but it has been much altered and is now used as offices by the Coal Board.

The passage through Harecastle Hill has also changed with the years, for in 1825 work was begun on a second tunnel under the direction of Telford. This was an altogether grander affair, with a wider bore and a towpath carried on piling down one side. Brindley's old, narrow tunnel is disused but can still be seen alongside the new. Comparison of the two indicates how rapidly canal engineering had developed in half a century. Brindley began his in 1766, but it was not completed until 1777. Boats were not towed through, for there was no towpath, but had to be legged. The horses had to be led over the top on a route still distinguished with the name Boat Horse Lane. Telford's wide tunnel with its towpath for horses was begun in October 1825 and was opened in March 1827. Poor Brindley never even lived long enough to see his tunnel completed.

The mark of Brindley's style can be seen throughout the route of the Trent and Mersey, particularly in the often tortuous line, and the steady sprinkling of locks. At its southern end, it meets the Trent and here the narrow canal boats met the wider river boats. Goods were transferred from one to the other, which meant warehouses and docks were needed. The trans-shipment point developed into the canal town of Shardlow, Derbyshire, still rich with reminders of earlier and busier canal days. The waterway is lined with handsome

Georgian houses and scarcely less handsome Georgian warehouses, one building being of particular interest, the Trent Corn Mill of 1780, also known as the Clock Warehouse. This was built over an arm of the canal, with a brick arch spanning the water so that boats could slide underneath the building for direct loading and unloading. There are no truly spectacular features along the way, no great aqueducts, for example, to rival that at Barton. Indeed, Brindley was never to build to that scale again, his later aqueducts being low, rather cumbersome affairs, suggesting that the influence of Gilbert on the construction of the Bridgewater Canal might have been crucial. There are, however, many other points of special interest on the Brindley canals.

The Trent and Mersey was conceived as part of a scheme to join four important rivers, the Trent, Mersey, Thames and Severn, in a watery cross. A vital part of that cross was the Staffordshire and Worcestershire Canal which offers today's boat travellers some beautiful scenery and a fascinating glimpse into the thinking of the early engineers. The canal falls quite sharply on its way down to the Severn, and has to negotiate some awkward terrain via some very Brindleyesque convolutions. A great deal of journey time could be saved by grouping locks together rather than by spreading them out over a wide area, and this idea is taken to extremes at the Bratch in Staffordshire. Here are three locks, topped by a very attractive octagonal toll house – a reminder that canals, like the turnpike roads, were expected to pay their way. They form a remarkable group, for there is literally a gap of just a few inches between one lock and the next. Going downhill, water flows out of the top lock and runs into a side pond terraced into the hillside, which acts as a reservoir from which water can be drawn to fill the next lock. It is remarkable that Brindley did not take the obvious step of removing the gaps altogether, simply allowing the water to run from the top lock straight into the one below, forming a continuous staircase of locks. Such staircases can be seen elsewhere on the canals where they make some of the most dramatic features of the whole system. Outstanding in this respect is the staircase at Bingley, West Yorkshire, on the Leeds and Liverpool Canal.

Work on the Leeds and Liverpool began in 1770, and Brindley was initially involved as engineer. This is not a narrow canal and the locks are fourteen foot wide. Unfortunately, however, they are only sixty foot long, which makes the canal impassable to the narrow boats of the Midlands. It is an early example of the lack of cooperation between different canal companies leading to serious disadvantages for all concerned. The Leeds and Liverpool took a long time to complete not because, as with the Trent and Mersey, there were major engineering problems, but because of the other great problem that beset canal builders – lack of funds. However, by 1780 the section from Leeds to Skipton was complete, including the Bingley staircase. Here five wide locks are joined together, lifting the canal up sixty feet from the Aire

Locks and toll house at the Bratch, Wombourne, Staffordshire, on the Staffordshire and Worcestershire Canal. Brindley planned these locks so that there is a gap of just a few inches between them rather than allowing the water from one lock to run straight into the one below.

valley. It is an amazing feat of engineering, made all the more remarkable by comparison with Brindley's somewhat tentative steps at the Bratch.

These early canals have many things in common. Canalside structures are built mainly of local materials – brick on the Staffordshire and Worcestershire, stone on the Leeds and Liverpool. There is a strong preference for going round obstacles rather than through or over them: even the Leeds and Liverpool, in spite of Bingley Five Rise, follows a corkscrew route on its way through the Pennines. And building progress tended to be slow: partly because of chronic cash shortages, and partly because of the fact that engineers and the men who worked for them were still comparatively inexperienced. In the early days, labourers were recruited locally for a specific job, after which they drifted back to their old employment. Some, however, stayed on, so that a hardened, experienced workforce gradually developed that moved around the country from one canal digging to the next. Known originally as 'navigators', the men who dug the navigations, they were soon popularly known as plain navvies – and by many a worse name, for their reputation for hard living soon exceeded their reputation for hard work. They were men of great strength and considerable skill, and all their qualities were to be needed in good measure as a second generation of canal engineers took over after the death of James Brindley. Three engineers, in particular, stand out: William Jessop, Thomas Telford and John Rennie.

The second canal age saw many profound changes, several of which are exemplified in one canal – the Ellesmere. This was one of the many canals begun in what were known as the 'Canal Mania' years of the 1790s. This was a time when investors, looking at the profits made by the early companies, rushed to buy shares in any venture with the magical name 'Canal' attached. Some schemes succeeded, others failed totally and a few, including the Ellesmere, were no more than modest successes in financial terms. But the Ellesmere was not the least bit modest in terms of engineering achievement.

The canal begins at a junction with the Chester Canal, north of Nantwich in Cheshire, continues on to Ellesmere, with a further junction with the Montgomeryshire Canal, and terminates at Llangollen, Clwyd. Looked at today, it seems to serve no obviously useful function, but when built the canal passed through coalfields and served the Plas Kynaston ironworks as well as a number of limestone quarries. From its beginning at Hurleston Junction where it leaves the Chester Canal, the Ellesmere announces itself as a modern waterway. It rises steeply through a flight of four locks, set very close together, and then proceeds on a reasonably straight line, punctuated by a few locks, until there is a sudden lift in level at Grindley Brook. Here the canal rises by thirty-nine feet through six locks, three very close together and a further three run together in a staircase. This is followed by a long, lock-free section, which maintains its level in spite of crossing some difficult and uneven terrain. The engineer, William Jessop, used a wide variety of techniques to achieve his aims. To the north of Ellesmere, he resorted to contour cutting in the best Brindley tradition, but elsewhere new techniques can be seen. The low-lying, boggy ground of Whixall Moss presented a particular problem which was solved by the construction of an embankment, taking the canal in an almost perfect straight line.

The new technology can be seen in even more dramatic form as the canal comes nearer to the hills of North Wales. Here the engineers were faced with two river crossings, the Ceiriog at Chirk and the Dee at Froncysyllte. The approach to the former shows the use of the

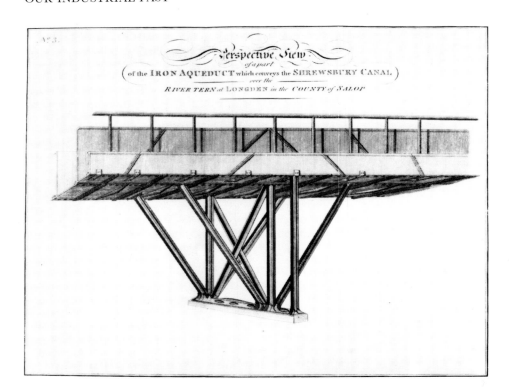

technique of 'cut and fill'. The initial section is via a cutting carved into the hillside, but as the ground begins to fall away the canal keeps its level raised up on a high embankment, a tremendous earthwork quite unlike anything seen on the earlier canals. The crossing itself is on a stone aqueduct, which again is on a new and massive scale. It carries the canal seventy feet above the Ceiriog on ten arches, each of forty-foot span. Once across the valley, the canal plunges straight into a tunnel to pierce the opposite hillside. This is followed by another deep cutting and a second short tunnel before the canal turns off to follow the valley of the Dee. So a whole panoply of techniques can be seen within a couple of miles: deep cuttings carved through hillsides, with the spoil being used to build up embankments in the valley, tunnels constructed and aqueducts built. But it is in the crossing of the next river valley that the Ellesmere Canal displays a major feat of engineering, an achievement that can only be appreciated in the context of canal history as a whole.

When Jessop was appointed chief engineer to the Ellesmere Canal Company, he took as assistant and general dogsbody the young Thomas Telford. Then, in February 1795, Telford was called away to take over the completion of the Shrewsbury Canal following the death of the engineer, Josiah Clowes. He found work was about to begin on a conventional aqueduct across the River Tern at Longdon, Shropshire. But among the canal's proprietors was the Shropshire iron master, William Reynolds. He suggested to Telford that the crossing could be made on a new type of aqueduct. Early aqueducts had been built to massive proportions because the stone work had to be lined with the mixture of clay, sand and water known as puddle, used to keep canals watertight. Reynolds' idea was to build an iron trough which would be light, for it would need no special lining. Telford enthusiastically accepted Reynolds' idea, and Longdon was duly built, the first iron trough aqueduct. The canal it carried has long since disappeared, but the aqueduct remains though it is, truth to tell, a somewhat ungainly structure. It is nevertheless an important extension of the use of iron, and was built only a few years after the first iron road bridge.

Telford returned to the Ellesmere Canal, where Jessop was still agonizing over what to do about the Dee crossing. Telford and Reynolds' work at Longdon offered the solution. The result was Pontcysyllte, an iron trough aqueduct over a thousand feet long, carrying the canal 120 feet above the Dee. It has been rightly acclaimed as the most impressive achievement of the canal age, and is a proud monument to the genius of three men – Reynolds, Jessop and Telford. Originally the canal then carried straight on towards the Plas Kynaston iron works, where the sections for the aqueduct were cast. Today, however, navigation is limited to the narrow feeder canal which hugs the side of the valley on its way to Llangollen. When the canal was used commercially there was some traffic on this line, but its main function was water supply. Follow it to the end and you arrive at the Horseshoe Falls, in fact a weir across the Dee, where water was diverted to supply the canal.

Jessop and Telford both worked on other canal schemes. Jessop's most significant work was the Grand Junction, now part of the Grand Union, a canal built to provide a direct route between London and the Midlands. Telford's most impressive English canal is the Birmingham and Liverpool Junction, now the Shropshire Union, work on which

One of the dramatic deep cuttings on the Shropshire Union Canal. This was originally the Birmingham and Liverpool Junction Canal, opened in 1835, and one of the last canals to be built in Britain.

began in 1825. Here 'cut and fill' can be seen at its most spectacular, with deep cuttings and high banks following in steady succession. The Birmingham and Liverpool joined the Chester Canal, and was then further extended northwards from Chester to the Mersey. Here a new port was established, Ellesmere Port, once famous for its extensive range of docks and warehouses. Sadly, many of those warehouses were destroyed by fire a few years ago, but what remains has been incorporated into a new boat museum, where a fine collection of inland waterways craft, both narrow boats and wide boats, is preserved.

The reputation of the third of the engineers, John Rennie, rests on a rather different basis to that of the other two. Where the latter could be described as engineers' engineers, Rennie was the architects' engineer. His most important single work, the Kennet and Avon Canal, suffers from a number of engineering drawbacks, not the least of which is a chronic shortage of water. This lack was alleviated by the construction of two pumping stations: one at Crofton, which was steam powered, the second at Claverton, containing pumps powered by a water wheel. Rennie also designed two quite outstanding stone aqueducts, at Avoncliff and Dundas. The Dundas aqueduct is a classical masterpiece built from rich Bath stone. The canal can also boast what must be the most impressive, if not the longest, flight of locks in the country. The prize for being the longest goes to Tardebigge on the Worcester and Birmingham Canal, but the thirty-one locks are narrow and spread over a considerable distance. The twenty-nine locks of the Caen Hill flight at Devizes are wide locks charging straight up the hillside and kept supplied with water by means of side ponds terraced into the slope to act as small reservoirs.

The canals served two principal functions: to provide cheap bulk transport between towns, and to link those towns to the sea and sea-going ships. The latter were included in the canal-builders' plans when the first ship canal, the Gloucester and Berkeley – now known as the Gloucester and Sharpness – was authorized in 1793. It was built to allow the ships that used the River Severn to bypass the shoals of the upper reaches to reach the heart of the city of Gloucester. Because it was used by big ships, the bridges across the canal were all built so that they could be swung out of the way, and they were looked after by bridge keepers whose little cottages with their pedimented porches are such a feature of the waterway. Following the canal's construction, Gloucester developed into a major inland port, and the docks surrounded by tall nineteenth-century warehouses remain a prominent feature of the city, even though their commercial importance has declined.

Other ship canals were constructed in Scotland. The Crinan cuts through a narrow neck of land to join Loch Fyne to the Sound of Jura, but the most impressive of the early ship canals is the Caledonian, joining Fort William on the west coast with Inverness on the east. As a piece of engineering it is magnificent: as a commercial venture it was a

Caen Hill Locks at Devizes, Wiltshire, on the Kennet and Avon Canal; a major headache for restorers. Side ponds can be seen to the left of the locks.

disaster. It remains in use, but has never carried the traffic for which it was designed: Baltic trade diminished, and ships became ever larger to the point where they would no longer fit into the locks. Nevertheless it is a fascinating canal to travel. The huge ship locks, known as Neptune's Staircase, lift the canal from sea level at the western end. On the east coast, the canal had to be pushed out on an artificial embankment away from the shore so that sea-going ships had sufficient depth of water under their keels to approach the sea lock. The chief engineer was Telford, a man associated in canal works with deep cuttings. These can be readily seen on the Birmingham and Liverpool, but are less immediately apparent on the Caledonian because they simply look less dramatic when set against the almost melodramatic

scenery of the Highlands. Yet cuttings such as that at Laggan must be counted among the great achievements of the canal age. The Caledonian represents the virtual end of canal building, though there was a brief revival of activity with the construction of the Manchester Ship Canal at the end of the nineteenth century.

The canals helped to create a whole series of new inland ports, starting with Stourport (Hereford and Worcester), which developed at the junction of the Staffordshire and Worcester Canal and the River Severn, and ending with the construction of the docks in Manchester following the completion of the Manchester Ship Canal. Other great dock complexes grew up along the banks of the major navigable rivers, ports such as Glasgow, Belfast, Newcastle, Liverpool and London. Their heyday came in the nineteenth century, when engineers began to construct enclosed docks, protected from the vagaries of the tides by lock gates. Before that ships had been forced to anchor in midstream where they were served by flotillas of lighters and barges. The new system meant that they could anchor alongside the wharves regardless of the state of the tides. The pattern was set with the construction of St Katharine's Dock in London, designed by the engineer Telford and the architect Philip Hardwick. In recent years the dock complex has been extensively redeveloped and much of the original character has been lost, though it does now form an appropriate home for the Maritime Trust's collection of historic ships. The finest surviving nineteenth-century dock complex is the Albert Dock in Liverpool, designed by Jesse Hartley. This, too, is an enclosed dock, providing security and first-class arrangements for loading and unloading at the wharves. The upper storeys of the warehouses are carried out over the quays on colonnades, so that goods could be hoisted straight out of a ship's hold and into a secure storage area. Remains of the hydraulic system that once powered cranes and hoists can still be seen, and this vast complex now forms one end of the new Merseyside Maritime Museum, itself based on an early dock complex.

The great age of water transport lasted well into the nineteenth century, but even by the end of the eighteenth century the seeds of change were being sown. It was apparent even in those early days that it was uneconomical in terms of both cash and water to build canals in very hilly country. One answer to the problem was the tub-boat canal, pioneered in Shropshire by William Reynolds in 1788. Here the tiny boats would be taken by canal to the foot of the hill and there floated on to wheeled trollies which would be hauled up a railed track to another section of canal at a higher level. These devices were known as inclined planes, and such a system has been preserved at Coalport, part of the Ironbridge Gorge Museum, where the tracks can be seen leading up from the Coalport Canal beside the River Severn. An alternative was to do away with the canal altogether in the hillier parts, and simply manage with the inclined plane and a rail

The Albert Dock, Liverpool, designed by Jesse Hartley in the 1840s and one of the finest examples of Victorian civil engineering skills.

system to link canal and works. These systems, known as tramways or plateways, were common in areas such as Wales, and a complex pattern of such routes can be traced out from canals such as the Brecon and Abergavenny. A particularly fine example can be seen at Llanfoist in Gwent, where the tramway can be followed down the hillside to a canalside warehouse. It was on such tramways that the railway age proper was born.

7 Iron Rails and Steam

The use of railed transport dates back to the end of the sixteenth century, when tracks were laid to join collieries to navigable rivers. The first such tramways were built from Broseley, Shropshire, to the Severn and from Wollaton, Nottingham, to the Trent. They were quite unlike any modern notion of a railway, for the rails themselves were wooden, and routes were organized so that laden trucks were sent on a steady, downhill line from colliery to river, their rate of descent controlled by a hand brake. The empty trucks were then pulled back up the slope by horses. It was a perfectly adequate system for a very limited task, and the tramways became immensely popular,

The Causey Arch which carried the Tanfield tramway, Co. Durham; by Joseph Atkinson, 1804.

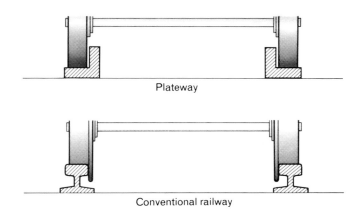

Plateway

Conventional railway

especially among the colliery owners of north-east England. A network of such tracks was soon built up, and tracing these old pathways can make a fascinating pursuit. Occasionally the builders found themselves faced by major obstacles: in the 1720s, for example, the builders of the Tanfield Tramway in Durham were confronted by the deep cleft cut by the Houghwell Burn. They turned to a local mason, Ralph Wood, who built them a bridge, the Causey Arch, which crossed the brook in a single 103-foot span. Today, Ralph Wood's bridge can claim the honour of being the world's oldest surviving railway bridge (NZ 200 560), but, although the trackbed of the railway has been cleared, all traces of the four-foot wide wooden railway have gone. Other early railway relics might be less dramatic, but are not necessarily less interesting. In Alloa, Central, a tramway was constructed in 1768 to join the local coal mines to the glass works and the distillery. As at Tanfield, the rails have gone, but here the two tunnels that carried the tracks right through the town centre have survived.

The first major improvement in construction came with the replacement of wooden rails by cast iron. The earliest recorded use of cast-iron rails was at Coalbrookdale in Shropshire in the 1760s, and within twenty years iron rails were becoming common. The most popular form worked on the opposite principle to that employed on modern railways. Today, we use edge rails, vehicles being kept on the track by flanged wheels: the earlier form were plateways with L-shaped rails, where the wheels were kept on track by running outside the verticals of the plates. Such rails can be seen at Coalbrookdale, running alongside the Severn outside the Darby warehouse. The rails were generally spiked to square, stone sleeper blocks and the presence of a line of such blocks is a sure indication of the presence of a tramway at some time in the past. The success of the tramways brought them to the attention of the canal companies, who saw them as useful extensions where the waterway ran into difficult country.

A particularly fine example of a tramway is the Cromford and High Peak Railway in Derbyshire, begun in 1825 to link the Cromford Canal near Cromford to the Peak Forest Canal at Whaley Bridge. The latter end is marked by a unique interchange shed, where boats

floated in at one end and rails led out at the other. Sections of the old rails can be seen embedded in the roadway outside the shed. The engineers had to build their line right across the spine of the Pennines, and had to overcome the sort of difficulties faced by canal engineers. In places they resorted to similar solutions, building a contour railway with extravagant curves, but they were also forced to build a number of inclines. Unlike the earliest tramways, this route was expected to carry two-way traffic, so loaded as well as empty trucks had to be hauled up the slopes, a task beyond even the most willing of horses. The engineers found their solution in a more powerful moving force, the steam engine. Engine houses were built at the tops of the inclines and stationary engines used to haul the trucks by cable. One such engine house and its engine has been preserved near the Cromford end – the Middleton Top Engine House. Inside are a pair of identical beam engines driving on to a common crank to work the winding mechanism. Two huge wheels, each fourteen foot in diameter, stand one above the other in the wheel pit, their motion controlled by a flywheel. Cable or rope was wound round these wheels, then passed out down the incline and back up again as a continuous line. Waggons were attached to the cable and hauled up the slope or lowered down it.

The Middleton Top engine still turns over, but the cable system has gone. However, a similar system can be seen on the Bowes Railway, which was built to join several collieries to the Tyne at Jarrow, Tyne and Wear. The first section was completed in 1826 and was the work of a gentleman who will feature largely in these pages, George Stephenson. The railway included a number of rope-worked inclines, which remained in use until quite recently. Here we have the complement to the Cromford and High Peak: there the engine survived but the haulage system is no more; here the engine has gone but the haulage system is demonstrated using modern engines. But before either of these lines was constructed, other experiments had begun with the idea of combining the iron rail and the steam engine to make a quite new transport system.

The Penydarren Tramway was opened in 1802, and was built to join the Penydarren ironworks near Merthyr Tydfil with the Glamorganshire Canal at Abercynon (Mid Glamorgan). It was typical of many such South Wales plateways, and much of its path can easily be followed with stone sleeper blocks appearing in a number of places. No physical trace, though, remains of the event that was to give this short tramway a permanent place in transport history. The Cornish engineer, Richard Trevithick, had spent some time experimenting with steam locomotives, first with road vehicles in Cornwall, and then briefly with a locomotive running on iron rails at Coalbrookdale. He had appreciated that a mobile steam engine would need to work at high pressure. The early beam engines of Boulton and Watt had all used steam at very low pressure, compensating for this with their immense size. There was no way in which such

Stone sleeper blocks marking the line of the Penydarren tramway in South Wales. It was on this tramway that Richard Trevithick ran his steam locomotive in 1804 and proved that iron wheels could grip smooth iron rails.

monsters could be set down to run along rails, so the small, high-pressure engine was essential. It was in South Wales that the notion was given its first major trial.

A local iron master, Samuel Homfray, backed Trevithick in more senses than one. He put money into the development, and then made a bet with a neighbour that Trevithick could produce an engine that would haul a ten-ton load over the tracks of the Penydarren Tramway. As the wager was for 500 guineas this shows either a remarkable faith in the engineer, or a last desperate attempt by Homfray to get some return on his investment. His opponent had popular opinion on his side, the general belief being that smooth iron wheels would not be able to grip smooth iron rails. The experiment was made on 21 February 1804, and Homfray duly collected his winnings. Trevithick waited impatiently for the orders to roll in for his new mechanical marvel, but waited in vain. Although the locomotive had worked well enough, the track had not: the heavy locomotive had proved too much for the fragile plates and many were cracked and broken. The engine was dismantled. One other Trevithick locomotive was built at Gateshead, Tyne and Wear, for the nearby Wylam colliery, but it too was a qualified success and finished its working days as a stationary engine.

The Penydarren locomotive no longer exists nor do we have any very detailed technical specifications. We do, however, know quite a lot about Trevithick locomotives in general and using this information the National Museum of Wales, Cardiff, has constructed a replica. It is a comparatively small engine, made to seem larger by the rather cumbersome mechanical arrangement. The single, horizontal cylinder is set in the end of the boiler, and drive transmitted to the wheels via a big transverse crosshead and slide rods which extend well in front of the boiler. At first glance, it would seem to be some form of mechanized trombone. The actual drive was through cogs, which only worked on one side of the engine, greatly reducing its efficiency. Trevithick also followed stationary engine practice of the time by adding a huge flywheel to keep the motion going, which further increased the size of the whole contraption. There is no means of knowing precisely how accurately the replica matches the original in detail, but by building it and running it the Museum has helped in creating an understanding of this important locomotive. It has also received a very practical insight into the problems involved in making the engine work! It is kept at the Welsh Industrial and Maritime Museum at Cardiff, where it is regularly steamed, and provides just one more reason for visiting this most excellent museum.

Trevithick made one further attempt to interest the world at large in his locomotives, by running an engine, *Catch me who can*, round a circular track in London. The fairground atmosphere did little to encourage serious, sober industrialists to take an interest. This was a pity, for it was quite an advance over the Penydarren engine. The power came from a vertical cylinder driving directly down to the rear wheels, making it a recognizable 2–2–0 direct drive locomotive. The times, however, were not propitious. The basic problem of breaking rails remained, and there was little that the locomotive could offer which could not be provided more cheaply and more easily by traditional horse power. This situation changed with the Napoleonic wars. The protracted conflict sent the cost of fodder ever higher, and colliery owners, in particular, began to look more favourably on a form of transport that could use the one fuel they had in plenty – coal.

The Middleton Colliery near Leeds in West Yorkshire was joined to the Aire and Calder Navigation by a tramway, constructed in 1758. The colliery manager, John Blenkinsop, set out to solve one of the problems that had plagued Trevithick – damage to rails. He designed a third, toothed rail to run alongside the existing track and asked a local engineer, Matthew Murray, to design a locomotive to run on it. This was to have a toothed cog, which would engage with the toothed rail – the system known as rack and pinion. It provided powerful traction, which meant that a very light locomotive could be built and the wear on the main track reduced to manageable proportions. The system worked, and in June 1812 the world's first commercial steam railway service duly went into operation.

Engine wheel arrangements. The numbers 2-4-2 tell us that there are two wheels supporting the front of the engine, four drive wheels and two wheels supporting the rear.

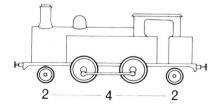

The Middleton Colliery Railway, West Yorkshire, in 1814, with a Blenkinsop locomotive hauling a train of coal waggons. R. & D. Havell after a plate from The Costumes of Yorkshire *by George Walker.*

The Middleton Colliery Railway continued in use for more than a century, but the introduction of tough, rolled iron rails soon made the rack and pinion system obsolete and it was replaced. A few remains of the old line are visible in the shape of stone sleeper blocks. And the railway itself is back in operation, preserved by enthusiasts who run a commercial diesel-hauled goods service as well as steam-hauled passenger trains. It has the distinction not just of being the world's oldest commercial steam line, but also the first preserved standard-gauge line in Britain as well. The Murray locomotives are no more, although a model can be seen in the Science Museum, London, but the rack and pinion system did not die with the removal of the Blenkinsop track at Middleton. It remained in use for mountain railways, though in somewhat different form, and can be seen on the Snowdon Mountain Railway, completed in 1896 to carry passengers to the summit. Four of the original locomotives are still in use on this line, all having been built at the Swiss locomotive works at Winterthur.

Interest in the Middleton experiment was widespread, and in 1813 a native of Wylam, where Trevithick had sent his first engine, came to look at the railway. His name was George Stephenson and within a year he was to begin his own career as a railway engineer. Wylam was already becoming an important centre for development. A local engineer, William Hedley, built two locomotives, known by the nicknames 'Wylam Dilly' and 'Puffing Billy', both of which are preserved – the former at the Royal Scottish Museum in Edinburgh, the latter in the Science Museum, London. They have vertical cylinders on either side of the boiler, and drive was transmitted through a beam mechanism, similar to that used in stationary engines. Stephenson's first engine, built for the Killingworth colliery, soon followed. It had little new to offer, and in some ways was inferior to Hedley's engines. The latter had return flue boilers – that is the flue carrying the hot gases from the fire was U-shaped, so that the fire box was at the same end of the boiler as the chimney. This looks a strange arrangement to modern eyes but it brought more of the heating surface into contact with the water in the boiler. Stephenson used a straight flue, a great expense in terms of fuel use. The main point about these early engines was not their efficiency, however, but the fact that they worked at all. It was this that was to lead to the establishment of the first public railway, the Stockton and Darlington Railway (S & DR), opened in 1825.

Work began in 1821 with Stephenson as chief engineer. The S & DR represented a major step forward, for the line was to be a public railway, carrying both freight and passenger traffic. Stephenson was responsible for both the civil engineering of the route and the provision of locomotives. The line he adopted showed very clearly that the influence of the older tramways still prevailed, and it made considerable use of inclined planes. Equally, the locomotives offered little that was new in engineering terms. Fortunately, as with the Penydarren

Drawing of George Stephenson's chain-drive locomotive built for Killingworth Colliery, c. 1815.

locomotive, we can learn a good deal about the first Stockton and Darlington Railway locomotives from the replica of the first *Locomotion*, built to celebrate the 150th anniversary of the official opening. This replica is regularly steamed at the North of England Open Air Museum at Beamish in Co. Durham. It is rather more difficult to assess the nature of the original line, if only because it has been absorbed and overwhelmed by later developments. Yet parts at least have remained. The railway was the first to employ an architect, Ignatius Bonomi, who was responsible for beautifying the Skerne Bridge at Darlington. Once it stood in all its glory amid open fields; today it lurks sadly in a gas works. The railway can also boast the first iron railway bridge, now removed to the National Railway Museum at York. But by far the most interesting aspect of the line is the area around Shildon, Co. Durham.

It is sometimes thought that the S & DR was built, from the first, as a line to be used exclusively by trains hauled along by steam engines. This was far from being the case. The inclines used stationary engines for haulage, and there was a good deal of horsedrawn traffic, including the famous passenger service. A special coach was built, very like the conventional stage coach but with iron wheels so that it could run on the rails, but this was considered a very minor part of the traffic. The main business, as with all colliery lines, was the haulage of coal, and here the steam locomotives showed their worth. They were worked hard, and the resident engineer, Timothy Hackworth, was kept desperately busy repairing and improving the engines. His headquarters was established at Shildon which, when he moved in, was no more than a few half-built cottages. It soon began to grow to the point where it could reasonably claim to be the first railway town. Hackworth himself went on to establish his own locomotive works, the Soho Works, in the town, and Shildon remains a railway town to this day. Happily, much of the Hackworth connection remains, including his house which is now home to a small museum where a model of one of his most successful locomotives for the S & DR, the *Royal George*, can be seen. Opposite the museum is all that remains of the Soho Works, the former paint shop, which now houses another replica, that of Hackworth's most famous engine, the *Sans Pareil*. This represents, in its way, the ultimate development of the early locomotive, with a return flue boiler and vertical cylinders. It is a fine, powerful engine, a point well demonstrated by the replica when seen under steam. It was built to take part in the Rainhill Trial on the Liverpool and Manchester Railway in 1829, a famous turning point in railway history.

The Liverpool and Manchester Railway (LMR) is, in many respects, of far greater importance than the Stockton and Darlington. It was agreed from the first that steam would provide the power, and that no horses should be allowed on the tracks. There was, however, a good deal of discussion about what form that steam power should take. Some, including the railway's chief engineer, George Stephenson, argued the case for locomotives, but as Stephenson was a locomotive builder his advice was not entirely unbiased. Others argued in favour of a series of stationary engines set at regular intervals all down the line. The Rainhill Trial was designed to test the worth of the steam locomotive. This was no colliery line where the cost of fuel was negligible, so the engines were required to do a good job of work, efficiently and economically. Engineers were asked to produce a locomotive that could pull a train on the equivalent of a return journey from Liverpool to Manchester at an average speed of ten miles an hour. There were three principal contenders, all of which were represented by replicas at the 150th anniversary celebrations: *Sans Pareil*; a curious lightweight locomotive, *Novelty*; and Stephenson's *Rocket*. The success of the latter ensured that it was to become world famous, and seeing the original in the London Science Museum or the replica under steam, it is easy to see that it deserves its place of honour.

The replica of Stephenson's Rocket *at the National Railway Museum, York.*

Rocket contains a number of important innovations. Externally, the most obvious are the cylinders set at a low angle instead of vertically, as in other Stephenson engines. The more important changes, though, are hidden from view. It was the boiler design that gave *Rocket* its advantage over the competitors. The separate fire box was surrounded by a water jacket in which the water was heated directly and the hot gases from the fire were carried through the boiler in twenty-five tubes. Finally, exhaust steam from the cylinders was led up the chimney rather than being allowed to pass straight out to the atmosphere. This dragged air across the fire box, ensuring a good draught.

It was the combination of so many important factors in the one engine that made *Rocket* unique. Separately, each element – fire box, multi-tubular boiler and blast-pipe exhaust – would have been an improvement, but taken together they were something more than the mere sum of their parts. *Rocket* could well be called the first modern locomotive, and not only did it put an end to any talk about stationary engines on the Liverpool and Manchester main line, but its success ensured that for the next century when people spoke of railways they would mean steam railways. Furthermore, those basic elements that made *Rocket* a success were all capable of development, and indeed were developed very rapidly. Many refinements were added, and some fundamental differences were to appear. Cylinder arrangements were changed. Devices such as superheating, whereby steam was reheated between leaving the boiler and reaching the cylinders, were introduced. Greatly improved mechanisms to work the valves on the cylinders were designed, notably the Walschaerts' valve gear, invented in Belgium in 1844 and giving greater efficiency. And, of course, locomotives got bigger: steam pressures rose higher; speed and power were increased. The changes were enormous, but the fundamentals were there in *Rocket*.

A visit to the National Railway Museum at York provides a view across more than a hundred years of development, with many great and famous locomotives on display. Look, for example, at the very last main-line steam locomotive built for British Railways, *Evening Star* of 1960. It is vast in comparison with tiny *Rocket*, and looking at the two together gives an idea of how far steam locomotives had progressed in terms of size and power. *Rocket* had a fire grate of six square feet, the heat from which passed through twenty-five tubes to provide steam at a pressure of at most fifty pounds per square inch (psi). The steam then passed to two 8-inch diameter cylinders which powered a pair of 4-foot-8-inch diameter driving wheels. The entire locomotive weighed just over four tons. *Evening Star* has a forty square foot grate from which the gases pass through 138 tubes to provide steam at 250 psi. That steam is then superheated before passing to two 20-inch cylinders and there are ten driving wheels. The total weight, with tender, is 142 tons. And, of course, *Evening Star* is not just bigger but is a good deal more efficient as well. Yet it would not be unreasonable to say that anyone who studied and thoroughly understood *Rocket* and its comparatively simple mechanisms would not find *Evening Star* baffling. So it is right to give *Rocket* a special place of honour. However, it is somewhat unfortunate that it is normally referred to as George Stephenson's engine, since he had little to do with either the design or the construction. The idea for the multi-tubular boiler came from Henry Booth, the Liverpool and Manchester Railway treasurer, while the design of the engine as a whole was the work of George Stephenson's son, Robert.

If advances in locomotive design were impressive and rapid in the years following Rainhill, the same could not be said of rolling stock. The LMR waggons were adaptations of the old coal waggons of tramway days, except that the frames were extended to form buffers and the waggons were sprung. Covered waggons were not introduced until the 1860s. The waggons were linked together by loose chains, so that starting up involved a series of clattering, jerky movements which were long the characteristic of the British goods train. Braking on the waggons was by means of a crude, hand-operated lever. The lack of a continuous braking system right through the train was to prove a major nuisance throughout the nineteenth century, as the long trains could scarcely be expected to dash around the country at high speed when a high proportion of the loose-coupled vehicles in the train had no working brakes whatsoever.

Passenger coaches in the early days, like freight waggons, showed their antecedents in their design. The poorer people who travelled third class had to make do with open trucks, little more than cattle trucks with benches, while the first-class coaches were very much adaptations of stage coach designs. The York Museum has a Stockton and Darlington coach of the 1840s where the lines of the stage coach are clearly reproduced in the curves of the compartment doors. The stage coach theme was taken even further, in that passenger luggage

A Stockton and Darlington Railway coach at the National Railway Museum, York. The influence of stage coach design can be clearly seen.

A vintage train on the Bluebell Railway, East Sussex; late nineteenth-century Metropolitan Railway coaches, hauled by a locomotive of 1909.

was piled on the roof and the guard had his airy perch in precisely the same position on top that he would have occupied in a horsedrawn vehicle. He needed to be a nimble fellow, for when the driver blew his whistle to indicate the train was to stop he had to nip down on to the buffers to haul on the handbrake. A major improvement that affected a large number of passengers came with the introduction of the composite coach in the 1870s on the Midland Railway. These coaches contained both first- and third-class compartments within the same carriage. This was a social rather than a technical revolution, but there were technical changes as well. The Midland also moved away from the four-wheel coach, borrowed from earlier times, and began to build six-wheel coaches. In 1872, the first bogie coach was built, in which the wheels were mounted on a movable frame beneath the carriage rather than being attached directly to the main frame, thus giving a smoother ride. It was built for the Ffestiniog Railway and remains in service.

It is not possible to travel in the oldest coaches, though many have now experienced the somewhat dubious pleasure of travelling in replica coaches behind replica locomotives such as *Rocket* and *Sans*

Pareil. Late nineteenth- and early twentieth-century carriages can be seen on several of the preserved lines in Britain, and apart from experiencing the pleasure of a steam-hauled ride, passengers can also enjoy travelling in these vintage coaches. Many lines are rightly proud of their rolling stock collection. The Bluebell Railway in East Sussex, for example, has a fine collection of early carriages, including a bogie carriage built for the directors of the Great Northern Railway in 1897. Other lines have tried to keep to 'local' coaches. The Great Western Railway, for example, is much favoured on several lines, including the Severn Valley, running from Bewdley to Bridgnorth, while the GWR collection at Didcot boasts a mail coach which is used to demonstrate the method of collecting mail on a moving train. It is still possible, thanks to the efforts of preservation societies, to travel on a wide variety of rolling stock of different periods.

Conservation and preservation societies have done an enormous amount to keep the world of the steam railway alive, and it would be unreasonable to attempt to give undue emphasis to any one group (a full list has been included in the gazetteer). Their efforts have, however, been concentrated on the preservation of locomotives and rolling stock. The lines on which these run are often quite short, and if all the preserved track was added together it would form only a tiny fraction of the total rail network in use in Britain. So looking at preserved lines gives an excellent picture of developments in mechanical engineering, but only a partial view of the equally important – and equally interesting – work of the civil engineers. Indeed, the two branches cannot really be separated, since improvement in services – which is, after all, the true measure of increased efficiency – depends on a combination of good track, good locomotives and good rolling stock. A large part of the network we use today is basically that laid down by our Victorian forebears. Recent developments in train design have had to take account of that fact: the Advanced Passenger Train introduced in the 1980s, for example, was given its unique tilting mechanism to cope with curved tracks set down when such speeds were not even contemplated. So, to pick up that side of the story, we must return to George Stephenson and the Liverpool and Manchester Railway.

If *Rocket* was the first modern locomotive, then the LMR was the first modern railway, used from its opening in 1830 entirely by steam locomotives, hauling both passengers and freight and using the company's own engines and rolling stock. The line itself contained a number of interesting features. The techniques of the latter-day canal engineers such as Telford were employed and Telford himself was called in to inspect the works, which turned out not to be much to his liking, for he was by then an old man and set in his ways. Although the engineers used his techniques, they did so on a far grander scale. At the Liverpool end there was a seventy-foot cutting carved out of the sandstone of Olive Mount. Near Newton-le-Willows there was a two-mile long cutting, spoil from which was used to build the adjoining embankment – the 'cut and fill' technique of the waterways. Two viaducts crossed these older routes – a minor one across the Bridge-water Canal and a splendid nine-arched viaduct across the Sankey Navigation. A wide tunnel provided the entrance into Liverpool, far wider and higher than anything that had ever been necessary in the canal age. The greatest obstacle faced by Stephenson does not look in the least menacing today but was a daunting barrier in the 1820s. Chat Moss was, in effect, a huge bog which had to be crossed on an embankment. The embankment is about five miles long, and seems quite unremarkable today for it stands only five foot above the surrounding land, which has now been drained. What we cannot see is the vast amount of material which had to be sunk into the bog to provide a foundation for the embankment.

The Liverpool and Manchester marked a beginning that was soon followed by more ambitious schemes – to link the LMR to London via

Construction work on the London and Birmingham Railway, by J.C. Bourne, 1839; here a retaining wall is being built near Park Street, Camden Town, London.

the Grand Junction and Liverpool and Birmingham Railways, and to link London to Bristol via the Great Western Railway. These schemes were followed by a flurry of activity and financial speculation, a railway mania comparable with the canal mania of the 1790s. Many new schemes were begun, some were completed but many collapsed.

The new schemes brought new men into prominence. Chief engineer on the Grand Junction was Joseph Locke, while the line from London to Birmingham was entrusted to the young Robert Stephenson. Another engineer of genius, Isambard Kingdom Brunel, took charge of the Great Western. It was a time for new men and new ideas. In one respect, however, the new men returned to older methods. Direct labour had been employed in the actual construction of the LMR, but on the Grand Junction the work was parcelled out, as it had been in canal-building days, between independent contractors employing their own workers. One contractor, Thomas Brassey, was to go on to become one of the richest and most powerful men in Britain, employing an army of thousands of navvies, an army that was steadily driving forward the railway frontiers.

The railway navvies earned for themselves a fearsome reputation as hard workers, hard drinkers and hard fighters. In the early days they performed seemingly Herculean labours, often both living and working in appalling conditions. Hardest and most dangerous of all the jobs they were called in to do was tunnelling. A memorial in Otley churchyard, West Yorkshire, commemorates the men who died in the completion of the Bramhope tunnel, built for the Leeds and Thirsk Railway between 1845 and 1849. The memorial copies the design of the tunnel itself, with its castellated entrance and tunnel-keeper's tower. No indication is given, however, of just how many men died in the work. Statistics are available for the Woodhead tunnel built between 1839 and 1845 on the line linking Sheffield to Manchester. Something like a thousand men were employed, and of these thirty were killed and a hundred and fifty seriously injured, casualties of the order one might expect to find in a war. Indeed, the men who joined up to dig the railway tunnel suffered a higher proportion of losses than those who served as ordinary soldiers at Waterloo. When viewing the undoubtedly fine structures of the railway age it is as well to remember that many of them were purchased at a high human price – a price that was paid because contractors preferred profits to safety.

The early works of Stephenson and Brunel provide ample evidence for the contention that they were men of genius. It is not always easy to interpret that evidence on the ground, for the routes they pioneered, though still in use, have been much altered over the years. Tring cutting on the London to Birmingham line, for example, is not quite the work as built by Robert Stephenson. But in the case of some of the more important structures, the original work can still be found standing. Two of Robert Stephenson's bridges are of special interest, for the Conwy and Menai Straits bridges stand alongside the earlier Telford

road bridges. Both the Stephenson bridges were built to a revolutionary new design, in which the trains actually ran inside square, wrought-iron tubes. The construction method was as daring as the conception, for the tubes were built on shore, then floated out into midstream and lifted into position by hydraulic rams. Conwy was something of a trial run for the mighty Britannia Bridge that was to link Anglesey to the mainland, and survives much as it was when built. Sadly, Britannia Bridge was seriously damaged by fire in 1970 and little of the original remains. Stephenson's other great achievement in bridge building was the High Level Bridge at Newcastle, built between 1845 and 1849. The superstructure is carried on five piers almost 150 foot above the river, and is built of bow-and-string girders, a form of construction in which the outward thrust of the arched girder, the bow, is counter-acted by the horizontal members, the strings. It has two decks, the upper carrying the railway tracks and the lower a roadway, and both remain in use today. The bridge also has the further distinction that the piling for the coffer-dam, still to be seen at the foot of the piers, was driven in using Nasmyth's newly-invented steam hammer.

Brunel was a man of broad vision in every sense. George Stephenson had established his lines on a 4 foot 8½ inch gauge, for no better reason than that that was the gauge in use at his local colliery. Brunel argued that a wider gauge would offer greater stability and set the gauge for the Great Western Railway at seven foot. There was a great deal to be said in favour of the broad gauge – but even more to be said in favour of a standard that would apply throughout mainland Britain. The first Irish railway, the Dublin to Kingstown, was also 4 foot 8½ inches, but the Irish standard was later to be changed to 5 foot 3 inches.

The second of the great tubes of Stephenson's Conwy railway bridge, Gwynedd, being floated into position on October 12, 1848. From The Britannia and Conway Tubular Bridges *by Edwin Clark, 1850.*

Brunel held out for his gauge, and it was to remain in use on the GWR until the last broad-gauge train ran on 20 May 1892. In retrospect, Brunel's decision to stand alone against the Stephenson gauge seems understandable but mistaken, but there are few other mistakes to record on the Great Western. Three particularly fine examples of his work are the Box tunnel and the bridges at Maidenhead and Saltash.

The Box tunnel, Wiltshire, was far and away the greatest rail tunnel of the day, with a length of almost two miles and reaching a depth of three hundred feet below the surface. A total of eight shafts were sunk down to the workings, and something like thirty million bricks were burned in a local brickyard to provide a lining for the tunnel. None of this registers on the traveller shooting through on a high speed express, but he can catch a glimpse of the superb stone portal which marks the western entrance. The bridges are a different matter, easy to see and easy to appreciate in the sense that they are immediately impressive. The first of the two, chronologically, was built across the Thames at Maidenhead, Berkshire. The Thames was and is a navigable river and the Thames Commissioners insisted that both navigation and towpath be kept clear. Brunel opted for a bold solution to the problem, a bridge of just two arches and one pier in the river, the arches to be 128 feet in span and to rise to just over 24 feet at the crown. The critics declared that such flat arches would never stand; but the critics, as so often in Brunel's career, were proved wrong.

OVERLEAF *Brunel's Royal Albert Bridge across the Tamar at Saltash, Cornwall. It was the engineer's last great work.*

The engine house at Camden Town, London; now the Round House theatre. From the Illustrated London News, *December 4, 1847.*

The second bridge was Brunel's last venture. It was to cross the Tamar at Saltash, joining Devon to Cornwall, and here the difficulties were even greater. Again the engineer was faced by a navigable river, this time a thousand feet wide, and now the Admiralty demanded a height of a hundred feet above the water to allow ships to pass beneath. Again Brunel planned for a single pier in the river, but this presented special problems for the river bed was soft, shifting sand and mud. He sank a 37-foot diameter iron cylinder down through the mud to the rock beneath. This was then pressurized so that masons could work inside the cylinder to construct the pier. The bridge itself was built in a manner pioneered by Brunel at Chepstow. The deck is suspended from two curved hollow tubes of elliptical cross section. It was originally intended that the bridge should carry two tracks but, as so often happened, the company, in this case the Cornwall Railway Company, ran out of cash. Work was held up for three years and when it eventually got started again the bridge was reduced to the present single track. It was opened in 1859 by Prince Albert, and named the Royal Albert Bridge, but Brunel was too ill to attend the ceremony. He was later taken across the bridge on a specially prepared truck, and a few months after that he died. The company placed an inscription on the bridge 'I.K. Brunel Engineer 1859': he would not have asked for a better memorial.

Other important bridges and viaducts continued to be built throughout the railway age, in brick, stone, iron and steel. Some are particularly noted for their elegance, a superb example being Balcombe Viaduct in West Sussex designed by the engineer John Rastrick and the architect David Mocatta to carry the London to Brighton line. Others impress by their sheer size, while some gain from the majesty of their setting. Scotland can claim a goodly share of structures where size and setting combine, and the many bridges along the old Highland Line are quite outstanding. But it is the most famous of all railway bridges that remains the finest, the bridge across the Firth of Forth. When work was started in 1873 this was originally planned to be a suspension bridge following the example of the bridge over the Tay, soon to be completed, which was the first of the major Scottish river crossings. Then, in 1879, the Tay Bridge collapsed, an event now chiefly remembered for the excruciatingly bad verse written for the occasion by William McGonagall. But there was nothing amusing about the reality, for seventy-four lives were lost in the disaster. The Forth Bridge Committee hastily revised their own plans. The idea of building a suspension bridge was abandoned and a new design adopted. This consisted of towers of tubular steel, from which cantilevers stretched out to be joined to cantilevers from adjoining towers by girders. It was a quite new concept and used a new construction material, mild steel. The bridge was opened in 1890 and, at over 8000 feet, was the longest bridge of any type in the world.

The most important bridges and structures could be aggrandized

by architectural embellishments, but the great majority of structures were left plain and unadorned. The railway architect only really came into his own in the design of stations, for these were the companies' showcases, the buildings that greeted all passengers at the very start of their journeys. Each company developed its own 'house style'. The 'Notty', the North Staffordshire Railway, favoured stations in the Jacobean manner – providing the railway equivalent of grand mansions at major stations such as Stoke-on-Trent, and homely, if somewhat elaborate, Jacobean houses elsewhere along the line. The most impressive stations were, not surprisingly, the termini.

The earliest passenger line, the Stockton and Darlington, originally had no stations as such at all and followed the stage-coach tradition of selling tickets at the local inn. Stations were added later, and one of the earliest at North Road, Darlington, is now a railway museum. As in so many other ways, the Liverpool and Manchester showed the way in the construction of purpose-built passenger stations. The Manchester station was soon replaced, and the original station was turned into a goods depot. This has survived, though much modified and it, too, now houses an important and developing industrial museum. Brunel's route from London to Bristol had two sharply contrasting termini. At Bristol Temple Meads the train shed was built in the style of a vast medieval hall, complete with hammer-beam roof. For a long time it survived only as a humble car park – a sad fate for one of the architectural glories of the railway age – but it is now being renovated by the Brunel Engineering Trust. Paddington, the London end, is quite different. It has no pretensions to masquerading as a medieval anything but is quite content to be judged as a railway station. There is not even an impressive street facade, but there is a hugely impressive train shed of glass raised up on slender pillars. It is a happy marriage between the arts of the engineer and those of the architect. The Great Western also has the dubious honour of introducing the station buffet to the travelling public, a service which Brunel found uniquely terrible and which passengers might claim has not improved a great deal since.

If Paddington has a rival as an example of engineers' architecture then that rival is King's Cross, the London terminus of the Great Northern Railway. This was the work of the Cubitt family and presents a compelling case for the attractions of functional design. There are two glass covered train sheds, one for outgoing and one for incoming traffic, and this stark simplicity is reflected in the twin arches of the facade. Other stations, such as St Pancras next door, might offer more ostentatious grandeur, but none can match King's Cross for simplicity combined with drama. Sadly, something of the rich diversity of station architecture has been lost in recent years with the British Rail policy of promoting a 'corporate image', a hideous phrase to describe a hideous practice in which rich diversity is smothered under acres of bland plastic. Enough diversity does remain to give some hope that, when the current grey thinking is eventually replaced, the old values will still be able to reassert themselves.

The railways had a profound effect on Victorian life, offering improved transport and helping to bring all parts of the country closer together. Journey times were cut dramatically. Before the railway age, the fastest means of transport was the mail coach, drawn by a team of horses which were changed at fifty-mile intervals. When the service was inaugurated in 1784, the mails were carried from London to Bristol at an average speed of just under seven mph. A century later, mail and passengers were being carried on the railways at ten times that speed. In the 1890s, rival companies were competing for the passenger traffic between London and Scotland: the Great Northern Railway following a route up the east coast from King's Cross and the London and North Western using the west coast route from Euston. The issue was decided in August 1895 in the famous 'Races to the North' with each company vying for the fastest time to Aberdeen. Victory went to the west, with the whole journey of 540 miles taking a mere 512 minutes. It was, and remains, a remarkable achievement, and one of the locomotives that took part in that historic run, *Hardwicke*, is preserved at the National Railway Museum in York. It is still in full working order, a tribute to the workmanship of Victorian engineers.

The effect of such fast times was immense. Letters no longer took days to reach their destination: news travelled fast as well as passengers. Time took on a new meaning. In the past, time on a local clock might have differed by several minutes from Greenwich time, but the railway timetables allowed for no such discrepancies. Railway time became the new standard: from 1852 signals were transmitted at noon by the new electric telegraph, so that all the stations in Britain could synchronize their clocks. The increased speed of communication did much to quicken the commercial life of the nation, but rather more important was the part played by the railways in moving freight. In the case of coal alone, for example, where the London Coal Exchange could record a mere 19,000 tons carried by rail in 1847, twenty years later the figure had risen to over 3 million tons. The coal fires of the London house were kept burning by the railways – not an unmixed blessing, as anyone with memories of the pea-soup fogs can testify.

The railways played a major part in changing the whole face of Britain – directly by adding new towns such as Shildon, Crewe and Swindon, with their works and housing estates; indirectly by providing a transport route for commuters, so making possible the spread of suburbs around the major towns and cities. But even by the end of the century, railways had still not penetrated all parts of the country. There was a demand for a number of small, branch lines to link the main routes together and to join them to remote regions. This would not have been possible had every would-be railway company been forced, as earlier companies had been, to go through the lengthy and expensive business of obtaining an Act of Parliament. In 1896, the Light Railways Act was passed which appointed commissioners empowered to authorize new lines without a separate Act being approved. One man in particular, Lt-Colonel Holman Fred Stephens, became associated with the new lines, acting as adviser to railway companies throughout Britain and administering several lines himself. The first that he instituted was the Kent and East Sussex Railway, running from Tenterden to Bodiam, part of which (to Wittersham Road) has been restored and now offers visitors time-travel back to the palmy days of the small country railway.

Throughout this period, industrial as well as passenger lines continued to be built and both play an important role in transport history. Paradoxically, today's industrial survivors are now among the more successful passenger lines, simply because the originals were often built through wild and beautiful scenery. The most famous examples are the narrow-gauge preserved railways of Wales. The first railway to be preserved, the forerunner of all preservation schemes, was the Talyllyn, a 2 foot 3 inch gauge line built to carry slate from the quarries at Bryn Eglwys down the hillside to the town of Tywyn. Passengers were carried from the early days, but they had a lower priority than slate. Today it is one of the more popular steam railways in Britain, using locomotives that date back to the nineteenth century, and the story of the line and

RIGHT *The iron bridge across the Severn at Ironbridge, Shropshire. This is the world's first iron bridge and the builders employed techniques traditionally used for wood.*

Holme packhorse bridge, Bakewell, Derbyshire. As they were not intended for use by vehicles, such bridges were narrow and high-arched.

Telford's Menai Straits suspension bridge, Gwynedd, completed in 1826 after seven years spent in its construction. A tablet to the men whose lives were lost in the work can be seen at the church of Llanfair PG.

LEFT *Dundas aqueduct, carrying the Kennet and Avon Canal across the Avon on the border between Wiltshire and Avon. This was the first canal structure to be scheduled as an ancient monument.*

BELOW LEFT *The iron trough aqueduct, Pontcysyllte, carrying the Ellesmere Canal across the Dee Valley, Clwyd. The tapering piers of stone are hollow towards the top to lighten the structure.*

RIGHT *One of the original locomotives built for the Talyllyn Railway, Gwynedd, in 1865 and still at work.*

its traffic is expounded in a small museum. Another popular and historically important line is the Ffestiniog, built in 1836, the first public narrow-gauge railway. It, like the Talyllyn, was originally built for the slate trade, linking the mines and quarries at Blaenau Ffestiniog with the port of Porthmadog. Steam locomotives were introduced in 1863, the unique double-ended Fairlies, two of which are still in use today, being brought in in 1869. After many years of struggle, the two towns were again reunited by steam railway in 1982.

The steam locomotive was less than a century old when a new form of traction was displayed at the Berlin Exhibition of 1879 by a small electric locomotive which gave demonstration runs around the grounds. In 1883, Magnus Volk built Britain's first electric railway, which ran for a mile and a half along the seafront at Brighton. It still runs but has been extended and modified over the years. The same is true in even greater measure of the next important application of electric power – to the London underground railway system. This began with the building of the first underground electric line, the City and South London Railway, between 1887 and 1890. Electrical power also began to play a part in town and city transport with the introduction of the electric tram.

The horsedrawn tram was introduced into Britain from America in the 1860s, though it might be more accurate to call it a re-introduction, since it was little more than an adaptation for passenger use of the old horsedrawn tramways of the eighteenth century. The electric tram followed quite soon afterwards in the 1880s. Both stages of development can be seen at Douglas in the Isle of Man where a tramway was opened in 1876 and later extended. Single-deck cars, some dating back to the 1880s, are still pulled by horse along the promenade to Derby Castle. There the tramway meets the electrified section of the 1890s. But far and away the most extensive collection of electric trams is to be found at the Tramway Museum at Crich in Derbyshire. Here is a splendid collection of vehicles, dating from the 1880s up to the 1950s, the great majority of which are used in regular passenger services along the mile and a half of track. Visitors can also see the electric sub-station and watch the dials register the sudden surge of power as the trams charge up the hillside. Trams have all but disappeared from commercial use, reserved now for museums and holiday towns. Electric power, however, is still very much with us, and electric power supply is just one of a number of public services which we tend to take for granted – until something goes wrong.

8 Pro Bono Publico

One effect of the Industrial Revolution was a large-scale movement of population away from the country and into the towns. Small towns grew into big towns and big towns grew into cities, often doubling in size in just a few years. The result was hideous overcrowding, atrociously insanitary conditions and, inevitably, disease. There was no lack of qualified observers to make plain what was happening. As early as 1792 a Manchester doctor, John Ferriar, was describing shocking conditions in the town, where grossly overcrowded lodging houses became breeding grounds for disease and 'a lodger from the country often lies down in a bed from which the corpse of a victim to fever has only been removed a few hours before'. He also described the total lack of sanitation, with dung heaps at every back door. There were a few half-hearted attempts at clearing up the town, usually instituted as a response to one of the several epidemics that marked the period, such as the cholera epidemics of 1796 and 1832. Yet as late as the 1840s, when cause and effect had been clearly established, the young Friedrich Engels came to Lancashire and found such wretched conditions that he was moved to write his famous book *Condition of the Working Class in England*. He described the courtyards on the banks of the Irk where 'the inhabitants can pass into and out of the court only by passing through foul pools of stagnant urine and excrement'.

In the villages which the new industrial workers had left behind there was no such pressure on resources. Water was generally available, either from streams or the village pump, and sewage disposal was crude but effective, while such matters as street lighting were simply not regarded as problems; many villages function quite happily without light to this day. The towns were different. The old ways no longer worked, the pressure of numbers was just too great – and no one was prepared to accept responsibility for the nightmarish conditions. Public health authorities when they did anything at all tried to alleviate the symptoms rather than tackle the causes and the nineteenth century was well under way before there was any concerted attempt to deal with even the most basic of problems – the supply of fresh water. Then there was a great rush of new schemes to try and make up for the years of neglect.

Despite this general picture, however, there had been some individual schemes to meet special demands. In 1591, for example, Francis Drake supervised the construction of a long, shallow leat to bring water down from Dartmoor to supply the Navy at Plymouth.

And an interesting and enterprising start was made in public water supply in the seventeenth century. In 1606 Parliament passed an Act authorizing the construction of the New River to bring 'a fresh stream of running water from the springs of Chadwell and Amwell in the County of Hertford, to the north parts of the City of London'. The work was carried out under the direction of Hugh Myddleton. Although the direct distance between Amwell and Clerkenwell, where the New River ended at the Round Pond, is only twenty miles, the river itself took forty miles for the journey. This was due to the elaborate contour cutting of the channel, which enabled Myddleton to devise a route which dropped a mere $15\frac{1}{2}$ feet in the whole forty miles. But just as the early contour canals were often straightened in the nineteenth century, so too the New River was to be much modified to reduce the length to just over twenty-four miles. Much of the old canal does remain, however, though it needs to be hunted down. There are several traces of the original line in Enfield, where the canal can be found winding its way round Forty Hill and on through Whitewebbs Park and Gough Park, while a further disused section around the present boundary to Theobalds Park shows very clearly how the old was built to far smaller dimensions than the New River we see today. Where the latter is over twenty foot wide, the old is just half that.

An important feature of both the old and the modernized route is the use of aqueducts to cross the various streams and rivers met with along the way. The most impressive was a wooden trough, nearly 700 foot long and lined with lead, that crossed the Salmon Brook. The original wooden piers that carried the trough across the brook itself were replaced in 1682 by a brick arch which can still be seen (TQ 324 951). Just to the north of Enfield (TQ 343 988) the Cuffley Brook is now crossed by a siphon pipe. This was the result of another nineteenth-century improvement, when the owner of an estate on nearby Clay Hill bought up the old loop and put in the new straight line. Before the present pipe was built, the water was carried in an iron trough aqueduct which is still visible.

This somewhat lengthy description of the New River has been included partly because it is important as the first major water-supply scheme to be introduced into Britain since Roman times, when numerous small aqueducts brought water to settlements and to industrial sites such as Dolaucothi, and partly as a demonstration of the difficulties in both planning and building the route that had to be overcome by the engineers and their workforce. This goes some way to explaining why there was no great enthusiasm for starting similar schemes. It was not, in fact, until the nineteenth century that there was to be any major improvement in the situation. Development followed two main lines: one was the construction of vast reservoirs, the other was the use of steam-powered pumps to draw water up from underground sources.

The early water-supply reservoirs were constructed in the Pennine valleys, where the techniques employed were those pioneered by the canal builders. William Jessop, for example, had built two major reservoirs at Hollingworth (Greater Manchester) and Blackstone Edge (West Yorkshire) to supply water for the Rochdale Canal. His original instructions to the builders have survived, so that we know the immensity of the earthworks involved. At the middle of the banks was to be puddled clay – clay mixed with sand and water to make an impervious lining – to a depth of nine feet. The earth was then piled around this, to form a bank on a 2:1 horizontal-vertical ratio, the top of the smallest of the banks being ten foot across. Jessop was well aware of the need for extreme care since if even a small crack were to appear the water 'may press with a force of 10,000 Tons'. Perhaps the most famous of all canal reservoirs is the 'Welsh Harp' in London, named after its shape and built to supply the Grand Union Canal. Early water-supply companies used the same techniques as Jessop but had very little understanding of the engineering principles involved. Reservoirs were built ever larger, and the water was contained behind ever more massive earthworks. A whole series of such dams was built to serve the city of Sheffield, one of which, Dale Dyke Reservoir, was created by the construction of a 100-foot high dam. In 1864, the nearly completed dam suddenly subsided and 200 million gallons of water bearing thousands of tons of earth swept down the valley. In the deluge 250 lives were lost and no more schemes of that type were ever attempted again.

Work on reservoirs only resumed in the 1880s, when new theories of masonry construction and Liverpool's increasing need for water led to the start of the biggest scheme of this sort ever undertaken. Liverpool represents a classic example of rapid development, starting as a small town in the eighteenth century and ending the nineteenth century as a principal city and seaport, a rate of growth that led to major water-supply problems. The city fathers looked southwards across the Mersey towards the hills of Wales, which could be clearly seen on a fine day. There were, however, few fine days and rather more when the mountains were lost from view behind heavy rain clouds – a happy state of affairs for those with water supply on their minds. In 1881, a scheme was begun to build a masonry dam across the River Vyrnwy. This was initially under the direction of Thomas Hawksley but he soon retired and the major part of the work was the responsibility of George Deacon. The dam was, and is, remarkable: nearly a quarter of a mile long and 145 foot high, it was built up of stone blocks weighing up to 12 tons each. Behind it a new lake was formed holding 12,000 million gallons of water. There was a certain amount of controversy over the desirability, not to mention the morality, of flooding Welsh valleys to supply English cities with water, and the controversy continues undiminished. Water-supply schemes in Scotland have been less controversial and one nineteenth-century project that deserves comment is that at Loch Katrine which has a dual function as a

recreational area and a reservoir. It was a famed beauty spot before the waters were tapped and led away thirty-five miles south to Glasgow in the 1860s and the new owners of the loch decided to make more use of it in this respect by starting a steamer service. The 1899 steamer *Sir Walter Scott* – what else could it be called? – continues in service. Its splendid triple expansion engine works as well as ever, and there is no fear of its replacement by a petrol or diesel engine since the lake waters must be kept free from pollution. The beauty spot has retained its beauty, and the citizens of Glasgow have their water; a public service is provided with no harm to the environment.

The alternative method of water supply that was to become increasingly important to the English Midlands and the London region was the use of the steam pump to raise water from rivers and underground sources. Londoners had been accustomed to having water pumped up from the Thames before the age of steam – though it was most certainly not drinking water they received. Steam engines

The Vyrnwy dam, Powys, under construction in 1887. This is the downstream face looking south-west.

162

increased the supply, and there was a distinct improvement in the product when legislators insisted that the water could only be taken from the non-tidal reaches and then had to be passed through filter beds. Steam engines were soon also involved in two other jobs: lifting water from deep wells to fill reservoirs, and lifting water from reservoirs up to storage tanks from where gravity could take over the task of delivery to the customers.

One of the most impressive collections of engines installed for such work can be seen at the Kew Bridge Waterworks at Brentford in West London (now the Kew Bridge Engines Trust and Water Supply Museum). The four Cornish engines worked right up to 1944. They include a beam engine built by Harveys of Hayle in 1869 which, with its 100-inch diameter cylinder, is the biggest in Britain. Other engines include a Boulton and Watt engine of 1820 and a Bull engine. The pumping station is now open to visitors, and engines are regularly steamed.

The great days of the Victorian pumping engines are done, but happily many have been taken over by volunteers and are regularly steamed. Their appeal is obvious. Many of the engines are especially fine examples of big beam engines and have been given quite extraordinarily elaborate engine houses. Two are particularly striking. Ryhope, near Sunderland in Tyne and Wear, has a quite magnificent gabled engine house, and a scarcely less elaborate boiler house alongside which is a tall stack. The two engines are equally stately, for they are big, compound engines, each having $27\frac{1}{2}$-inch bore high-pressure cylinders and 45-inch bore low-pressure cylinders. They were built in 1868 by Hawthorns of Newcastle. Papplewick Pumping Station in Nottingham is even more elaborate and fantastic in design than Ryhope. The engine house has pillars decorated with fish and water plants and ending in capitals in the form of ibises, while the watery theme is continued in the stained glass windows that decorate the house. It is interesting to note that all this magnificence existed in a remote pumping station which must have seen very few visitors once the official opening ceremony was out of the way. The splendour remained and was kept splendid by the diligent staff, for it was a source of pride to all who worked there. And the same is true today, for the building is as carefully tended as the two 1884 beam engines, believed to be the last ever delivered from the famous James Watt Company.

The beam engine is very much the machine that is associated with early water-pumping stations, but other types were installed. The Mill Meece Pumping Station in Staffordshire was completed in 1915 and has a pair of horizontal tandem compound engines which have been restored to steam for visitors. Even more recently two vertical triple expansion engines were installed in Kempton Park Waterworks in Hounslow in London in 1928. Coming down in scale from these giants, the biggest engines of their type in Britain, there are also

examples of pumping engines using a quite different principle. In 1859 a Frenchman, Etienne Lenoir, built a gas engine in which a gas-air mixture was introduced into a cylinder and ignited, the resulting expansion of the gas driving the piston. By introducing the mixture alternately on either side of the piston, something that worked very like a horizontal steam engine could be produced. Such an engine can be seen in the basement of Abingdon Town Hall, Oxfordshire, where it was used to power a pump for local water supply.

Other features associated with water supply can often be of considerable interest. For example, one necessarily large and often dominant feature in any landscape is the water tower. Designers often sought to disguise this very functional object in a number of ways. The Perth Waterworks' engineer and architect, Adam Anderson, devised a classical building in 1832 in which the water tank was built as a rotunda with domed roof and Ionic pilasters, the whole thing being constructed out of cast iron. Equally remarkable is the Appleton water tower in Norfolk, which was disguised as a prospect tower. The man in charge had a cottage built in under the tank and the flue from

The splendid 1891 steam pumping engines in their ornate engine house at the Abbey Sewage Works, Leicester, now form the centre-piece of the Leicestershire Museum of Technology.

his hearth went up through the tank itself to keep the water from freezing in winter. The tower has, by a curious quirk, ended up by becoming what it at first only pretended to be – a prospect tower and holiday home.

Improvements in water supply were paralleled by improvements in sewage disposal – and, by the nineteenth century, such improvements were desperately needed. It is a sad reflection on our concept of progress that sewage treatment at the beginning of the nineteenth century was far worse than it had been in the first century of Roman occupation. Excavations at York under the old Roman fortress have revealed a superbly constructed sewer system, consisting of low, narrow tunnels lined with dressed stone. In eighteenth-century London, sewage went straight into the River Fleet from where it was washed into the Thames. In theory, the tide then carried the rubbish out to sea. That theory was well and truly divorced from practice was dramatically demonstrated in the 1850s when a series of hot summers brought such a stench from the river that the curtains at Westminster were daily soaked in disinfectant in a vain attempt to protect the sensitive nostrils of Members of Parliament. It was generally agreed that something needed to be done, and something was done.

Building the London sewers. The illustration shows one of the branches of the main northern sewer under construction in 1859. From the Illustrated London News, *August 27, 1859.*

The engineer, Joseph Bazalgette, who was already at work on the construction of the new Thames embankment, was the man chosen for the task. He built an entire new sewer system for London, one of the most remarkable examples of civil engineering in the entire Victorian age. A complex system of small sewers led down to the main sewers which ran along the bank of the Thames to what is now Thamesmead. The statistics give some idea of the work involved: 1300 miles of sewer were constructed using over 300 million bricks. At the terminus of the system, the sewage was run into settling tanks, where the solid matter could be removed and loaded into barges for dumping at sea. The liquid was pumped out into the Thames on the ebb tide to be carried away. The Crossness Pumping Station, built in 1864, is yet another splendidly ornate Victorian building. Four Watt beam engines were installed which were later converted to triple expansion. Great improvements though they were in their day, the Victorian pumping engines can, however, no longer cope with modern needs. As with water-supply engines, a number of sewage pumping engines have been preserved. The former Abbey Lane Pumping Station in Leicester, for example, is now home to an industrial museum and the 1891 engines are regularly steamed.

One new, ingenious use was found for London's sewage. In 1895, J.E. Webb patented a sewer gas lamp which quite simply used the gas generated naturally in the sewers to provide light for the streets above. An example of one of Webb's lamps can be seen in Carting Lane, London, just off the Strand, though it is no longer in use. Nor indeed are other, more conventional, gas lamps in general use, although the station buildings and approach roads of the Keighley and Worth Valley Railway are gaslit. But not long ago it was the gas lamp that provided the lighting for streets and houses in any town which had any pretensions to importance.

The story of the gas industry begins with the story of coke. As early as the thirteenth century, it was recognized that the residue left after heating coal in a closed hearth had quite different properties from the coal itself. Uses were found for this substance, coke, especially in the iron industry after the introduction of the coke-fired blast furnace. The essential feature of coke production is that the coal should not come into contact with the atmosphere, and should smoulder rather than burn – much as wood smoulders to produce charcoal. The simplest method was to cover a huge heap of coal with damp straw or hay and earth and leave it to smoulder gently for several days. In the north-east of England coke making was put on to a more systematic basis with the introduction of the beehive oven. These stone-built ovens, whose shape gave them their name, were arranged in long rows or batteries, which were fed with coal from trucks that ran along a track at the top of the battery. Coke was drawn out at the bottom. This system remained in use from the middle of the eighteenth century until the 1950s, when the last set at Rowland's Gill in Tyne and Wear

Charging a battery of coke ovens with coal at Rowland's Gill, Tyne and Wear, in the 1950s.

Scraping coke from the back of the oven, Rowland's Gill.

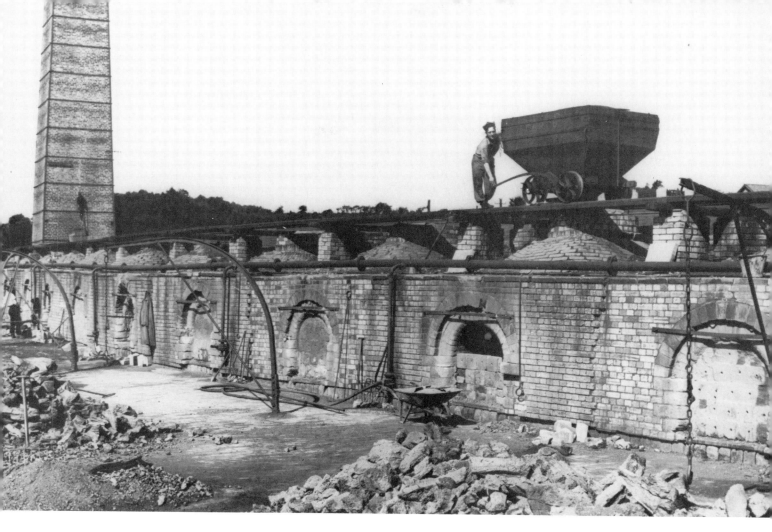

was closed down. There were originally almost two hundred beehive ovens in the battery, and they stopped work in 1958 just two years short of celebrating a century of use. The vast majority are now in ruins, but four ovens have been preserved as an industrial monument.

During the manufacture of coke, gas was given off which burned with a bright flame. In the 1790s William Murdock, an engineer employed in Cornwall by Boulton and Watt, began a series of experiments on the controlled heating of coal to produce gas. He was sufficiently successful to be able to leave his home in Redruth and set up in business. In 1802 he built a gas plant for Boulton and Watt who used it to illuminate the factory, and then proceeded to use the factory to manufacture gas plant for others. Gas was produced by a simple process in which coal was packed into horizontal tubes or retorts and then heated by a furnace. The gas rose up from the retorts and then passed to a condenser, where jets of water condensed out the tar and washed it away into a pit. After that the gas was ready for use. It proved immensely popular with manufacturers who could now keep their factories open night and day, and it played an important part in changing the pattern of life of the industrial worker. Where, in the past, work had been regulated by the hours of daylight, the new light meant that work could be continuous. In the cotton mills it became a common practice for apprentice children to work twelve-hour shifts: as one set of children rose from their beds, the next shift took their places. So it came to be said that the beds of Lancashire never grew cold.

In 1812, the Gas Light and Coke Company was formed in London, the first gas works as we know it, producing gas for a large number of customers by piping it from the works via cast-iron mains. Other gas companies were soon formed in other towns, so that gas lighting became a familiar part of the urban scene with lamps in the streets, in public buildings and, increasingly, in private houses. Few of these town gas works have survived the arrival of North Sea gas, but one small works has been preserved at Biggar in Strathclyde. It was established in 1839 as the Biggar Gas Light Company and continued in use until 1973, the works taking on their present form in a major reconstruction in 1914. It was a typical small horizontal retort works, the retorts themselves being hand fired. The process was still basically that invented by Murdock, though the cleaning of the gas was much more efficient. The gas passed through a whole series of scrubbers and washers so that by-products such as ammonia and coal tar could be reclaimed. The gas was then pumped into one of two gas holders popularly, but erroneously, known as gasometers. The simplest gas holders rest on water, which seals the bottom of the holder, and they rise up as gas is pumped in. The larger holders consist of several cylinders, which fit one inside the other, so that the entire holder gradually opens out like a giant telescope. These are still the structures which are universally associated with gas works and are still to be seen

Charging the retorts at a gas works. From the Illustrated London News, *November 2, 1878.*

throughout the country. The story of the use of gas is told in the John Doran Museum, housed in part of the old Aylestone Road gasworks in Leicester.

Gas lighting had a long reign, in spite of the discovery of electro-magnetism by Faraday in 1831 which offered an alternative. The first experiments with electric light were not in fact carried out until twenty years later when F.H. Holmes demonstrated an arc lamp at Trinity House in which the light was supplied by an electric arc struck between two electrodes. After that successful experiment, arc lamps were installed in the South Foreland Lighthouse in 1858, but it took until 1872 for final approval to be given for the use of electricity in the place of the old oil lamps. South Foreland also achieved distinction as the first place at which radio was used as a navigation aid, when Marconi used it to contact the East Goodwin Lightship in 1898. Lighthouses still need their own electric generators to ensure operation whatever happens elsewhere, and a fascinating collection of early generating equipment can be seen in the museum attached to the Lizard Lighthouse in Cornwall.

The generation of electricity depends on a wire moving through the force field of a magnet, so that the essential feature of all generators is that some form of movement must be produced. Either the wire can be moved in the force field, or the field itself can be moved by rotating the magnet. At first it seemed sensible to turn to the familiar steam engine to power the generator, but the old engines proved unsuitable. It was Sir Charles Parsons who appreciated that the problem could be solved by using a turbine instead of the conventional steam engine. His first turbines consisted of a shaft fitted with blades, the rotor, set inside a fixed case lined with blades, the stator. Steam was passed in at one end and, as it moved between the two sets of blades, so it caused the rotor to spin. He installed his system at the Forth Banks Power Station in Newcastle in 1884. He then went on to adapt the turbine to other uses, notably marine propulsion. His experimental vessel *Turbinia* of 1894 was an immediate success and has been preserved in its own museum at Newcastle. It was built with a three-stage turbine and proved far faster than any other vessel on the water at that date. In the generation of electricity, however, the turbine could also be adapted to run from a different form of power. Instead of being turned by steam it could be moved by water in the hydroelectric power station.

Few early power stations survive but one excellent early example can be seen in the Roe Valley Country Park in Londonderry. Water power had been brought to the valley in the seventeenth and eighteenth centuries to work both grain and textile mills. By the end of the nineteenth century, however, the linen industry was in a sorry state and when J.E. Ritter took over part of the valley in the 1890s he decided to use the water power to turn a small generator so that he could light his home of Roe Park. The scheme was successful, and in 1896 he built a far larger turbine to provide power and light for the

Battersea Power Station, London (1932): a famous landmark beside the Thames, the question of its future is still to be resolved.

LEFT *One of Britain's first hydroelectric power stations at Roe Valley, Londonderry.*

nearby town of Limavady, the original equipment for which can be seen today. One of the earliest generating stations to survive in England is the Kensington Court Generating Station of 1889 in West London, built to serve a new housing development. But although the building with its inscription 'Electric Lighting Station' can still be seen, the machinery has gone. Although few very early sites remain, there are many later ones which are destined to provide huge problems for the conservationists of the future. Battersea Power Station, such a dominant feature of London's riverside, was listed as a building of outstanding historic importance in 1981. In many ways this is splendid news, but leaves one question unanswered. What is to be done with such a vast building? Electric power is a vital ingredient in the story of industrial development in the twentieth century, but the preservation of its more important memorials will be no easy matter, and already many of the old, coal-fired power stations have been destroyed.

RIGHT *The steam winding engine used to haul trucks up the Middleton incline on the Cromford and High Peak Railway, Derbyshire.*

BELOW *Getting up steam on the Ffestiniog Railway, Gwynedd.*

RIGHT *The rail bridge across the Firth of Forth. Opened in 1890, it was one of the great engineering feats of its day. The bridge is just over 1½ miles long and the railway track runs 157 feet above the water.*

BELOW *The working replica of Stephenson's* Locomotion *at the North of England Open Air Museum, Beamish, Co. Durham. The original was built for the opening of the Stockton and Darlington Railway in 1825.*

Cheddleton Flint Mill, Staffordshire. There are two mills, each powered by a breastshot water wheel fed by a leat from the River Churnet. The mills are of uncertain origin but reached their present form in the 1780s.

BELOW *The majestic ruins of the Cwmystradllyn slate factory, Gwynedd. It was here that slates from the nearby quarry were cut and shaped.*

9 Back to Basics

Any survey of industrial history, unless it extends to encyclopaedic proportions, will contain gaps and this is no exception. There are, nevertheless, some industrial activities which are so closely related to the everyday life of everyone in the country that they cannot be ignored, even though they cannot be made to fit into some neat, pre-ordained pattern. Early on, we looked at some of the special minerals extracted from the earth and used by man. Here we shall return to a similar topic, but look at much more direct uses of natural resources.

Amongst the earliest industrial activities known to man are those which use the materials found in the ground beneath his feet: stone for building, clay for ceramic ware and sand for glass. Indeed, this sort of activity was very common and it was frequently carried out on such a small scale that it scarcely registers as an industrial activity at all. The simple labourer's cottage could be built out of stone literally picked up from the surrounding land. In some areas, pots could be manufactured from nothing more than the clay found outside the front door, moulded by a skilled pair of hands. Such processes only count as industrial activity when the stone is of such exceptionally good quality that it can be quarried commercially, or when the simple pots are being manufactured for sale over a wide area. Glass is the exception, in that its manufacture always depended on a comparatively high level of organization.

Of all these varied activities, the quarrying of stone has been the most widespread, the method by which it was won varying according to the nature of the stone. Small quarries can be found throughout Britain, but some areas are of special interest because the particular qualities of the stone made it especially valuable to builders, Bath stone and Portland stone being excellent examples. Bath stone has certainly been quarried since Roman times but, unlike most other building stones, much of it had to be taken from underground workings. Extensive deposits of first-rate building stone were found to occur in layers beneath other, less durable stone strata. The area round Box Hill in Wiltshire is riddled with tunnels leading to these underground quarries, now mostly closed off for safety. At Monk's Park, just south of Corsham, one of the last of these mines can be found, its underground workings so extensive that during the Second World War it was used as a secure site for building aircraft. The stone from Portland, Dorset, offered no such problems and conventional quarries were and are in use. The great quarried blocks can be seen piled up along the eastern cliff like a succession of prehistoric monuments. Moving such blocks was an immense labour, much eased by the construction of a tramway, the Merchants' Railway, in 1825. The track was later taken over by a conventional steam railway and can be easily followed from a point above the harbour where the line of an inclined plane is clearly visible. This was used to connect the tramway to the ships which formed the only trade route between the island and the mainland until the construction of a causeway and the opening of the Weymouth and Portland Railway.

The difficulties of transporting stone from remote quarries led to the construction of a variety of different transport systems, one of which is of special interest. The quarries of Haytor on Dartmoor in Devon provided excellent granite but also presented considerable problems when it came to transporting the stone. A tramway was the obvious answer, but iron for the rails was difficult to come by and very expensive. Stone, on the other hand, was readily available and cheap, so in 1820 the Haytor granite tramway was constructed using stone rails. On this route the rails were themselves made out of the local granite, and proved remarkably durable as the many lengths that can still be followed across the moor testify.

Not all quarried stone was intended for use as a building material. Lime was a valuable commodity which found a variety of applications, from the making of quicklime to its use in agriculture for the treatment of acid soils. Wherever limestone was found, there you will find lime kilns. Many are built up against hillsides, on the same principle as blast furnaces, so that stone and fuel can be loaded in at the top and the burned lime drawn off at the bottom. And because lime was a commodity that found so many uses in so many areas, the kilns were often built close to a convenient transport route. The tiny quay at Cotehele (NT) on the River Tamar, for example, is all but surrounded by kilns, and a very well-preserved group of big kilns can be seen by the harbour at Beadnell (NT) in Northumberland where they are now used as stores by the local fishermen. Inland waterways also provided attractive sites and there is a particularly interesting spot at Dudley in the West Midlands where quarries, canal and kilns form a coherent group. Dudley Hill itself was honeycombed with limestone workings, and in 1792 the Dudley Canal tunnel was completed, piercing the hill and connecting the various underground workings. The tunnel is itself a remarkable piece of engineering; visitors who take the boat trip through the tunnel find it alternating between low, narrow passages and the wide expanses of the underground quarries. At the northern end, in what is now the Black Country Museum, is an impressive range of lime kilns built alongside a wharf for ease of transport.

One particular type of quarry, the slate quarry, has proved of

Lime kilns on the quay at Beadnell, Northumberland (NT). They are now used as stores by local fishermen.

An intersection on the Haytor granite tramway, Devon. This Dartmoor railway was entirely constructed of stone.

special interest to conservationists in recent years. Slate is found in many regions, and workings are often of considerable antiquity, though most of the visible remains date from the eighteenth and nineteenth centuries. In Cornwall, for example, the deeds of the Delabole Slate Company go right back to the fourteenth century. Since then the Delabole quarry has seen a great many changes. There was a period of considerable expansion in the late eighteenth century when complex machinery was first used. The quarry was sunk to a great depth and pumps had to be introduced to keep the workings dry. Inclined planes were constructed to join the quarry floor to the surface, and steam engines were soon in use for winding. This machinery has now all been replaced, for the quarry is still at work and can boast of being the largest man-made hole in Britain, five hundred foot deep with a circumference of over a mile and a half.

It was the growth of the industrial town that created a demand for slate to roof the new town houses, a demand that was met in good measure by the slate quarries and mines of North Wales. Then, as cheap composites came to replace the more expensive slates, the demand died away and the industry began to die, leaving behind ravaged mountains lapped by a tide of broken slate. Blaenau Ffestiniog, Gwynedd, the slate town par excellence, is ringed by workings, by hills that have been sliced away and bored through. It is quite possible to see this as no more than despoliation on a massive scale, but there is grandeur here as well, for the magnitude of the work was immense. It is this that has ensured a continuing life for many of the old workings as industrial museums. Trains take visitors into underground passages to see how the slate was blasted, and back above ground there are demonstrations of how the craftsmen cut and shaped the blocks of slate by machine and by hand.

Perhaps the most impressive of all the quarries is the Dinorwic quarry of Llanberis further to the north. Here the side of the mountain has been sliced off to create a cliff of sheer faces, crossed by terraces joined to one another by steep inclines. At the foot of the cliff a narrow-gauge railway runs along the side of the lake, though now the traffic is limited to holidaymakers. The quarry's workshops now form the Welsh Slate Museum, and here can be seen a full range of machinery for repairing and maintaining virtually everything needed in the quarries. Here, too, visitors can learn something of the often dangerous life of the men who worked on the high faces. But for anyone of a romantic disposition, who wishes not just to see an industrial building that is in itself fascinating but also to feel that special melancholy produced by the sight of something that was once great but whose majesty is now in ruin, then the place to visit is Cwmystradllyn in the hills above Dolbenmaen in Gwynedd (SH 550 434). In a spot as remote from industrial life as one could imagine stands a slate factory, a huge granite shell. It has been called the Cathedral of the Slate Industry and the name seems apt enough for it is easier to imagine

The largest man-made hole in Britain, with a circumference of more than a mile and half: Delabole slate quarry, Cornwall.

The vast Penrhyn slate quarries, Gwynedd, in 1852, by Alfred Sumners. At the beginning of the nineteenth century the quarry employed several thousand men and the slate was shipped by sea to other parts of the country.

that one has stumbled across some old monastery than a factory for cutting slate. Yet all the evidence for the old workings is still here. The dam that retained the waters of the millpond area can be seen, as can the pit where the wheel turned to power the machinery of the factory. And from the factory, the line of a tramway can be traced leading away to the remote quarry.

Britain is a small land, but its geology is extraordinarily rich and varied, so that where one area provides stone for building, just a few miles away there might be pits from which clay is dug for bricks or tiles. Brick making was, until well into the nineteenth century, often a very local affair. Bricks are, in essence, blocks of burned clay and at a myriad of small sites, especially in the Midlands and Southern England, the clay was moulded by hand and burned in improvised kilns. Even major users, such as the canal companies, with their heavy demand for bricks for bridges, tunnel linings, locks and water-side buildings, would frequently dig their own pits and fire their own bricks rather than go to the expense of transporting them from else-where. Some of these sites proved particularly successful and continued as brickworks after the immediate task was completed. At Devizes, on the Kennet and Avon Canal in Wiltshire, a brickworks was established during the building of the Caen Hill locks and continued in use until the middle of the present century. A happy result of this diversity of sites can be seen in early brick buildings. Local clays have their own characteristics and produce quite distinctive bricks, while the lack of proper temperature control in the simple kilns added still more colour variations. The phrase 'red brick', has, in more recent times, been associated with dull uniformity, but early brick buildings offer delightful richness and variety.

Few early brickworks survive with anything much in the way of recognizable structures. One notable exception is at Nettlebed in Oxfordshire, where a thirty-foot tall conical kiln can be seen. It is of somewhat uncertain date, but may well be as early as the seventeenth century. There is a bricked-in arch, clearly distinguishable at the base, through which the kiln could be loaded and unloaded. Standardization arrived in the 1850s with the introduction of the Hoffman kiln, named after its designer, Friedrich Hoffman. It was circular with chambers radiating out from a central chimney, and was worked as a continuous process. The heating flues were made of the unfired bricks themselves. After firing, the hot gases were admitted to the next flue and cold air sucked into the hearth was passed over the fired bricks to cool them before removal. The circular kiln was soon followed by a continuous long-chamber kiln. Few such structures survive at all, even in a ruinous state, but the Cove Bottom Brickworks at South Cove, Suffolk, dating from the mid nineteenth century, only stopped working recently.

Tile manufacture is closely associated with brick making and buildings connected with major manufacturers survive at Jackfield in the Ironbridge Gorge in Shropshire. But perhaps the best of the early works is the Blackpots Brick and Tile Works at Boyndie in Grampian. Dating back to the late eighteenth century, but with many additions and replacements, the buildings are now falling into decay, though the plateway can still be traced back to the clay pits themselves. One major museum which is specializing to quite a large extent on building materials is the Chalk Pits Museum at Houghton Bridge, West Sussex. Here a brickworks is being established, a small kiln is being rebuilt, and a brickworks drying shed from Petersfield in Hampshire has already been re-erected. The shed protected newly-made ware such as tiles and pipes as they were slowly hardened in the warmth of the underfloor heating system.

Local clays suitable for brick making could often also be used for pot making. This might appear, at first glance, to be a somewhat tenuous connection, but in fact the nature of the raw material makes it equally fitted for either purpose. Baked clay can be made impervious to water, so that it can be used just as well to keep rain out of a house as to keep liquid in a pitcher or bowl. Pot works and brick and tile works are therefore often found in close proximity. Brickworks were established in many parts of Britain, and where the clay appeared particularly well suited to other purposes, a small country pottery was often set up to produce simple earthenware items.

Wetheriggs Pottery, Cumbria, in 1906; the kiln and engine house can be seen on the left.

A fine example of a nineteenth-century pottery of this type is Wetheriggs at Clifton Dykes, near Penrith in Cumbria. Clay was dug from adjoining pits, over sixty foot deep, the tunnel entrance to which can still be seen, and from there it was taken on a short tramway to the works. The trucks were hauled by a stationary steam engine, which also worked the other machinery on site. The original engine was scrapped and replaced by an 1890 horizontal engine early this century. Before the clay could be shaped into pots it had to be cleaned and prepared. It was put into a round pit, known as the blunger, where it was mixed with water and broken down into a slurry by rotating blades. Stones and impurities sank to the bottom of the pit and the slurry was run off into settling tanks to be dried by the sun. When it had reached the right consistency, the clay was chopped up into forty pound lumps and taken away to the store. When enough clay was ready to make a complete load of ware it was taken to the pugmill where the individual lumps were forced together into a continuous length, a great clay sausage. Finally, to ensure consistency and to get rid of any small air bubbles, the clay was 'wedged'. The wedger took a length of clay from the pugmill, cut it in half and then reunited the two halves by slamming one half down on the other. This was done several times with each lump of clay. When that process was complete the clay was at last ready for shaping into pots.

The potters' wheels were kept turning at a steady rate by the steam engine, and potteries such as Wetheriggs depended more on speed of manufacture than on artistry for their profits. The nineteenth-century potter might well spend an entire day turning flower pots at the rate of three a minute. When shaped, the pots were set to dry and a glaze added. Then they were taken to the kiln which in this case is one of the comparatively rare beehive kilns, a domed structure as the name suggests. The pots were stacked inside on shelves made of a clay and fireclay mixture, or placed in saggars, boxes made of the same material. The kiln was coal-fired and stoked through arches in the outer wall. When the kiln was full, it was bricked up and the fire stoked up all round. Then the fireboxes were also bricked up, leaving just enough space for stoking. The fires burned for up to thirty-six hours, and then the kiln was slowly cooled to prevent the ware from cracking. Finally, the kiln was reopened, the ware removed, packed and sent on its way. All these different aspects of manufacture can be seen at the works, though today the pottery produces ware using more modern methods. The old works represent a complex series of processes, even if each process was in itself somewhat crude. Similar methods were also in use in the major centres of the industry: the difference lay in the increased scale of the operations and in the organization of the work.

The modern pottery industry developed from changes brought about in the Stoke-on-Trent area in the eighteenth century, and those changes were largely initiated by one man, Josiah Wedgwood. He was determined to bring high-quality ware to a wide market, both in Britain and abroad. This involved him in the vigorous promotion of the Trent and Mersey Canal, which would enable him to send out ware to other regions and, just as importantly, bring in raw materials from different parts of the country. The potter no longer had to rely on what he found on his own doorstep – literally, according to popular tradition, which tells of Staffordshire potters making good deficiencies in their supplies by digging up the road outside the works. When local residents complained of potholes in their roads they meant just that. The introduction of a greater variety of raw materials led to a greater complexity in the works, and Wedgwood's move towards mass production and standardization called for rigorous controls at all stages of production. Old methods of working had essentially been those of the medieval craft, of the journeyman who could, and did, control all aspects of the work, helped by assistants and apprentices. Wedgwood changed all that. Manufacture was broken down into stages. Instead of a craft-based industry in which individuals controlled everything, there was now a flow system, where the ware moved from specialist department to specialist department, starting with the preparation of raw material and ending with the finished product. It was, in effect, an assembly line.

Wedgwood put his new system to work in the Etruria factory built beside the canal. His inspiration came from the classical pottery of Greece and Rome, so he gave his buildings an appropriate classical facade. Behind this facade, everything was organized on a regular plan to facilitate the smooth production line. Very little now remains of the original works, the Wedgwood company having moved to Barlaston, further south in Staffordshire, but the Wedgwood plan was soon followed by other manufacturers and his influence can be seen in their works, which show similar classical facades to the world. The logical arrangement of the works can also be seen in a typical small nineteenth-century pottery, now the Gladstone Pottery Museum, in Longton, Staffordshire.

Bottle kilns at the Gladstone Pottery, Staffordshire. The inner furnace can be seen through the entrance to the nearest kiln.

The Gladstone Pottery followed the basic Wedgwood pattern. Access from the street is through a tunnel under the manager's office to a courtyard around which are grouped the various workshops. The processes are very similar to those at Wetheriggs, starting with a steam-powered blunger. The main 'production line' is at ground-floor level, where ware was made both by throwing on the wheel and by moulding. The upper floors were used for other parts of the process, such as hand painting and design, which stood apart from the main line. The kilns at Gladstone are bottle kilns. These were once found in profusion throughout the region and are notably different from the kiln at Wetheriggs. As with the beehive kiln, the ware is held in saggars which are then stacked round a central furnace. But the tall bottle kilns ensured a better draught to the furnace than was possible in the beehive kilns, and so higher temperatures could be reached. There are two big kilns, one for the unglazed 'biscuit' ware and one for glazed ware, and there is also a small enamelling kiln used for the most expensive, gilded ware. One of Wedgwood's principal contributions to the development of the Stoke region was the introduction of a new type of earthenware; in contrast to the traditional dark, heavy earthenware he began producing light, delicately-coloured ware that was acceptable to the rapidly developing middle-class market. To do this he had to introduce new materials, which were mixed with the local clays. If pottery has a dark body it can only be given a light colour by covering with a thick glaze; but if the body colour can be made lighter, then a thinner glaze can be used and the resulting ware will be more delicate. The first agent to be used for lightening the clay body was powdered flint, the powdering being done in special flint mills in the area.

There is a fine eighteenth-century flint mill at Cheddleton, Staffordshire, a small town linked to the main pottery centres by the Caldon Canal that joins the Trent and Mersey at Etruria. The flints were brought to the canal wharf into which was built a pair of small kilns. Here the flints were heated (calcined) to make them brittle and easier to crush. The system is similar to that used in lime kilns, the material being fed in at the top and removed at the bottom, when the heated flint was taken on a short plateway to the mill. There are actually two main mill buildings, each with its own water wheel. The grinding takes place on the upper floors, where the flints were loaded into circular pans. Water was added and the flints crushed under heavy stones attached to rotating arms. The flint slurry was then run down into settling tanks, finally dried off in a kiln and sent off to the potter. Later, the water-powered mill was replaced by the steam mill, and just such a mill is currently being restored to its original form at Etruria. The Etruscan Bone and Flint Mill was built into the angle formed by the junction of the Caldon and Trent and Mersey Canals, and the engine house of 1857 with its shaped gables is a prominent feature of the site. Everything is on a far larger scale than at

The Etruscan Bone and Flint Mill, Staffordshire, on the Trent and Mersey Canal. The gabled building is the steam engine house.

Cheddleton, with twelve grinding pans instead of two, but the principle is exactly the same.

An alternative method of producing a white clay body is to start with a light coloured clay, such as china clay. Using this material, however, posed a problem: the deposits are in Devon and Cornwall, while the coal for firing – and the expertise in pot making – was in Staffordshire. There were attempts to take pot making to the clay, and one fine early Cornish pottery survives at Truro, but in general it was found to be far better to carry the clay to the Midlands. Once again the advantages of a sound transport system were demonstrated.

The Cornish china clay region fans out from St Austell and dominates this part of the country with an eerie landscape all its own, scarred by deep clay pits and strange, unnaturally white mountains of spoil. One of the older clay works, Wheal Martyn, has been preserved and is now the museum of the industry. Wheal Martyn was established when the Martyn family moved to the area in the 1790s. Today it provides an excellent example of the way in which china clay was won and treated in the early years of the industry. The clay, or kaolin, was removed from the pits as a slurry by a pump. The pump and its source of power were often a long way apart, and at Wheal Martyn they were a mile away from each other. Power came from a 35-foot diameter water wheel and was transmitted to the pump itself by a system of flat rods worked through a crank. In many cases, once the slurry reached the works, gravity could be relied on to take over the job of moving it from process to process. At Wheal Martyn, however, the site is small and awkward so a second water-powered pump had to be installed to carry the slurry up the hillside. It could then be run down through a series of sand traps and settling tanks so that impurities could be removed. Those impurities were eventually carried away to form the huge tips which dominate the area while the slurry was run into tanks to be dried out. Once it reached the consistency of a thick, glutinous mass it was loaded into trucks and taken to the 'dry', in effect a vast kiln. This was immensely hard work, for each of the tanks held something like 250 tons of wet clay, all of which was loaded by hand. The dry is a long building with a furnace at one end and a chimney at the other. The gases from the fire passed through flues under the floor, on which the clay was laid to be dried. Finally, the dried clay was carried away to one of the clay ports, such as Par or Charlestown, for shipment to the potteries.

The pottery industry uses a large number of different raw materials to produce an immense variety of products, from delicate table ware to industrial ceramics. A very important part of the treatment of basic pottery is the addition of a glaze – the covering of the porous pot with an impervious, hard shell. This can be done for purely practical reasons or as a decoration, but the glaze itself is simply a form of glass. Indeed, the production of pottery glazes occurred long before glass came to be used in its own right: glazing dates back to at least 4000 BC while the first glass vessels were not produced until around 1500 BC. In both cases, the basic materials are the same – sand, lime and soda fused together at high temperature. The process is more involved than the production of pottery from clay and, for a long time, glass remained an expensive luxury. The poorer people took their drinks from earthenware pots not glasses, and their windows were holes in the wall covered by wooden shutters. Until comparatively recently, only the rich could afford glass windows.

Glass making is complicated by several factors. Glass itself is a poor conductor of heat – a great advantage when it is used in windows but a problem in manufacture, for the surface of the glass from the furnace would cool very rapidly if allowed to do so, setting up strains and tensions. So, a glass furnace uses a two-stage process – frittering, where the ingredients are first heated together, and annealing, where they are slowly cooled in controlled conditions. In some respects, the glass furnace has much in common with the pottery kiln, but with the essential difference that the glass workers needed to work within the cover of the furnace itself.

We are fortunate in that one early furnace does remain. It was built at Rosedale in the heart of the North Yorkshire moors in the sixteenth century, using a design introduced at that time by Flemish glass makers. It has been dismantled and re-erected at the Ryedale Folk Museum at Hutton-le-Hole, North Yorkshire. At the centre of the furnace is the hearth which held the wood fire, flanked by crucibles containing the raw materials for glass making. This central area could be closed off during firing, but holes were left so that the glass makers could push their pipes into the molten glass, withdrawing globules for blowing and shaping. The glass objects were then annealed in side chambers, kept at a high temperature by the central furnace.

The same general idea was adapted in the coal-fired furnaces of the eighteenth and nineteenth centuries. Here the main structure was in the form of a tall cone and a few of these impressive features have survived. Two especially fine examples are the Catcliffe cone near Sheffield in South Yorkshire, and the cone at the still active glass works of Stuart & Sons at Stourbridge in West Midlands.

All the materials discussed so far in this chapter have played an important part in the construction industry, so this is an appropriate point to introduce one of the earliest materials used by man the builder – timber. Like stone, timber requires no complicated processing before use, other than weathering and shaping to size. And the industrial element is further reduced in that timber felling involves no works on the scale required for quarrying. So physical remains of the industry are necessarily limited to the last stage, that of cutting the timber to size. For centuries, the saw pit answered the need as far as cutting the large logs into manageable planks was concerned. The timber was placed across the pit and cut by a saw worked by two men: one stood on top of the timber holding one end of the saw, while the second man was down in the pit, where he received all the sawdust full in the face. This arduous and unpleasant task was relieved, as so many other hard tasks had been, by the introduction of power from water wheel and steam engine.

Dunham Massey Mill, part of the Dunham Massey estate (NT) in Greater Manchester, was built *c.* 1600 as a corn mill. Externally it has changed little over the years, and is a most charming building with its gabled stone roof and rich brickwork. However, late in the nineteenth century the mill was converted and refitted as a sawmill and workshop. Power came from an overshot water wheel, 15 feet 4 inches in diameter, and was transmitted to the machinery through line-shafting. Perhaps the most interesting machine is the frame saw which is the mechanical equivalent of the old pit saw. This is the oldest type of mechanical saw and was first introduced *c.* 1600. Later developments can be seen in the circular saw and band saw, and there are other woodworking implements, including a boring machine, a lathe and a crane, used for moving heavy timber around the workshop. All the machines have been restored to working order.

The Blackgang Sawmill Museum on the Isle of Wight shows the development of the timber trade in the steam age. A steam winch was used to haul the logs, while a portable Ruston Proctor engine was used in conjunction with a small sawbench. Inside the main sawmill building there is a much larger sawbench, built more than a century ago, the main iron frame for which was cast as a single piece. The drive for the rotary saw blades came via flat belts from a 1939 oil engine. Such engines were designed to work on the cheapest oil even, according to the makers, 'palm or cotton seed oil'. The sawmill is now a museum and there are also displays showing how timber was used by coopers, carpenters and wheelwrights. In a specially con-

structed hovel, a bodger's tools can be seen. To the uninitiated, the term 'bodger's hovel' might suggest a filthy workshop used by an incompetent carpenter. In fact, hovel is simply another name for a wooden hut and, although the bodger worked with simple tools producing simple objects, he was by no means incompetent. He worked in the woodland itself, producing such items as the bevelled legs for Windsor chairs.

Some large estates combined woodworking and ironworking, and such a workshop was built at Combe in Oxfordshire to serve the adjoining Blenheim estate. Here there was a smithy, carpenters' shop and sawmill under one roof. What makes Combe Mill so fascinating is the arrangement made to power the machinery. The line-shafting and belt drive are conventional enough, but here the shafting is connected to two sources of power – a water wheel at one end and a small beam engine at the other. It is something of a belt-and-braces job, for the steam engine was there to take over in dry weather when there was insufficient water for the wheel.

We have followed a long and seemingly complex road from materials used in construction to those used for domestic objects. Yet the connections are more than simply a device enabling an author to tidy up a few industrial odds and ends. Just as the structural properties of baked clay have ensured that it could be used in building and pot making, so too the strength and transparency of glass have been utilized for a variety of tasks from providing windows to the manufacture of drinking receptacles and the qualities of timber have made it equally suitable for house building and furniture manufacture. Now, however, we must break the chain, and turn to industries which are included in this chapter primarily because they are too important to leave out. A case could be made for turning from glassware to the drinks that fill the glasses, but the temptation will be firmly resisted. Brewing and distilling are included because they are industries which have remarkable histories and some remarkable remains, though the origins were in many cases domestic. It was, for example, common for the bigger houses to have their own brewhouses for the manufacture of beer. One, at least, has survived and is still occasionally used for brewing, at Traquair House near Innerleithen, Borders. This fine little eighteenth-century brewhouse contains, in small scale, all the basic elements found in the major breweries of Britain.

The most important of the raw materials for brewing is malted barley, and maltings can be among the most impressive of all industrial buildings. Malting consists of soaking barley grains in water so that they

Langley Maltings on the Birmingham Canal Navigations, where barley is malted for the brewing industry.

begin to germinate, and stopping the process at the right moment by heating in a kiln. The malt has to be spread thinly on the malting floor, which accounts for the large scale of the buildings, such as Langley Maltings beside the Titford Canal in Birmingham. One malting is of especial interest, although it was originally built in 1796 as a flax mill. It stands at Ditherington in Shropshire and is the world's first iron-framed factory building.

The big breweries, such as Guinness in Dublin and Bass in Burton-on-Trent, have long histories and often have sections of great historical interest. The Bass Brewery now has an excellent museum, which includes reminders of how the big breweries really have been major industrial plants for a very long time. For example, the locomotive and carriage in a siding by the entrance are left over from the days when there were seventeen miles of railway track within the brewery complex. Like most of the major companies, Bass has been much

The model brewery at the Bass Museum, Burton-on-Trent, Staffordshire.

modernized, but there are still a few, smaller breweries where methods and equipment have not changed since the last century. The Hook Norton Brewery in Oxfordshire works on the tower principle. Water – liquor in brewers' language – is pumped to the top of the building by a small, horizontal steam engine. The rest of the processes follow on down the tower. The liquor is heated and mixed with malt, hops are added and the liquor is then reheated and fermented with yeast. It is left for a final conditioning process before being racked into casks.

Malted barley is also the basis for Britain's other great drink – whisky or whiskey, depending on whether you are referring to the Scottish or the Irish variety. Each has its adherents, but whichever is preferred connoisseurs agree that it is only in those two countries that the true product can be found. The distillery shares the first stages of malting and fermenting with the breweries, but after that the processes part company. The liquor is heated in great coppers, and the more volatile alcoholic spirits are distilled off and collected, and then redistilled. The resulting liquid then needs to mature for many years before it reaches the glass. The distilleries often have their own maltings within the complex, recognizable by a pyramidal or pagoda roof over the kiln. Many of the distilleries allow visitors, and a number have small museums.

Our survey of the industrial scene is nearly complete, but it must be obvious that it is far from comprehensive. Many of the omissions have little to do with choice or personal preferences and rather more to do with a lack of preserved material. This can be seen, in particular, in those areas which show a continuity of development. The most exciting industrial remains usually belong to those regions where the tide of industry lapped briefly round the shores and then retreated, leaving rich pickings for the industrial beachcomber. In industries which show a greater continuity of activity, the old has been constantly swept aside to make way for the new and the dynamism of change has ensured that little of the old has been retained through the processes of renewal. This is true, for example, of the engineering and chemical industries where, until recently, there has been little attempt at conservation. Now, somewhat belatedly, the attempt has been made. In the field of engineering, the Garrett Works at Leiston in Suffolk, established in 1778, became well known for their later work as manufacturers of steam traction engines. Much of the works has decayed, but the Long Shop, formerly the erecting shop, has been restored. It is a tall, handsome building with a fine queen-post roof with iron trusses bearing Richard Garrett's initials and the date 1853. This is now home to a new steam and engineering museum, which is excellent news, for the building itself was well worth preserving. In the chemical industry, a number of buildings have survived, notably the dye works of the textile regions, but few of the buildings show many distinguishing features. One more specialized, but nevertheless important branch of the chemical industry was the manufacture of gunpowder. It is ironic that a gunpowder mill should feature in a list of preserved buildings, since historically they tended to disappear faster than most – often very fast indeed. Gunpowder is a mixture of sulphur, potassium nitrate and charcoal which react chemically when ignited. Chart Gunpowder Mills at Faversham in Kent was once part of the Royal Gunpowder Factory established there three centuries ago. The surviving machinery consists of water-powered edge rollers contained in a flimsy, wooden building. The flimsiness is deliberate, for explosions were by no means uncommon and the damage likely to be caused by disintegrating timber was a lot less than that from flying bricks.

Not only could the list of industries be extended to cover many other subjects, but so too could the list of important preservation schemes. New schemes are constantly being started and old schemes extended. One can safely say that even as these words are written someone, somewhere, is hard at work on a new project. Long may the process of renewal and revitalization continue.

Conclusion

In previous chapters, we have looked at what has been preserved of our industrial past and the emphasis has inevitably been on that great period of change that began in the eighteenth century. Yet we too live in an age of rapid and accelerating change. It is true that Britain no longer holds a position in centre stage as she did during the earlier industrial drama but, nevertheless, Britain's contribution to the technology of the twentieth century has been by no means negligible. Perhaps it is not too soon to start looking at our own world to see what might be of interest to future generations, especially as there are enormous problems in deciding what, if anything, should be preserved for posterity. We have numerous museums with collections of old motor vehicles, but what should be done about the engineering works that produced them? And what about other modern factories? When so much of production takes place in standardized units on the ubiquitous industrial estate, it is very difficult to see what future generations would find interesting. On the other hand, there will always be buildings, such as the Hoover factory on Western Avenue in London, for which strong conservation arguments will be advanced on the basis of their architectural merit rather than because of their importance to the history of industry. These matters need to be considered, for as we go off to early industrial sites, whether to study them in detail or simply to enjoy a recreation of life in another age, we should perhaps remember that our present will be someone else's past.

It is always comparatively simple to make out a case for preserving the very old – antiquity is its own justification. No one now, one would hope, would dream of proposing the wholesale demolition of Hadrian's Wall. And if one were to suggest pulling down Windsor Castle, there would be a nationwide howl of outrage. Yet looked at in the context of world history, both these sites, splendid as they are, are of no more than marginal importance. Hadrian's Wall is merely a barrier, marking the outer limits of a great empire, a small-scale affair in comparison with the Great Wall of China. Windsor Castle is but one of many castles that played so vital a role in the economic, social and political life of medieval Europe. It is important in English history, but its significance stretches very little beyond a relatively parochial setting.

Our industrial remains are far more modern, but their importance to world history is far greater. We are only just beginning to appreciate the truth of this and to understand that, measured on this world scale, the old furnace at Coalbrookdale or Arkwright's mill at Cromford hold a place comparable to that occupied by the Parthenon and the pyramids of Egypt. Perhaps such claims seem exaggerated: I do not believe this is so. It can be argued that the monuments of the ancient world have a beauty which touches the heart of the beholder in a way that the mundane monuments of the industrial world can never do. Yet we are now coming to realize that aesthetics and social considerations cannot be divorced. The pyramids are astonishing sights – they are also astonishing monuments to technological expertise, and they represent an equally astonishing use of human labour. But the pyramids have had little influence on the great current of human affairs. The Industrial Revolution can offer nothing to match them for sheer visual grandeur – though I hope to have shown that grandeur is by no means absent from early industrial remains. The Industrial Revolution has, however, profoundly changed the whole nature of life on this planet. The revolution occurred in Britain, and the physical remains are its monuments. They are not always grand, though sometimes they may be; they are by no means always beautiful, but then beauty is an abstract concept, defined anew by each generation, and many of us do find beauty there. They are, however, of the greatest importance, and that importance can only grow as time goes on.

In this book an attempt has been made to evaluate the significance of the physical remains of Britain's industrial heritage. This is not in itself enough. The remains speak not only to our intellects but to our hearts as well. There was life here once – a way of life which was quite new in the history of the world. Those who can teach themselves to see will find that life breathing again. And that is the true significance of the remains of our industrial past.

Gazetteer

The sites listed below are all open to the general public, although in some cases openings may be somewhat infrequent, or by appointment only. They represent only a fraction of the total remains of our industrial past. A number of other sites have already been mentioned in the body of the text, and readers who wish thoroughly to explore a particular area should consult one of the regional guides listed in the bibliography. As site and museum opening times are constantly changing, no attempt has been made to give details here. A number of museum guides are, however, published at regular intervals, and many of the sites appear in their pages. The following are especially recommended:

A Glimpse of the Past (Wales Tourist Board)
Association of Railway Societies' Official Year Book
Museums and Art Galleries in Great Britain and Ireland (published annually)
National Trust for Scotland Year Book (published annually)
Properties of the National Trust (published quinquennially)
Properties Open (National Trust, published annually)
Stately Homes, Museums, Castles and Gardens in Britain (AA, published annually)

ABBREVIATIONS

AT	An Taisce
DoE	Department of the Environment
NT	National Trust
NTS	National Trust for Scotland
ONOP	Oifig Na n Oibreacha Poibli – Commissioners of Public Works, Eire
SDD	Scottish Development Department
WO	Welsh Office

Ordnance Survey map references have been given for those sites which would otherwise prove difficult to locate. Properties of The National Trust and The National Trust for Scotland are marked with an asterisk. All places listed in the gazetteer are shown on the maps at the end of this book.

The replica of Trevithick's Penydarren locomotive at the Welsh Industrial and Maritime Museum.

ENGLAND

AVON

Bath
Bath Carriage Museum, Circus Mews. Collection of horsedrawn carriages and early road vehicles in eighteenth-century mews.
Camden Works, Julian Road. The building, originally a real tennis court, now houses the works of J.B. Bowler, brass founder, engineer and aerated mineral water manufacturer, founded 1872. These have been restored as The Museum of Bath at Work.

Bristol
Bitton Railway Centre, Bitton Station. Steam railway with preserved locos and rolling stock.
Bristol Industrial Museum, Prince's Wharf. Housed in converted wharf building; manufacturing and transport including Grenville steam carriage of 1875.
SS Great Britain, Great Western Dock, Gas Ferry Road. Brunel's famous screw steamer, undergoing restoration.
Stratford Mill, Blaise Castle House, Henbury. Water mill moved to this site from Chew Valley.
Temple Meads Station The original 1841 GWR station is now being renovated by the Brunel Engineering Trust.

Claverton
Restored water-powered beam pumps on Kennet and Avon Canal. (ST 792 645)

Priston
Priston Mill, Priston Farm. Water-powered corn mill still in use today. A mill has stood on this site since Domesday but present buildings mainly eighteenth-century. (ST 695 615)

Weston-super-Mare
Woodspring Museum, Burlington Street. Museum housed in workshops of Edwardian gaslight company. Exhibits include local mining and transport.

BEDFORDSHIRE

Leighton Buzzard
Leighton Buzzard Narrow Gauge Railway, Page's Park Station, Billington Road. Narrow-gauge railway with 1½ miles of line. Passenger trains hauled by steam and diesel locos.

Stevington
Eighteenth-century post windmill. Keys available from Royal George, Silver Street.

BUCKINGHAMSHIRE

Brill
Restored post mill: main structure dates from seventeenth century.

Chalfont St Giles
The Chiltern Open Air Museum, Newland Park. Open-air museum of buildings which include the 1724 castellated toll house from High Wycombe.

High Wycombe
Wycombe Chair and Local History Museum, Castle Hill House, Priory Avenue. Museum devoted to chairs, tools and chair making.

Ivinghoe
Ford End Water Mill, Ford End Farm, Station Road. Grain mill of 1773 with overshot wheel.

Loosley Row
Lacey Green Windmill Smock mill built *c.* 1650 with early wooden machinery.

Milton Keynes
Stacey Hill Collection of Industry and Rural Life, Stacey Hill Farm, Southern Way, Wolverton, Milton Keynes. Museum depicting industrial and agricultural life of area before establishment of New Town, including working industrial machines.

New Bradwell
Bradwell Tower Mill Three-storey tower mill of 1876. 3 miles south-east of Stony Stratford on A422.

Pitstone
Pitstone Windmill (NT) Post mill with carved date 1627 on interior timber.

Quainton
Quainton Mill Tower windmill of 1830s in grounds of 16 The Green, being restored.
Quainton Railway Centre, The Railway Station. Large collection of standard-gauge locomotives and rolling stock including many nineteenth-century items.

CAMBRIDGESHIRE

Barnack
Barnack Windmill, Windmill Farm. Tower mill with machinery but no sails.

Bourn
Bourn Windmill, Caxton Road. Post mill dating from 1630s and one of the best examples of seventeenth-century mills in Britain. Off B1046.

Cambridge
Cheddars Lane Sewage Pumping Station Built 1894, now houses Cheddars Lane Museum of Technology. Contains pair of tandem compound steam engines and pair of 1909 gas engines.

Great Chishill
Great Chishill Windmill Post windmill on B1039 built in 1819.

Houghton
Houghton Water Mill (NT) Timber mill on the River Ouse, south of A1123 between Huntingdon and St Ives. Leased to YHA.

Lode
Anglesey Abbey (NT) Eighteenth-century water mill in grounds. Machinery restored to working order in 1982.

Maxey
Three-storey water-powered mill of 1779, still in use as grinding mill.

Over
Over Windmill, Longstanton Road. Restored tower mill built *c.* 1860; used for grinding.

Soham
Downfield Windmill Eighteenth-century smock mill rebuilt as tower mill in 1887. 1½ miles south-east of town on Fordham Road.

Wicken Fen Windpump (NT), showing the casing of the scoop wheel which is powered by the sails.

Stretham
Stretham Old Engine Scoop wheel powered by beam pumping engine of 1831.

Thornhaugh
Sacrewell Mill A small estate water mill dated 1755 with pitchback wheel. Machinery run for demonstrations. Collection of rural bygones.

Wansford
Nene Valley Railway, Wansford Station, Old North Road, Stibbington, Wansford. Large collection of main line passenger and industrial locomotives. Regular passenger service on 5½ mile track.

Wicken Fen
*Wicken Fen Windpump (NT), Lode Lane, Wicken, Ely. Small smock mill built early this century and used for drainage.

CHESHIRE

Bunbury
Bunbury Water Mill, Mill Lane. Fully restored mill of 1850. Machinery demonstrations.
See also two-lock riser and stable block on Chester Canal, 1 mile north of town.

Ellesmere Port
The Ellesmere Port Boat Museum, Oil Sites Road. Large collection of canal and river boats in old Shropshire Union Canal port complex. Also steam engine for hydraulic power system.

Nether Alderley
*Alderley Old Mill (NT) Fifteenth-century corn mill with two wooden overshot water wheels and restored mill machinery. On west side of A34.

Northwich
Salt Museum, London Road. Museum tracing history of the salt industry since Roman times.

Stretton
Stretton Mill Water-powered corn mill dating from seventeenth to nineteenth centuries, restored to working order. Turn south off A534 at Barton.

Styal
*Quarry Bank Mill and Mill Village (NT) A complete mill complex with eighteenth-century cotton mill, apprentices' house and village. The mill is now home to a developing textile museum. 1½ miles north of Wilmslow off B5166.

CLEVELAND

Guisborough
Tockett's Mill Restored water-powered grain mill. 2 miles east of Guisborough on the Skelton road (A173).

Hartlepool
Maritime Museum, Northgate. Maritime history of the town and shipbuilding industry.
HMS Warrior, Coal Dock. The first iron-clad warship, being restored.

Stockton-on-Tees
Preston Hall Museum, Yarm Road. Social history museum; includes reconstructed street with craftsmen's and tradesmen's workshops.

CORNWALL

Ashton
*Wheal Prosper (NT) The engine house of this former copper mine,

which worked 1832–49, stands above Rinsey Cove. (SW 592 272)

Bude
Bude Historical and Folk Exhibition, The Wharf. Housed in warehouse alongside Bude Canal. Traces history of canal, including tub boats.

Camborne
Agar Mine (NT) Taylor's Shaft pumping engine, massive beam engine of 1892 with 90-inch diameter cylinder.
Camborne School of Mines Geological Museum, Pool. Collection of minerals, ores and artefacts connected with local mining industry.
East Pool Mine (NT) Steam winding engine of 1887 in original engine house.
Trevithick's Cottage (NT), Lower Penponds. Birthplace of Richard Trevithick, the steam engine pioneer.

Carthew
Wheal Martyn Museum Museum of the china clay industry based on a restored clay works of *c.* 1800. On A391 2 miles north of St Austell.

*Chapel Porth (NT)
The deep valley of Chapel Coombe contains remains of Towanroath, Wheal Charlotte and Charlotte Un-

RIGHT *The preserved kiln at Truro Pottery, with the Cathedral in the background.*

ited engine houses, together with a set of ore stamps (SW 701 493). 1½ miles south of St Agnes.

Cotehele
Cotehele Quay (NT) Includes maritime museum in warehouse, restored Tamar sailing barge *Shamrock* and lime kilns. Also eighteenth-century grain mill with overshot water wheel.

Delabole
Slate Quarry and Museum Slate quarry worked continuously since fourteenth century and is now largest man-made hole in Britain.

Falmouth
Falmouth Maritime Museum Housed in the 1930 steam tug *St Denys* berthed at Custom House Quay.

The Royal Albert Bridge, Saltash, Cornwall, under construction (1858).

Lizard
Working lighthouse with a museum showing development of generators and lights.

Newlyn East
Lappa Valley Railway 15-inch gauge steam railway on line of former Newquay–Chacewater GWR line. Trains run to East Wheal Rose Halt with engine house of former silver-lead mine.

Pendeen
Geevor Tin Mine A working mine with museum illustrating history of Cornish tin mining.

Redruth
Tolgus Tin Company, Portreath Road. Last remaining tin streaming works and set of Cornish ore stamps.

St Agnes
Wheal Coates (NT) Engine house of Wheal Coates mine on cliffs. (SW 700 501)

St Ives
St Ives Museum, Wheal Dream. Museum housed in former pilchard cellar with material on mines and Great Western Railway.

St Neot
Carnglaze Slate Caverns Slate mine with underground tours for visitors.

Truro
Truro Pottery and Old Kiln Museum, Chapel Hill. The oldest pottery in Cornwall and still working. The old kiln was built in the eighteenth century and modified in the nineteenth century. Demonstrations of hand-throwing of pots.

Wendron
Poldark Mine and Wendron Forge Tin-mining museum which includes the Greensplat beam engine of 1830 that worked until 1959. Also contains former Holman Museum collection including 1850 beam engine (NT). 2 miles north of Helston on B3297.

Zennor
Zennor Water Mill Eighteenth-century grain mill with internal machinery but no wheel.

CUMBRIA

Beetham
Heron Corn Mill Restored eighteenth-century water-powered mill with small milling museum.

Boot
Eskdale Mill and Museum Restored corn mill, part dating back to sixteenth century, and small museum.

*Borrowdale
Remains of eighteenth-century graphite mines, adits and spoil heaps (NT) can be seen on fells, 1000 feet above hamlet of Seathwaite.

Clifton Dykes
Wetheriggs Country Pottery Working pottery uses modern methods but nineteenth-century remains have been preserved, including coal-fired kiln, steam engine, blunger, clay pit and tramway. To the east of Clifton, 3 miles south-east of Penrith, on the Cliburn road.

Coniston
Steam Yacht Gondola (NT) Built 1859 and recently restored. Carries up to 86 passengers on Lake Coniston.

Embleton
Wythop Mill Water powered, originally used for corn, but converted to a sawmill 1860. Woodworking machinery intact.

Great Langdale
Pike o' Stickle Axe Factory (NT) Remains of Neolithic flint quarry and location where flints were dressed. (NY 274 070)

Haverthwaite
Lakeside and Haverthwaite Railway Preserved passenger railway with steam-hauled trains on $3\frac{1}{2}$ mile run to Lake Side and lake steamer connection to Windermere.

Kendal
Abbot Hall Museum of Lakeland Life and Industry Housed in Abbot Hall stable block.

Keswick
Cumberland Pencil Museum, Southey Works, Greta Bridge. Museum showing pencil manufacture from sixteenth century to present day.

Lake Side
Stott Park Bobbin Mill (DoE) Used to manufacture bobbins for cotton mills and now an industrial museum. 1 mile north of Lake Side pier.

Levens
Levens Hall Steam Collection A collection of steam engines housed in the brew house of the Elizabethan manor.

Little Salkeld
Eighteenth-century water-powered corn mill with two overshot wheels restored to working condition and producing flour. 1 mile from Langwathby, off A686.

Maryport
Maritime Museum, Shipping Brow, 1 Senhouse Street. Models and artefacts dealing with local maritime history.

Millom
Millom Folk Museum, St George's Road. Contains full-scale model of drift of the Hodbarrow Iron Ore Mine. Extensive remains of mine can still be seen on the coast 1 mile south of the town.

Ravenglass
Muncaster Mill Working flour mill with water brought $\frac{3}{4}$ mile from River Mite to overshot wheel. Site in use since fifteenth century.
Ravenglass and Eskdale Railway Narrow-gauge (15 inch) railway offers steam-hauled passenger service on 7 mile track to Dalegarth.

Whitehaven
Whitehaven Museum, Market Place. Local museum with emphasis on coal mining and shipbuilding.
See also remains of mining to the south of the harbour including twisted candlestick chimney of 1850.

Windermere
Windermere Steamboat Museum, Rayrigg Road. Unique collection of steam launches dating from the 1850s.

DERBYSHIRE

Bakewell
The Old House Museum, Cunningham Place. Museum contains early Arkwright machinery.

Crich

The National Tramway Museum, Matlock Road. Large collection of electric trams dating back to the 1880s, many giving passenger rides.

Cromford

Arkwright's Cromford Mill The world's first successful cotton mill, at present undergoing restoration. See also houses built in North Street by Arkwright.

Cromford Canal Museum at canal wharf and trips by horsedrawn boat. See also Leawood pumping station by the aqueduct which contains 1849 beam engine (occasionally steamed).

Good Luck Lead Mine Lead mine with surface remains and conducted underground tours. Via Gellia, 2 miles from Cromford by A5012.

Dale

Dale Abbey Windmill Also known as Cat and Fiddle Mill. A post mill built in 1788.

Derby

Derby Industrial Museum, Silk Mill, off Full Street. Museum housed in early eighteenth-century silk mill contains exhibits on local industries and Rolls Royce collection of aero engines.

Royal Crown Derby Porcelain Company Ltd, Osmaston Road. Porcelain factory established to incorporate the old Derby workhouse in 1877. Museum of Royal Crown Derby china. On A514 1 mile from town centre.

Glossop

Dinting Railway Centre Collection of steam locomotives and freight vehicles. Centre for steam-hauled main-line rail tours. 1½ miles west of Glossop, off A57.

Matlock

Peak Railway Society, Matlock Railway Station. Collection of steam locomotives.

Matlock Bath

Peak District Mining Museum, The Pavilion. Museum of Derbyshire lead-mining industry. Exhibits include nineteenth-century water pres-

The eighteenth-century corn mill built over an arm of the Trent and Mersey Canal at Shardlow.

sure pump.
See also Arkwright's Masson Mill.

Middleton by Wirksworth

Middleton Top Engine House Steam winding engine at top of incline on Cromford and High Peak Railway. Pair of beam engines now worked by compressed air.

Ripley

The Midland Railway Centre, Butterley Station. Collection of steam locomotives. Centre is being developed as a working museum to demonstrate LMS practice. 1 mile north of Ripley.

Morley Park Blast Furnaces Remains of two furnaces built 1780 and 1818 for Morley Park Ironworks. (SK 380 492)

Rowsley

Caudwell's Mill Water-powered mill of 1874. Uses rollers instead of stones for grinding. Still in use.

Shardlow

The Canal Story Exhibition, Clock Warehouse, London Road. Canal museum housed in eighteenth-century mill built over spur of Trent and Mersey Canal.

LEFT *Part of the surface remains of Magpie Mine: the ruins of the pumping engine house and the headstock gear over the shaft.*

Sheldon
Magpie Mine The lead mine has extensive surface remains including two engine houses and is headquarters of Peak District Mines Historical Society. (SK 172 682)

Whaley Bridge
Restored canal basin on Peak Forest Canal with quarry, tramroad tracks and lime kilns. See also canal-rail interchange shed.

DEVON

Appledore
North Devon Maritime Museum, Odun House, Odun Road. Museum depicting history of famous schooner port.

Arlington
Arlington Court (NT) Collection of horsedrawn vehicles in stable block. Off A39 7 miles from Barnstaple.

Bickleigh
Bickleigh Mill Craft centre in waterpowered corn mill. 4 miles south of Tiverton.

Bideford
North Devon Maritime Museum Special emphasis on transatlantic trade.

Buckfastleigh
Dart Valley Railway Preserved railway offering steam-hauled passenger service along 7 mile track beside the River Dart. Museum at station.

Dartmouth
Newcomen Engine, Royal Avenue Gardens. This 1725 engine last worked as a pumping engine on Coventry Canal.

Dawlish Warren
South Devon Railway Museum and Model Railway, Dawlish Warren Station. Large collection of railway relics and model railway.

Dunsford
Dunsford Edge Toolworks Edge tools are being made here as they have been for over two hundred years. Museum shows tools and traditional methods of working. North of B3212 Exeter to Moretonhampstead road.

Exeter
Exeter Maritime Museum, The Quay. Large collection of boats and ships from around the world, some on the water, others housed in old warehouses. Exhibits include Brunel's steam dredger, *Bertha*.

Honiton
Allhallows Museum, High Street. Display of Honiton lace and demonstrations of lace making.

Ilfracombe
Bicclescombe Water Mill Late eighteenth-century mill with just one pair of stones.
Hele Mill Restored corn mill powered by 18-foot overshot wheel, and producing flour. The mill dates back to sixteenth century. 1 mile east of Ilfracombe on A399.

Lynmouth
Lynton and Lynmouth Cliff Railway The railway, built in 1890, takes passengers up the 900-foot cliff. It works on the water-balance principle.

Mary Tavy
Wheal Betsy (NT) Engine house of former lead mine on Black Down, east of A386.

Morwellham
Morwellham Open Air Museum Large museum complex incorporating many features including extensive dock area by Tamar linked to Tavistock Canal by inclined plane. Copper mine with underground railway for visitors, water wheel and kilns.

Okehampton
The Old Mill, Mill Road. Restored water mill with plans for waterpower museum.

Otterton
Otterton Mill, Fore Street. Restored water-powered corn mill with two wheels, still used for grinding, and craft centre. A corn mill has stood on this site since medieval times; present remains mainly nineteenth-century.

Paignton
Dart Valley Railway, Torbay and Dartmouth Line, Queen's Park Station. Preserved railway offering steam-hauled passenger service on 7 mile route to Kingswear.

Plymouth
Devonport Dockyard and Dockyard Museum Tours of the Royal Dockyard take in covered slip of 1816, graving (repair) docks and rope walk.

Starcross
Brunel's Atmospheric Railway Engine House The remains of one of the engine houses originally intended to create the vacuum which would draw trains along an underground system. The system failed.

Sticklepath
Finch Foundry Museum Nineteenth-century water-powered scythe works. A series of three overshot wheels, the first of which drives a fan for the furnace, the second powers trip hammers and the third turns the grindstone. Everything is in working condition.

Tiverton
Tiverton Museum, St Andrew Street. General museum with industrial exhibits including display on the Grand Western Canal, steam locomotive and Heathcoat lace-making machine.

Topsham
Topsham Museum, 25 The Strand. Maritime museum in sail loft of seventeenth-century house.

Uffculme
Coldharbour Mill Late eighteenth-century mill, originally used for spinning and combing worsted, powered by 18-foot breastshot wheel and 1910 cross-compound steam engine. Retains original machinery including mule spinner and carding engine; all still in use.

DORSET

Poole
Maritime Museum, Paradise Street, The Quay. The museum occupies part of the medieval town cellars.

Swanage
Swanage Railway Centre, Swanage Station. Collection of locomotives and rolling stock.

DURHAM

Darlington

Darlington Railway Museum, North Road Station. Museum housed in the Stockton and Darlington Railway Station of 1842. Exhibits include rolling stock and locomotives with pride of place going to Stephenson's *Locomotion*.

Tees Cottage Pumping Station, Coniscliffe Road. Water pumping station dating back to 1840s with 1903 compound beam engine and gas engine with its own gas plant. Regular steamings. 2 miles from Darlington on A67 Barnard Castle road.

Hamsterley

Cementation Furnace The remains of this important early furnace for the manufacture of steel stand beside a rough track, north of the A694. Preserved by the North of England Open Air Museum, Beamish. (NZ 131 565)

Haswell

Preserved colliery engine house built c. 1800. (NZ 374 423)

Shildon

Timothy Hackworth Museum, Hackworth Close. Museum housed in home of Timothy Hackworth, first manager of Stockton and Darlington Railway. Opposite the house is an SDR shed with a replica of Hackworth's locomotive *Sans Pareil*. Also railway trail.

Timothy Hackworth's business card.

Stanley

North of England Open Air Museum, Beamish Hall. This major museum occupies a 200-acre site. Industrial remains include a pit head, with vertical steam winding engine and screens for grading the coal, railway with working replica of Stephenson's *Locomotion* and working tramway.

Tanfield

Tanfield Railway Preserved steam railway running on trackbed of plateway, opened 1725. The route continues over Causey Arch, world's oldest surviving railway bridge (NZ 200 560). Off A6076.

Weardale

Killhope Lead Mine The ore-crushing mill of Killhope Mine has a 34-foot diameter overshot water wheel. By A689 8 miles south-east of Alston.

EAST SUSSEX

Brighton

Volks Railway Britain's first public electric railway, opened 1883, still runs $1\frac{1}{4}$ miles from Palace Pier to Brighton marina (2 foot $8\frac{1}{2}$ inch gauge).

Burwash

Bateman's Mill (NT) Eighteenth-century water mill on the Bateman estate, former home of Rudyard Kipling. Restored and producing flour. Adjacent is turbine installed by Kipling in 1903 to generate electricity. $\frac{1}{2}$ mile south of village.

Hastings

The Fisherman's Museum, Rock-a-Nore Road. Museum contains two-masted fishing lugger.
See also Rock-a-Nore passenger lift of 1903.

Hove

British Engineerium, off Nevill Road. Museum housed in former Goldstone Pumping Station, with two restored beam engines of 1866 and 1876. Exhibition hall has extensive collection of engines demonstrating history of steam power, many in working order.

West Blatchington Mill, Holmes Avenue. Six-storey smock mill, built c. 1820, currently being restored.

Nutley

Nutley Windmill Seventeenth-century open-trestle post mill, restored and regularly used. 1 mile north of village on Crowborough road.

Polegate

Polegate Windmill Tower mill of 1817 in working order with museum attached. 4 miles north of Eastbourne, south of A27.

Sheffield Park

Bluebell Railway Preserved steam passenger line running between restored stations at Sheffield Park and Horsted Keynes (West Sussex). Large collection of steam locomotives and vintage rolling stock. On A275, 10 miles north of Lewes.

Upper Dicker

Michelham Priory Mill Restored eighteenth-century water mill, supplied with water from Priory moat. Also wheelwright and blacksmith in Priory grounds.

ESSEX

Aythorpe Roding

Eighteenth-century post mill with fan tail mounted on ladder; recently restored.

Battlesbridge

Late eighteenth-century tide mill on River Crouch and nineteenth-century granary with pyramidal kiln.

Bocking
Post windmill built *c.* 1700, in working order and now a museum.

Castle Hedingham
Colne Valley Railway, Castle Hedingham Station, Yeldham Road. Collection of locomotives with regular steamings.

Chappel
Stour Valley Railway Centre, Chappel and Wakes Colne Station. Collection of locomotives and vintage rolling stock; regular steamings.

Colchester
Bourne Mill (NT) Two-storey water-powered corn mill of 1591 with Dutch gables. 1 mile south of town centre off Mersea road.

Harwich
Treadwheel crane from naval yard, re-erected Harwich Green. See also navigation light towers.

Mountnessing
Early nineteenth-century post mill, currently being restored.

Rayleigh
Rayleigh Windmill, The Mount. Tower windmill of *c.* 1800, restored externally but with no internal machinery. Used as museum by local history society.

Stansted Mountfitchet
Five-storey tower windmill built 1787. Machinery complete, including flour-dressing floor.

Thaxted
John Webb's Windmill Tower windmill of 1804 under restoration. Museum on ground floor.

GLOUCESTERSHIRE

Ashchurch
Dowty Railway Preservation Society, Northway Lane. Collection of industrial standard-gauge and narrow-gauge locomotives and rolling stock with occasional steamings. 2 miles east of Tewkesbury.

Bibury
Arlington Mill Museum Seventeenth-century water mill used at various times for grain and textiles. Collection of agricultural implements.

Bourton-on-the-Water
Motor Museum The museum is housed in an eighteenth-century water mill.

Clearwell
Clearwell Caves Ancient iron mines heavily worked in Middle Ages. Underground workings and museum with exhibits on local history.

King's Stanley
Stanley Mill A woollen mill of 1813 of outstanding architectural interest, still producing woollen cloth.

Lydney
Norchard Steam Centre Collection of steam locomotives with occasional steamings; also small museum. On B4234 ½ mile off A48 at Lydney.

Soudley
Dean Heritage Museum Trust, Camp Mill. A nineteenth-century mill on the site of a seventeenth-century forge. Centre being developed for interpretation of local history. On B4227 between Cinderford and Blakeney.

Stroud
Stroud and District Museum, Lansdown. Exhibits deal with local woollen industry. See also many remaining mills along A46 and A419 Chalford and Nailsworth roads.

Tewkesbury
Abbey Mill Former grain mill. Exterior has been restored with two water wheels; interior now in use as restaurant.

Winchcombe
Winchcombe Railway Museum, Gloucester Street. Museum specializing in signalling, lineside features, tickets, lamps etc. On A46 north-east of Cheltenham.

GREATER MANCHESTER

Blackstone Edge
Roman road made up of stone setts with central groove. 5 miles north-east of Rochdale off A58. (SD 973 170 to 988 184)

Bolton
Atlas Mills, Chorley Old Road. Northern Mill Engine Society Collection housed in former mill engine house.

Four engines including horizontal tandem compound of 1902 and twin beam engine of *c.* 1840 are steamed on open days.
Bolton Industrial Museum, Tonge Moor Road. Textile machinery museum, including machines by Hargreaves, Arkwright and Crompton.
Hall i' th' Wood Museum Fifteenth-century house, home of Samuel Crompton, inventor of spinning mule. North of Crompton bypass.

Bury
Transport Museum, Castlecroft Road. Locomotives and rolling stock with railway exhibition and road vehicles.

Dunham Massey (NT)
Sixteenth-century house with Elizabethan mill in working order in the grounds. 3 miles south-west of Altrincham off A56.

Eccles
Monks Hall Museum, Wellington Road. Sixteenth-century building contains collection of machinery associated with the nineteenth-century machine tool designer James Nasmyth.

Manchester
Liverpool Road Station Originally passenger station on Liverpool and Manchester Railway, now occupied by Greater Manchester Science and Railway Museum.
North Western Museum of Science and Industry, 97 Grosvenor Street. Large collection of textile, paper-making and printing machinery.

Salford
Museum of Mining, Buile Hill Park, Eccles Old Road. Technology of mining museum including reproductions of mines.

Shaw
Dee Mill Horizontal twin tandem compound mill engine built in 1907 and housed in original engine house. Mill demolished 1982 and future of engine under discussion.

Stockport
Stockport Museum, Vernon Park, Turncroft Lane. Includes an industrial gallery and hat block making workshop.

Uppermill

Saddleworth Museum Local museum housed in former woollen mill beside Huddersfield Canal.

HAMPSHIRE

Bordon

Headley Mill Grain mill with breast-shot wheel and 4-acre millpond, still working commercially. Original building twelfth century, but much changed over the years.

Breamore

Breamore House Countryside and Carriage Museum Collection of horsedrawn carriages. On A338.

Buckler's Hard

Maritime Museum Site of eighteenth-century ship-building centre and museum.

Liphook

Hollycombe House Steam Collection Narrow-gauge (2 foot) steam railway and demonstrations of fairground and agricultural engines. $1\frac{1}{2}$ miles south-east on Midhurst Road, off A3.

New Alresford

Mid Hants Railway, Alresford Station. Steam-hauled passenger trains on 3 mile line.

Portsmouth

Eastney Pumping Station, Henderson Road, Southsea. Engine house contains two 1887 Boulton and Watt beam engines in working order and Crossley gas engine.

Southampton

Maritime Museum, Wool House, Bugle Street. Museum housed in fourteenth-century wool store.

Totton

Eling Mill Tide mill dating from eighteenth and nineteenth centuries, now a working museum, with demonstrations of grinding.

Whitchurch

Whitchurch Silk Mill, Winchester Street. Late eighteenth-century silk mill, still at work; originally water-powered.

Winchester

City Mill (NT) Water-powered grain mill, built in 1744. Now leased to YHA. At foot of High Street, beside Soke Bridge.

HEREFORD AND WORCESTER

Bewdley

Bewdley Museum, The Shambles, Lode Street. Includes brass foundry, parts of which date back to eighteenth century. It has been restored to working order and visitors can see castings from coke-fired furnace. Also exhibition of history of brass working.
Severn Valley Railway, The Railway Station. Steam-hauled passenger service on $12\frac{1}{2}$ mile route to Bridgnorth. Rolling stock kept at Bewdley, locomotives at Bridgnorth. Line features restored GWR stations and Severn Viaduct.

Blakedown

Churchill Forge Water-powered forge with two overshot wheels providing power for manufacture of spades. Converted from corn mill in sixteenth century. 4 miles north-east of Kidderminster, north of A456.

Bromsgrove

The Avoncroft Museum of Buildings, Redditch Road, Stoke Heath. Open-air museum, with buildings re-erected on site, including working windmill, nailer's workshop and chain works.

Hereford

Bulmer Railway Centre, Whitecross Road. Collection of steam locomotives, and centre for rail tours.
Herefordshire Waterworks Museum, Broomy Hill. Museum housed in pumping station which contains two working steam engines of 1895 and 1906.
Museum of Cider, The Cider Mills, Ryelands Street. Exhibits show facets of cider making from sixteenth century. Museum incorporates 1920s cider factory.

Lucton

Mortimers Cross Water Mill Eighteenth-century grain mill with undershot wheel.

Newnham Bridge

Newnham Water Mill, Mill Lane. Seventeenth-century grain mill with undershot wheel.

Redditch

Forge Mill, Bordesley Lane. Water-powered factory for the manufacture of needles, converted from grain mill in 1720s. Much original equipment remains. 2 miles north of town, off A441.

Worcester

Dyson Perrins Museum of Worcester Porcelain, Severn Street. Porcelain collection housed in part of Worcester Royal Porcelain Works of 1751.

HERTFORDSHIRE

Hatfield

The Old Mill House Museum, Mill Green. Local history museum housed in seventeenth-century water mill, being restored.

St Albans

Kingsbury Watermill Museum, St Michael's Street. Three-storey sixteenth-century corn mill, housing collection of farm implements.

HUMBERSIDE

Hull

Springhead Pumping Station, Springhead Avenue, Willerby Road. 1876 building containing Cornish engine with 90-inch diameter cylinder. Also display of waterworks equipment. North of A164, $1\frac{1}{2}$ miles west of junction with A63.
Town Docks Museum, Queen Victoria Square. Local maritime history. See also Humber keel, *Comrade*, and sloop, *Amy Howson*, moored locally and regularly sailed on Humber.
Transport and Archaeological Museum, 36 High Street. Mostly devoted to road transport.

Humberston

Lincolnshire Coast Light Railway, North Sea Lane Station. Narrow-gauge steam passenger railway (1 foot $11\frac{5}{8}$ inch) with vintage rolling stock.

Skidby

Tower windmill of 1821, now an agricultural museum. Also subsidiary buildings, including roller plant.

Wrawby

Post windmill built *c.* 1780 and restored to working order. 1 mile north-east of Brigg.

ISLE OF MAN

Castletown
Nautical Museum (Manx Museum and National Trust), Bridge Street. Eighteenth-century armed, schooner-rigged yacht *Peggy* in original boathouse.

Cregneish
The Folk Museum (Manx Museum and National Trust) Based on original buildings, including a loom shed and turner's shed with treadle lathe. Near Port St Mary.

Douglas
Horse Tramway Last horsedrawn tramway in Britain still in use, built between 1876 and 1890, connects up to electric tramway of 1893–9. Both use many nineteenth-century cars.
Isle of Man Railway Steam-hauled passenger service on narrow-gauge (3 foot) line from Douglas to Port Erin. Locomotives include original Bayer Peacocks of nineteenth century.

Laxey
Lady Isabella Wheel Built in 1854 to power mine drainage pumps. The 72-foot diameter wheel is largest in Britain.
Snaefell Mountain Railway 3 foot 6 inch gauge electric tramway, opened in 1895 from Laxey to summit of Snaefell.

ISLE OF WIGHT

Bembridge
Bembridge Windmill (NT) Stone tower windmill, built *c.* 1700. Original wooden machinery preserved.

Calbourne
Calbourne Water Mill and Museum Seventeenth-century grain mill in working order. Rural museum.

Carisbrooke Castle (DoE)
Working donkey wheel raises water from 160-foot deep well. Rebuilt in 1587 over a well sunk in 1150.

Haven Street
Isle of Wight Steam Railway Passenger service to Wootton. Railway museum at Haven Street, 3 miles south-west of Ryde.

Ventnor
Blackgang Sawmill Museum, Blackgang Chine. Museum of timber industry, including sawmill powered by steam and oil engines and craft workshops with bodger and wheelwright.

Yafford
Yafford Water Mill Farm Park Museum based on nineteenth-century grain mill.

KENT

Chillenden
Chillenden Mill Post windmill of 1868.

Cranbrook
Union Mill Octagonal smock windmill of 1814, in the centre of town. Still produces animal feed, but by electric motor.

Dover
Crabble Mill, Lower Road. Six-storey water mill built in 1812 to provide flour for army. Restored to working order. 2 miles north-west of Dover, by River Dour. (TR 297 432)
Transport Museum, Connaught Pumping Station, Connaught Road. Museum housed in Dover Waterworks buildings. Original equipment includes a Worthington-Simpson vertical triple-expansion steam engine.

Faversham
Chart Gunpowder Mills, Westbrook Walk. Restored water-powered powder grinding mill of late eighteenth century, sole survivor of once thriving local industry.

Folkestone
Cliff Lift, The Leas. Cliff railway completed in 1885, with 5 foot 10 inch gauge track and still using hydraulic power.

Maidstone
Tyrwhitt-Drake Museum of Carriages, Archbishop's Stable, Mill Street. Collection of horsedrawn vehicles in medieval stable block.

Margate
Draper's Windmill, St Peter's Footpath, College Road. Smock mill of 1847, restored to working order.

Meopham
Small hexagonal smock windmill, built in 1801 and fully restored.

Mersham
Swanton or Hanover Mill Water-powered grain mill of 1879.

New Romney
Romney, Hythe and Dymchurch Railway Narrow-gauge (15 inch) railway, providing regular steam-hauled passenger service between Hythe and Dungeness. Museum and depot at New Romney.

Sandwich
The White Mill Eighteenth-century restored smock windmill, north of A257, ½ mile west of town.

Sittingbourne
Dolphin Yard Sailing Barge Museum Based on barge maintenance yard, with old machinery still in use for sailing barge repair and restoration.
Sittingbourne and Kelmsley Light Railway 2 foot 6 inch gauge industrial line, now provides passenger service over 2 mile route.

Stelling Minnis
Stelling Minnis Windmill Windmill of 1866, restored to working order.

Tenterden
Kent and East Sussex Railway Preserved railway offering steam-hauled passenger service to Wittersham Road, with extension planned to Bodiam.
Tenterden and District Museum, Station Road. Contains the Colonel Stephens Railway Collection.

West Kingsdown
Kingsdown Mill Smock windmill with much machinery intact. Moved to present site 1880.

LANCASHIRE

Blackburn
Lewis Museum of Textile Machinery, Exchange Street. An important collection, tracing development of textile machinery from eighteenth century.

Burnley
Toll House Museum, Manchester Road. Museum of textile industry,

Cotton mills and warehouses lining the Leeds and Liverpool Canal in the area of Burnley known as the Weavers' Triangle.

housed in Leeds and Liverpool Canal toll house.

Carnforth
Steamtown Railway Museum, Warton Road. Large collection of steam locomotives, including *Flying Scotsman* and *Sir Nigel Gresley*, in former motive power depot. Steam excursion centre.

Earby
Museum of Mines, Old Grammar School, School Lane. Collection of miners' tools and artefacts and working models.

Fleetwood
Fleetwood Museum, Dock Street. History of port with special emphasis on fishing industry.

Gisburn
Tom Varley's Museum of Steam, Todber Caravan Park. Collection of traction engines, steam waggons and fairground organs.

Helmshore
Higher Mill Textile Museum, Holcombe Road. Museum of textile machinery, based on restored mill complex with spinning mill and fulling mill, fulling stocks and water wheel.

Thornton
Marsh Mill Five-storey tower windmill, built in late eighteenth century and fully restored. On A585.

LEICESTERSHIRE

Cadeby
Cadeby Light Railway, Cadeby Rectory. 2 foot gauge railway and traction engines.

Cottesmore
Rutland Railway Museum, Cottesmore Ironstone Sidings, Ashwell Road. Collection of industrial locomotives and rolling stock, steam crane. ¾ mile track. Off B668, north of Oakham.

Leicester
John Doran Museum, Aylestone Road. Small museum devoted to the history of gas.
Leicestershire Museum of Technology, Abbey Lane Pumping Station, Corporation Road. Originally a sewage pumping station, it retains four beam engines of 1891. Engines and steam shovel regularly steamed. Also collection of machinery and vehicles.

Loughborough
Great Central Railway, Central Station. Steam-hauled passenger service on 5½ mile route. Locomotives include 1919 Norwegian engine.

Moira
The Moira Trail Follows line of Ashby Canal and tramways and includes massive blast furnace of *c.* 1800, complete with charge house.

Shackerstone
Market Bosworth Light Railway, Shackerstone Station. Preserved steam-hauled passenger railway to Market Bosworth (2¾ miles). Museum at Shackerstone Station.

LINCOLNSHIRE

Alford
Hoyles Mill, East Street. Five-sailed tower windmill built in 1813. Has bakehouse attached.

Alvingham
Alvingham Water Mill, Church Lane. Eighteenth-century grain mill with breastshot wheel, now a working museum.

Burgh le Marsh
Dobson's Windmill Five-sailed tower mill of 1833, with exhibition of Lincolnshire milling.

Heckington
Tower windmill built in 1830, and only surviving eight-sailed mill in Britain. South of village on B1394.

Lincoln
Ellis Mill, Mill Road. Last surviving windmill in city. Interior viewable by appointment only. Off B1398.

Sibsey
Sibsey Trader Mill (DoE) Tower windmill of 1877; last six-sailed mill in Britain. 1 mile west of Sibsey on B1184.

Stamford
Stamford Brewery Museum, All Saints Street. Museum based on nineteenth-century brewery with original equipment and demonstrations of crafts, such as coopering.

Tattershall
Dog Dyke Pump Drainage pumping station with scoop wheel powered by 1855 beam engine. Occasional steamings. By Tattershall Bridge, A153.

LONDON

Brentford
Kew Bridge Engines Trust and Water Supply Museum, Green Dragon Lane. Largest in situ collection of beam engines in the world. These include an early Boulton and Watt, a Bull engine and a Cornish engine of 1869 with 100-inch diameter cylinder. Regular steamings.

Bromley-by-Bow
Three Mills Conservation Area, Three Mills Lane, E3. Two tide mills. The

earlier is dated 1776, the Clock Mill, 1817 (though clock tower *c.* 1750). Exterior only viewable. Third mill demolished.

Chalk Farm

Round House, Chalk Farm Road, NW1. Built by Robert Stephenson as engine shed for London and North Western Railway, 1847. Now a theatre.

Covent Garden

The London Transport Museum, WC2. Large collection of road and rail

Tower Bridge. The walkway has recently been reopened, providing a spectacular view across the Thames.

transport housed in former flower market.

Greenwich

National Maritime Museum, Romney Road, SE10. This major museum covers all aspects of Britain's maritime past from prehistoric times to the present day. See also preserved clipper ship, *Cutty Sark.*

Gunnersbury

Gunnersbury Park Museum, Pope's Lane, W3. Collection of restored road vehicles and some smaller items.

Rotherhithe

Brunel Engine House Originally held steam engine used during construction of Thames tunnel to Wap-

ping. Now houses museum and horizontal compound engine. Next to Rotherhithe Underground Station, SE16. See also original shaft, Wapping Underground Station.

South Kensington

The Science Museum, Exhibition Road, SW7. Britain's principal museum of science and technology, covering all aspects of the subject.

Southall

Great Western Railway Preservation Group, Bridge Road, SW19. Collection of steam and diesel locomotives.

Tower

St Katharine's Dock, E1. Dock built by Telford 1825–8, with warehouses by Hardwick, extensively redeveloped. Now houses Maritime Trust collection of historic ships, including both sailing ships and steamers and Scott's vessel *Discovery.*
Tower Bridge, E1. Built 1888–94. One of original steam engines with hydraulic pump for lifting bridge preserved.

Upminster

Upminster Windmill Large smock mill, with adjoining cottage and bakery, north of A124.

Wimbledon

Wimbledon Common Windmill, Windmill Road, SW19. Hollow post mill, built in 1817, with windmill museum.

MERSEYSIDE

Liverpool

Merseyside County Museum, William Brown Street. General museum with technology section, including major collection of ship models.
Merseyside Maritime Museum, Pierhead. Important new museum based on port complex. Vessels displayed in former graving (repair) docks. Other exhibits in pilotage building and new boat hall. Adjoins Albert Dock.

Prescot

Prescot Museum of Clock- and Watch-making, 34 Church Street. Museum tells the history of the local industry, with reconstructed workshops.

St Helens

Pilkington Glass Museum, Prescot Road. History of glass making from earliest times to present day.

Southport

Steamport, Derby Road. Large collection of steam locomotives; occasional steamings.

NORFOLK

Acle

Stacey Arms Wind Pump Three-storey tower mill of 1883, used for powering drainage pumps. $2\frac{1}{2}$ miles east on A47.

Billingford Common

Billingford Windmill Tower mill of 1860, with much of its original machinery. 1 mile east of Scole, on A140.

Bressingham

Bressingham Live Steam Museum Large collection of locomotives, regularly steamed. Standard- and narrow-gauge track ($9\frac{1}{2}$ inch, 15 inch and 24 inch) to a total of 5 miles. Also museum and steam fair.

Denver

Denver Windmill Six-storey tower mill, c. 1835, with two-storey former steam mill attached.

Forncett St Mary

Forncett Industrial Steam Museum, Low Road. Collection of stationary steam engines, including one of original engines from Tower Bridge, London. Regular steamings.

Great Bircham

Bircham Mill Tower windmill of 1846 with bakery from earlier mill.

Great Yarmouth

Maritime Museum for East Anglia, Marine Parade. Housed in former home for shipwrecked sailors.

Horsey

Horsey Mere Wind Pump (NT) Tower windmill built in 1912 on eighteenth-century foundations to work drainage pumps.

Norwich

Bridewell Museum of Local Industries, Bridewell Alley. Displays of all aspects of local industry in medieval house, former gaol or bridewell.

Colman's Mustard Museum, Bridewell Alley. Museum of mustard manufacture, based on nineteenth-century shop.

Paston

Stow Windmill Tower windmill with little internal machinery. On B1159, 1 mile south of Mundesley.

Reedham

Berney Arms Windmill (DoE) Seven-storey drainage mill of 1840 in Halvergate Marshes. Accessible by boat or from Berney Arms railway halt. Exhibition in mill. (TG 465 051)

Sheringham

North Norfolk Railway Preserved steam railway with passenger service to Weybourne and extension under construction. Steam locomotives and vintage rolling stock.

Stalham

Sutton Windmill Nine-storey tower mill, tallest in Britain. Originally built 1789, rebuilt following fire in 1857. 1 mile east of village, south of B1151.

Thurne

Thurne Dyke Wind Pump Small pumping mill of 1820 at end of dyke. The working wherry *Albion* has moorings alongside.

Thursford Green

The Thursford Collection, Laurel Farm. Large collection of traction engines, steam waggons and stationary engines. Also fairground and theatre organs. 5 miles north-east of Fakenham.

Weeting

Grimes Graves (DoE) Neolithic flint mines; extensive site with many pits, one of which is open to public. South of B1108, east of A1065.

Wolferton

Wolferton Station Museum, Sandringham Estate. Railway museum in former Royal Retiring Room.

NORTHAMPTONSHIRE

Kettering

Westfield Museum, West Street. General museum with section devoted to boot and shoe manufacture.

Little Billing

Billing Mill, Billing Aquadrome. Nineteenth-century water-powered grain mill and mill museum. 4 miles east of Northampton on A45.

Northampton

Hunsbury Hill Industrial Museum Museum of the ironstone industry in former ironstone quarries and railway exhibits on former tramway trackbed. Near Rothersthorpe Road. *Museum of Leathercraft*, Old Blue Coat School, 60 Bridge Street. Leather industry from ancient times to present day.

Stoke Bruerne

Waterways Museum Housed in lockside warehouse building on Grand Union Canal. Historic craft moored outside.

NORTHUMBERLAND

Beadnell

Beadnell Lime Kilns (NT) A group of preserved eighteenth-century lime kilns by the harbour.

Ford

Heatherslaw Mill One nineteenth-century building houses two grain mills, each originally powered by undershot water wheels. One mill restored. Between Ford and Etal, near B6354.

Newton

Hunday National Tractor and Farm Museum Museum includes stationary engines of all kinds – steam, oil and gas – and early agricultural machinery. North of A69, 3 miles west of Corbridge.

Otterburn

Otterburn Mill This traditional tweed mill was adapted from a corn mill in 1821. Only the showroom is now open but visitors can see tenter field with tentering frames in use.

Rothbury

Cragside House and Country Park (NT) The house was built for the pioneer hydraulic and general engineer Sir William Armstrong in the late nineteenth century. It was the first private house to be lit by electricity produced by water power.

Wylam-on-Tyne
George Stephenson's Cottage (NT) A small stone cottage built about 1750 where the railway pioneer was born in 1781. Open by appointment with tenant.

NORTH YORKSHIRE

Aysgarth
The Yorkshire Museum of Carriages and Horsedrawn Vehicles The collection is housed in a nineteenth-century cloth mill.

Crakehall
Crakehall Mill Water mill, mostly dating from seventeenth century, with additions of c. 1800. 2 miles west of Bedale on A684.

Embsay
Yorkshire Dales Railway Large collection of industrial locomotives and vintage rolling stock. Passenger rides on 1½ mile track (to be extended).

Goathland
Wade's Causeway (DoE) Well preserved and partially restored section of Roman road across the moor. (SE 793 938 to 812 988)

Grosmont
North Yorkshire Moors Railway Preserved steam passenger line, running through National Park to Pickering (18 miles). Adjoining Grosmont station is tunnel of Whitby and Pickering Railway of 1835 with castellated portals.

Hawes
Upper Dales Folk Museum, Station Yard. Regional museum with many exhibits relating to Wensleydale Railway.

Hutton-le-Hole
Ryedale Folk Museum Large collection, which includes nineteenth-century tools and the unique Elizabethan glass furnace.

Pickering
North Yorkshire Moors Railway See **Grosmont** above.

Reeth
Swaledale Folk Museum, Reeth Green. Museum includes section dealing with lead industry.

*Robin Hood's Bay
Extensive remains of alum mines and quarries *(NT)*, worked since the early seventeenth century. On the cliffs at Ravenscar, 2 miles south of town.

Scarborough
South Cliff Tramway The first seaside cliff tramway in Britain, built in 1875. Originally worked on water balance principle, then by steam and now by electric motor. 284 feet long.

Skipton
George Leatt Industrial and Folk Museum, High Corn Mills, Mill Bridge. Museum in restored water mill. Milling and agricultural exhibits.

York
Castle Museum, Tower Street. The Raindale water-powered mill from North Yorkshire Moors re-erected.
National Railway Museum, Leeman Road. Britain's principal railway museum housed in former motive power depot. Important collection of locomotives dating back to 1829 and historic rolling stock, including royal coaches.

NOTTINGHAMSHIRE

Bestwood
Colliery steam winding engine of 1873, with engine house and headstock. 5 miles north of Nottingham to east of A611.

Calverton
Folk Museum, Main Square. Exhibits of local hosiery industry. Framework knitters' cottages survive in Windles Square.

Carlton-in-Lindrick
Carlton Mill, Church Lane. Grain mill with undershot wheel. Now houses museum.

East Retford
National Mining Museum, Lound Hall, Haughton. Major museum, devoted to history of coal mining. 5½ miles south-west of East Retford, off B6387.

North Leverton
Three-storey tower windmill of 1813, still in use. Originally a 'subscription' mill, bought and worked by shareholders.

Nottingham
Canal Museum, Canal Street. Waterways museum housed in warehouse of famous carrying company, Fellows, Morton and Clayton.
Greens Mill, Belvoir Hill, Sneinton. Windmill undergoing restoration.
Industrial Museum, Wollaton Road. Housed in former stable block of Wollaton Hall, includes machinery of local industries, nineteenth-century beam engine and horse gin.

Ravenshead
Papplewick Pumping Station, off Longdale Lane. Ornate Victorian pumping station with two 1884 Watt beam engines. Occasional steamings. East off A60 at Seven Mile House.

Ruddington
Framework Knitters' Museum, Chapel Street. A group of cottages and workshops built for hosiery industry in 1820s. One workshop and two cottages restored.

OXFORDSHIRE

Abingdon
Town Hall Nineteenth-century gas engine in basement, originally used to power water pump.

Combe
Combe Mill Maintenance works for Blenheim Estate, built mid nineteenth century. Wood- and metal-working machinery with shaft drive from water wheel and beam engine. Engine regularly steamed.

Didcot
Railway Centre, adjacent to BR station. Preserved GWR locomotives and rolling stock, including broad-gauge demonstration track.

Garford
Venn Mill Water-powered corn mill of c. 1800 under restoration. Display of mill equipment. On A338.

Mapledurham
Working water-powered grain mill, largely eighteenth century. Last working mill on the Thames.

Rotherfield Greys
*Greys Court (NT) Donkey wheel to raise water from well in Tudor wheelhouse.

SHROPSHIRE

Bridgnorth
Castle Hill Railway Funicular railway of 1892, originally worked on water-balance principle, now electric.
Severn Valley Railway See **Bewdley**, Hereford and Worcester.

Broseley
Willey Iron Works Site where John Wilkinson first used steam-powered blowing engine for blast furnace. Cottages and furnace remains. (SO 674 006)

Coalbrookdale See **Ironbridge**

Coalport See **Ironbridge**

Ironbridge
Ironbridge Gorge Museum This is arguably the most exciting museum in Britain, for it has been built up around several existing sites of immense importance in Britain's industrial history. Coalbrookdale, home of the first experiments with the coke-fired blast furnace, must take pride of place but by no means represents the whole story. Here, within the one valley, are iron works, canal, tramways, inclined plane, potteries and much more. To complete the scene is the famous iron bridge which gave the town its name. Many of the sites have working exhibits, and more material is added with each passing year. The Ironbridge complex includes: Severn Wharf and Warehouse, Coalbrookdale Museum of Iron and Furnace Site, Blists Hill Open Air Museum and Coalport China Works Museum.

Longdon-upon-Tern
The first iron-trough canal aqueduct is preserved here, although the canal has gone. Off B5063 at Longdon.

Oswestry
Cambrian Railways Society, Oswestry Station yard, Oswald Road. Collection of industrial locomotives and rolling stock.

Shrewsbury
Coleham Pumping Station, Old Coleham. Former sewage pumping station with two compound beam engines of 1897, turned by electric motor. $\frac{1}{4}$ mile south-east of town centre, on A49.

Darby's Gothic warehouse beside the Severn at Ironbridge, built like a medieval fortress.

SOMERSET

Burrow Bridge
Pumping Station Museum Former water-pumping station, with two preserved steam engines of 1864 and 1869. Turn south off A361 opposite King Alfred Hotel.

Chard
Chard and District Museum, Godworthy House, High Street. Contains cider press, once worked by horse, now by water wheel.
Hornsbury Mill, Ilminster Road. Grain mill powered by overshot wheel. Houses small museum.

Charterhouse
Blackmoor Educational Nature Reserve The reserve occupies former lead-mining area. A battery of eight nineteenth-century condensing flues has been preserved.

Cranmore
East Somerset Railway Preserved railway offering passenger service on $1\frac{1}{2}$ mile route with passenger and industrial steam locomotives. 4 miles east of Shepton Mallet.

Dunster Castle
Dunster Castle Mill (NT) The water mill, thought to be late seventeenth-century, is in working order and produces wholemeal flour. 3 miles south-east of Minehead.

High Ham
Stembridge Windmill (NT) Tower mill of 1822. Last mainland British windmill to retain a thatched cap. $\frac{1}{2}$ mile east of village. Admission by appointment with tenant.

Minehead
West Somerset Railway, The Railway Station. Passenger railway operating between Minehead and Bishop's Lydeard (20 miles) worked with both steam and diesel locomotives. Large collection of locos and rolling stock.

Street
Street Shoe Museum, C. & J. Clark Ltd, High Street. Housed in the oldest part of the shoe factory. Museum contains shoes of all periods and nineteenth-century machinery.

Westonzoyland
Westonzoyland Pumping Station Land drainage pump for Somerset levels,

first established here in 1830. The present preserved machinery consists of a two-cylinder vertical steam engine of 1861 geared to a centrifugal pump, instead of the more familiar pump rods.

Williton

Orchard Water Mill Late nineteenth-century mill, originally used for grinding alabaster for cement. West of B3191.

Wookey Hole

Water-powered paper mill, part dating back to seventeenth century but largely rebuilt in nineteenth century. Demonstrations of paper-making by hand. Now owned by Madame Tussaud's. 2 miles north-west of Wells.

SOUTH YORKSHIRE

Catcliffe

Catcliffe Glass Works Preserved glass cone of c. 1740. 4 miles east of Sheffield, off A630.

Elsecar

Elsecar Colliery Eighteenth-century Newcomen-type colliery pumping engine in original engine house.

Sheffield

Abbeydale Industrial Hamlet, Abbeydale Road South. Major industrial museum based on eighteenth-century scythe works. All processes are represented from manufacture of crucible steel to shaping of blades by water-powered hammers and finishing processes.
Sheffield Industrial Museum, Kelham Island. Based on 1899 electricity-generating station for trams, exhibits include Bessemer converter, steam engine for rolling mill and 'little mesters' workshops.
Shepherd Wheel, Whiteley Wood, Hangingwater Road. Nineteenth-century water-powered grinding shop.

Worsbrough

Worsbrough Mill Museum, Worsbrough Country Park. Working mill museum, housed in two adjoining buildings – a seventeenth-century water mill and nineteenth-century steam mill. 2½ miles south of Barnsley, on A61.

Wortley

Wortley Top Forge Iron-making site dating back to seventeenth century. Machinery mainly nineteenth century, including water-powered hammers and rollers. Off A629. (SK 294 998)

STAFFORDSHIRE

Barlaston

Wedgwood Museum and Visitor Centre Museum housed in modern factory traces history of works; many items relating to first Josiah Wedgwood.

Burton-on-Trent

Bass Museum of Brewing, Horninglow Street. Housed in nineteenth-century joiners' shop, the museum has many brewing exhibits, including model brewery, steam engine and Company train.

Cheddleton

Cheddleton Flint Mill, Leek Road. Flint-grinding mill, restored to working order, alongside Caldon Canal. Original water-powered machinery includes pumps, grinding pans and hoists.
North Staffordshire Railway, Cheddleton Station. Preserved locomotives and small museum.

Dilhorne

Foxfield Light Railway Former colliery line, offering steam-hauled passenger service to Blythe Bridge (4 miles).

Froghall

Froghall Wharf Conservation area at terminus of Caldon Canal with lime kilns and tramway remains. Canal trips by horsedrawn narrow boat. Off A52.

Hanley

Etruscan Bone and Flint Mill Nineteenth-century works situated between Caldon and Trent and Mersey Canals, originally used for grinding bones and flint for the pottery industry. Small preserved beam engine of c. 1840. 200 yards south of Etruria Park.

Leek

Brindley Mill and Museum, Mill Street. Water-powered grain mill of 1752, originally built by the canal engineer, James Brindley.

Longton

Gladstone Pottery Museum, Uttoxeter Road. Museum based on nineteenth-century pottery works. Original buildings, including bottle ovens, have been retained. Working steam engine and displays of pottery crafts.

Millmeece

Mill Meece Pumping Station Water-supply pumping station with two preserved horizontal tandem compound steam engines of 1914 and 1927, regularly steamed. Off A519, 3 miles north of Eccleshall.

Shugborough

Staffordshire County Museum (NT) Former coach-houses holding collection of horsedrawn vehicles, and brewhouse. See also elaborate railway viaduct over Lichfield Drive.

Tunstall

Chatterley Whitfield Mining Museum The museum is based on former colliery. Many surface buildings are retained, including engine house with horizontal steam winding engine of 1914. Visitors are taken underground. On A527, Congleton road.

SUFFOLK

Carlton Colville

East Anglia Transport Museum, Chapel Road. Collection of road vehicles and narrow-gauge railway exhibits. 3 miles south-west of Lowestoft.

Flatford

Flatford Mill (NT) This eighteenth-century water mill, once owned by John Constable's father and featuring in many paintings, is a Field Studies Centre (not open). Adjoining lock on Stour Navigation has been restored.

Herringfleet

Herringfleet Marsh Mill Smock drainage mill of 1823 with scoop wheel. Occasional working demonstrations. (TM 465 974)

Leiston

The East Anglian Steam and Industrial Museum A museum of steam engines and engineering housed in The Long Shop, formerly part of Garrett's engineering works.

Little Welnetham

The Rake Factory, Station Yard. A working museum, based on factory of *c.*1900 for manufacture of agricultural tools. Original machinery powered by belting from overhead shafts turned by oil engine. To the east of A134, Long Melford to Bury St Edmunds road.

Lowestoft

Lowestoft Maritime Museum, Fisherman's Cottage, Sparrow's Nest Park. Museum mostly dealing with local fishing industry.

Pakenham

Pakenham Water Mill, Grimstone End. Eighteenth-century water-powered grain mill with fine Georgian frontage, built on foundations of Tudor mill.

Pakenham Windmill Five-storey tower mill, *c.*1830. Still in use for animal feeds, but most grinding by electric motor.

Saxtead Green

Well-preserved eighteenth-century post mill *(DoE)*, winded by fan tail mounted on the end of the ladder.

Stowmarket

Museum of East Anglian Life An open-air museum containing a collection of horsedrawn vehicles. Also the Alton water mill and Eastbridge wind pump have been re-erected on site.

Thorington Street

Thorington Mill Water mill undergoing restoration, 1½ miles east of Bramfield on River Stour.

Thorpeness

Thorpeness Windmill Post mill of 1824, originally a grain mill and brought to present site in 1920s to pump water.

Woodbridge

Buttrums Windmill, Burkitt Road. Six-storey tower mill of 1835.

Tide Mill Built in 1793, on site in use since twelfth century. The mill worked until 1957 and has now been restored.

Robert Stephenson's High Level Bridge, Newcastle, in the days of steam. Built in the 1840s, it has two decks, the upper carrying the railway tracks and the lower a roadway.

SURREY

Guildford

Treadmill Crane Wharf crane powered by treadmill on quayside on east bank of River Wey.

Haxted

Haxted Watermill Museum The mill is part sixteenth-century on fourteenth-century foundations. Houses museum and exhibition by Wealden Iron Research Group. 2 miles west of Edenbridge.

Ockham

Telegraph Tower Admiralty telegraph tower of 1848, part of a chain linking London to Portsmouth. Signalling equipment at County Hall, Kingston upon Thames.

Outwood

Outwood Windmill A post mill of 1665, restored and occasionally used for grinding flour.

Reigate

Reigate Heath Windmill A post mill of 1765 with round house converted for use as a chapel in nineteenth century. Stands on golf course, 1½ miles southwest of Reigate, south of A25.

Shalford

*Shalford Water Mill (NT) An eighteenth-century grain mill. Off The Street.

TYNE AND WEAR

Newcastle upon Tyne

Museum of the Department of Mining Engineering, Queen Victoria Road. Collection of mine safety lamps and other exhibits.

Museum of Science and Engineering, Blandford House, West Blandford Street. Large collection covering industrial history of region.

Turbinia Hall, Exhibition Park. Houses *Turbinia*, the world's first steam turbine powered ship of 1894. See also Tyne bridges.

RIGHT *Engine house and headstock, Washington F Pit.*

Rowland's Gill

Whinfield Coke Ovens A range of preserved beehive coke ovens, built 1861. Off A694. (NZ 152 580)

Ryhope

Ryhope Pumping Station 1868 station containing two beam engines, both regularly steamed, and waterworks museum. Next to General Hospital, off Stockton Road.

Springwell

Bowes Railway Preserved section ($1\frac{1}{4}$ miles) of railway engineered by George Stephenson, opened 1826. Demonstrations of rope-hauled incline, also locomotives, rolling stock and museum.

Sunderland

Monkwearmouth Station Museum, North Bridge Street. Railway museum in 1848 station built in classical style.

Washington

Washington F Pit, Albany Way. Preserved colliery steam winder of 1888 with headstock, now run on electric motor.

Winlaton

Cottage Forge A small nail-making shop attached to the cottage.

WARWICKSHIRE

Charlecote

*Charlecote Park (NT) Sixteenth-century house with domestic brew house. 5 miles east of Stratford-upon-Avon, north side of B4086.

Chesterton Green

Chesterton Windmill Unusual tower windmill of 1632, carried on six-arched base. Design attributed to Inigo Jones. 4 miles south of Leamington, east of A41.

Great Alne

Water-powered grain mill of *c.* 1800, worked by turbine installed 1904. 2 miles north-east of Alcester, south of B4089.

Hawkesbury

Canal complex at junction of Coventry and Oxford Canals includes restored pumping engine house, which once held Newcomen engine now preserved at Dartmouth. 4 miles north of Coventry, west of B4109.

Stratford-upon-Avon

Stratford-upon-Avon and Moreton-in-the-Marsh Tramway of 1826 crosses the Avon on nine-arched viaduct. Restored section of line and waggon at town end. ¼ mile south-east of town centre.

WEST MIDLANDS

Balsall Common

Berkswell or Balsall Windmill, Windmill Lane. Tower mill of 1826, with restored machinery.

Birmingham

Avery Historical Museum, Foundry Street, Smethwick. Museum devoted to weighing machines occupies part of Soho foundry established by Boulton and Watt in 1776.
Birmingham Railway Museum, Warwick Road, Tyseley. Large collection of steam locomotives and rolling stock housed in former motive power depot. Centre for rail tours.
The Museum of Science and Industry, Newhall Street. Exhibits in this major museum include machine tools, Boulton and Watt beam engine of 1779, regularly steamed, and locomotive *City of Birmingham.* Stands beside locks on Birmingham and Fazeley Canal.
Sarehole Mill, Cole Bank Road, Hall Green. Eighteenth-century water-powered mill used at various times as grain mill and for metal working. Now a milling museum.

See also Telford's Galton Bridge and Engine Arm Aqueduct, Birmingham Canal.

Brownhills

Chasewater Light Railway, Chasewater Pleasure Park. Collection of industrial locomotives and rolling stock.

Dudley

The Black Country Museum, Tipton Road. Extensive and still developing open-air museum, based on canal dock site. Canal features include workshop and lime kilns. Buildings re-erected on site include a working chain shop. Regular boat trips to Dudley Canal tunnel and underground limestone workings.
Bumble Hole, Netherton. Preserved Windmill End Colliery engine house at south end of Netherton Canal tunnel.

Stourbridge

Stuart & Sons, Wordsley. Glass works with preserved 90-foot high glass cone of *c.* 1780.

WEST SUSSEX

Amberley

Chalk Pits Museum, Houghton Bridge Industrial museum based on 36-acre chalk-pit site. Original features include lime kilns and narrow-gauge railway with steam and diesel locomotives. Also brickworks, iron working, tannery and transport exhibits. Off B2139.

Clayton

Jack and Jill Windmills Jack, a privately owned tower mill of 1876; Jill, a preserved post mill of 1821. See also castellated portals of railway tunnel and tunnel-keeper's house.

Ebernoe Common

Brickworks dating from late eighteenth century. Preserved remains include an open-topped kiln with twin stoke holes and moulding shed. To be found in Nature Reserve (SU 979 274), 1½ miles south-east of North Chapel.

Henfield

Woods Water Mill Four-storey eighteenth-century grain mill, restored to working order and now

The magnificent Balcombe viaduct, West Sussex, on the London to Brighton line designed by the engineer John Rastrick and the architect David Mocatta.

housing countryside exhibition. 1 mile south on Shoreham road.

Horsted Keynes

Bluebell Railway See under **Sheffield Park** (East Sussex).

Ifield

Ifield Mill, off Hyde Drive, Rusper Road. Restored water-powered grain mill of 1817 houses the Crawley Museum. 1½ miles north-west of Crawley.

Petworth

Burton Water Mill Mill of *c.* 1920, water-powered by turbine and occasionally worked. 2 miles south of Petworth.

Coultershaw Water Pump Water-driven beam pump of 1782, possibly first pumped water supply for British town. Now powers fountain. Coultershaw Bridge, 1½ miles south-west of Petworth, off A285.

Sharpthorne
Medieval tanyard with museum of leather industry attached to manor house. 1 mile south on Horsted Keynes road.

Shipley
Belloc's Mill Smock mill of 1879, preserved as memorial to Hilaire Belloc who owned the mill.

Singleton
Weald and Downland Open Air Museum Historic buildings re-erected on site include a wind pump and working water mill producing flour, also charcoal-burner's camp showing various stages in production of charcoal.

WEST YORKSHIRE

Bradford
Industrial Museum, Moorside Road, Eccleshill. The museum is housed in large nineteenth-century woollen mill and concentrates on local textile industry.

Dewsbury
The Canal Museum, Savile Town Wharf, Mill Street East. Canal museum housed in former stable block on canal basin of Calder and Hebble Navigation.

Golcar
Colne Valley Museum, Cliffe Ash. Museum based on nineteenth-century weavers' cottages, refurbished with hand looms and spinning wheels.

Halifax
Piece Hall The Hall of 1775 was built for cloth merchants and now houses a textile museum and craft workshops.

Haworth
Keighley and Worth Valley Railway Preserved steam railway offering passenger service between Keighley and Oxenhope (5 miles). Large collection of locomotives and rolling stock, with museums at Haworth and Oxenhope. Restored stations on line.

Huddersfield
Museum of Hand Tools, Banney Royd Teacher's Centre, Halifax Road. Collection of tools from many trades. *Tolson Memorial Museum*, Ravensknowle Park, Wakefield Road. General museum with large

*The five-lock staircase at Bingley,
West Yorkshire, on the Leeds and
Liverpool Canal, lifting the canal sixty
feet from the Aire valley.*

industrial collection, especially
relating to woollen industry and
transport.

Keighley
Keighley and Worth Valley Railway. See
Haworth above.

Leeds
Armley Mills, Canal Road. Early
nineteenth-century woollen mill
associated with Benjamin Gott, the
pioneer of mechanization in the
woollen industry. Now home to the
new Leeds Industrial Museum.
Middleton Colliery Railway, Garnet
Road. Preserved steam railway with
passenger rides over 1 mile track.
Original line dates back to 1758 and
was used for Blenkinsop's rack and
pinion railway.
Thwaite Mills Putty mills dating from

1820s, with complete range of
buildings from mill house to fully
equipped engineering workshop.
Adjoining locks on River Aire at
Stourton.
See also *Temple Works*, Marshall
Street. Flax mill built in Egyptian
style.

Shipley
Shipley Glen Tramway, Baildon. Cable-
hauled tramway, built in 1895 ($\frac{1}{4}$
mile). Originally powered by gas
engine, now electric.

WILTSHIRE

Devizes
Canal Centre, The Wharf. Small
museum with items relating to the
history of the Kennet and Avon
Canal. See also flight of twenty-
nine locks with side ponds.

Great Bedwyn
Crofton Pumping Station Pumping
station built to provide water for

Kennet and Avon Canal. Two beam
engines, 1812 and 1845, regularly
steamed.

Malmesbury
Avon Mill Water-powered woollen
mill of 1790, now an antiques
showroom.

Swindon
Great Western Railway Museum,
Faringdon Road. Museum houses
GWR locomotives, including broad-
gauge models, in former GWR
workers' hostel.
Railway Village Museum, 34 Faringdon
Road. Original GWR worker's
cottage, restored and furnished.

Wilton
Wilton Windmill Restored tower mill
of 1820s; working demonstrations of
wholemeal flour production.

IRELAND
Eire

DONEGAL

Glencolumbkille
Glencolumbkille Folk Museum Museum is based on three cottages of eighteenth, nineteenth and twentieth centuries and includes features on tools and equipment used for manufacturing Donegal tweed.

DUBLIN

Dublin
Guinness Museum, James's Gate, James's Street. Museum displaying brewing equipment and machinery and also brewery transport.

Dun Laoghaire
National Maritime Museum of Ireland, Mariner's Church, Haigh Terrace. Museum housed in former church. Exhibits include lighthouse optic and steam engine from dredger.

GALWAY

Tuam
Mill Museum, Shop Street. 300-year-old corn mill and exhibits illustrating history of milling.

KILDARE

Robertstown
Canal and Transport Museum, Grand Canal Hotel. Museum devoted mainly to Irish canals, especially Grand Canal.

LAOIS

Stradbally
Irish Steam Preservation Society, Stradbally Hall. Collection of standard- and narrow-gauge locomotives.

MEATH

Navan
Athlumney Mill (AT) The Boyne Canal runs for 19 miles from here to Drogheda. 1½ miles from town it is straddled by Athlumney Mill.

MONAGHAN

Monaghan
Monaghan County Museum, The Courthouse. General museum with transport exhibits and section on lace making.

WEXFORD

Screen
Garrylough Mill (AT) A small, well-preserved corn mill housing a museum of milling. On L29 Gorey road.

Tacumshane
Tacumshane Windmill (ONOP) Tower mill of 1846 with thatched cap and tail pole. North shore of Lake Tacumshane, 7 miles south of Wexford.

Wexford
Wexford Maritime Museum, lightship Guillemot, Wexford Harbour. Ship models and relics of schooner trade.

WICKLOW

Ashford
Mount Usher Museum Collection of carriages by Dublin coach builder.

Donard
Transport Museum Society of Ireland, Castle Ruddery Depot. Large collection of commercial road vehicles and transport history displays.

Northern Ireland

ANTRIM

Antrim
Shanes Castle Railway 3 foot gauge line (1½ miles) with steam locomotives, the earliest a Peckett of 1904. Includes 1949 loco from Bord-na-Mona turf railway.

Belfast
The Transport Museum, Witham Street, Belfast 4. Transport collection covering land, sea and air transport. Part of collection is housed in Ulster Folk and Transport Museum, **Holywood** (see below under **Down**).

Brockley, Rathlin Island
Doonmore This prehistoric mound fort marks site of Neolithic axe factory.

Bushmills
Old Bushmills Distillery The whiskey distillery, first licensed in 1609, is the oldest distillery in the world and can be visited. See also two water mills by the bridge over the Bush.

Carnanee
This eighteenth-century water-powered forge is still run by the Patterson family and produces spades and shovels. 3 miles east of Templepatrick, north of the Belfast road.

Carnlough
The limestone bridge over the main street carried the railway built in 1854 to link limestone quarries to the harbour. Eighteenth-century lime kiln preserved by Carnlough River, reached by Waterfall Road.

Crumlin
Old Woollen Mill Water-powered mill producing Ulster tweed. Contains craft centre.

Parkgate
Ballywee Corn Mill Water-powered and still in use. North of Templepatrick.

Whitehead
Whitehead Excursion Station Railway Preservation Society of Ireland's

collection of steam locomotives and rolling stock. Regularly used for steam excursions.

ARMAGH

Armagh

Armagh County Museum, The Mall East. Numerous exhibits dealing with transport history.

Bessbrook

Mill and mill village built by Quaker linen manufacturer Richardson between 1846 and 1855. Linen still woven. Remains of tramway from Bessbrook to Newry. Railway viaduct longest in Ireland.

Tassagh

Tassagh Mill Large water mill on Callan River. Also eleven-arched railway viaduct.

DOWN

Aghagallon

Riverdale Mill Nineteenth-century water-powered mill with mixed machinery including grindstones, milk churner and potato sorter.

Annalong

Water-powered grain mill by quayside of busy fishing harbour.

Ballydugan

Remains of eight-storey flour mill with engine house and stack of 1792. ½ mile north of A22, between Downpatrick and Clough, by Lake Ballydugan.

Ballynahinch

Harris's Mill Water-powered grain mill of 1830 still using original wheel. Now grinds animal feed. Flax mill alongside used for drying grain.

Gilford

Flax spinning town. At Tullyish, 1½ miles east, is Bleach Green watch house for guardian of linen spread on bleach field. Pottery and chandlery in former spinning mill.

Holywood

Ulster Folk and Transport Museum, Cultra Manor. Large open-air museum, which includes industrial buildings removed to this site. The

Old warehouses lining the banks of the Newry Canal.

Coalisland Spade Mill is a water-powered forge with two wheels: one for powering the fan for the hearth, and the second for the tilt hammer under which spade blades were shaped. The 1850s Gortichashel flax-scutching mill used water power for rollers that broke the flax and blades to separate flax from outer casing.

Millisle

Ballycopeland Windmill Tower mill of the 1780s, fully restored. 1½ miles west of town.

Newry

Quays lined with preserved warehouses on canal completed 1741, the first canal in the British Isles.

Strangford

Castle Ward Water Mill (NT) Water-powered mill in castle grounds. Also Victorian laundry.

FERMANAGH

Belleek

Belleek Pottery Founded 1857 to produce porcelain and still working.

LONDONDERRY

Limavady

Roe Valley Country Park, Dog Leap. The valley contains many remains of water mills, including a mill adapted in 1896 as a private hydroelectric plant. Original machinery still intact.

TYRONE

Cookstown

Wellbrook Beetling Mill (NT) A water-powered mill of 1765 for the final stage of linen processing, beating the cloth under hammers to produce a sheen. 3 miles west on A505.

Sion Mills

Mill village built by Herdman family in the 1840s. Linen mill still at work and preserved mill cottages. See also suspension footbridge over River Mourne. 3 miles south of Strabane.

Strabane

Gray's Printing Press (NT), 49 Main Street. Eighteenth-century printing press. John Dunlap worked here before emigrating to found America's first newspaper and print the Declaration of Independence.

SCOTLAND

BORDERS

Innerleithen (Peebles)
Traquair House A brewhouse was installed 1739 and is still used. See also late nineteenth-century woollen mill in town.

Walkerburn (Peebles)
The Scottish Museum of Woollen Textiles Housed in the mill established by the Ballantyne family in the 1850s. Shows development from cottage industry to modern times.

CENTRAL

Bo'ness (West Lothian)
Bo'ness and Kinneil Railway Preserved railway centred on rebuilt station from Wormit, Fife. Opened 1981 with plans for line to Kinneil.
Bo'ness Museum Museum of local industry, housed in seventeenth-century stable block.

Callander (Perth)
Kilmahog Woollen Mill Early nineteenth-century water-powered woollen mill famous for tweeds and blankets. Hand looms still in use.

Deanston (Perth)
One of the first Scottish cotton towns, founded 1785. Mill and mill houses currently being renovated.

Falkirk (Stirling)
Scottish Railway Preservation Society, Springfield Yard, off Wallace Street. Collection of locomotives and rolling stock with occasional steamings.

Grangemouth (Stirling)
Grangemouth Museum, Victoria Library, Bo'ness Road. Display centres on canals and relics of early steamer *Charlotte Dundas*. Local industry collection held separately, viewable on special open days.

DUMFRIES AND GALLOWAY

Wanlockhead (Dumfries)
Museum of the Scottish Leadmining Industry, Goldscaur Road. A small museum devoted to the local industry. Visitors' walk includes such important remains as the preserved beam pump *(SDD)*.

FIFE

Anstruther
The Scottish Fisheries Museum, St Ayles, Harbourhead. Museum housed in buildings dating from fourteenth to eighteenth centuries. Also two examples of local classes of preserved craft in harbour, a sailing 'fifie' and motorized 'zulu'. See also North Carr lightship moored in harbour.

Ceres
Fife Folk Museum Housed in seventeenth-century weigh house. Exhibits deal with local weaving industry.

Kirkcaldy
Kirkcaldy Industrial Museum, Forth House, War Memorial Grounds. Displays relate to local industries, including linoleum and coal. Collection of horsedrawn vehicles and blacksmith's forge.

Lochty
Lochty Railway Private standard-gauge railway offering steam-hauled passenger trips through the estate of J. B. Cameron.

GRAMPIAN

Alford (Aberdeen)
Alford Transport Museum and Alford Valley Railway Purpose-built museum containing a variety of vehicles from bicycles to steam-rollers. Also Alford Station, rebuilt in situ, and 2 foot gauge passenger line.

Ballindalloch (Moray)
Glenfarclas Distillery, Marypark. Traditional whisky distillery (established 1836) producing malt whisky; and whisky museum.

Buckie (Banff)
Buckie Museum and Peter Anson Gallery Maritime museum dealing with fishing industry.

Dufftown (Banff)
Glenfiddich Distillery Working distillery, founded 1887, and Scotch Whisky Museum.

Fordyce (Banff)
Mill of Dern Late nineteenth-century water-powered grain mill and central kiln.

Glenlivet (Banff)
Glenlivet Distillery Traditional distillery, founded 1824, with Gothic bonded stores of 1890s. Museum of whisky-making equipment. On B9008, 10 miles north of Tomintoul.

Rothes (Moray)
Glen Grant Distillery Whisky distillery, established 1840, with visitors' centre and traditional stills at work.

HIGHLAND

Boat of Garten (Inverness)
Strathspey Railway, The Station. Steam-hauled passenger service on 5 mile route to Aviemore.

Kingussie (Inverness)
Highland Folk Museum Buildings re-erected on site include click mill from Lewis.

Lephin, Isle of Skye
Glendale Water Mill Nineteenth-century grain mill and kiln in working order.

LOTHIAN

East Linton (East Lothian)
Preston Mill (NTS) Water-powered grain mill, possibly sixteenth-century, with attached conical-roofed kiln. Oldest working water mill in Scotland.

Edinburgh (Midlothian)
Mr Purves' Lighting Emporium and Museum Shop, 59 St Stephen Street. Collection of domestic and marine lights.
Royal Scottish Museum, Chambers Street. General museum with many technological exhibits, including colliery locomotive *Wylam Dilly*, 1813. Main hall, built 1860s, excellent example of iron and glass construction.
St Cuthbert's Co-operative Association Transport Collection, Grove Street. Extensive collection of horsedrawn vehicles.

ABOVE *The Forth railway bridge, Lothian, under construction in the summer of 1888. The cantilevered design was revolutionary and used a new construction material: mild steel.*

Linlithgow (West Lothian)
Canal Museum, Manse Road Basin. Museum is housed in former Union Canal stables and tells story of Union Canal. Replica Victorian steam packet boat *Victoria* gives pleasure cruises.

Tranent (East Lothian)
Prestongrange Historical Site and Mining Museum Museum based on former colliery and 1874 beam pumping engine with 70-inch diameter cylinder. Mining exhibits. Colliery locomotives and steam navvy regularly steamed.

ORKNEY ISLANDS

Dounby, Mainland
Click Mill (SDD) The only surviving Norse mill in Orkney. It differs from conventional water-powered grain mills in having a horizontal water wheel. Off A986.

Bonawe iron furnace. The furnace and hearth are on the left, the charge house on the right.

Stenness, Mainland

Tormiston Mill Nineteenth-century grain mill with overshot wheel. Now craft centre. On Kirkwall to Stenness road.

SHETLAND ISLANDS

Lerwick, Mainland

Shetland Museum, Lower Hillhead. General museum with strong maritime emphasis.

Southvoe, Mainland

A group of three Norse mills, one of which has been restored by the adjoining Croft House Museum. (HU 401 145)

STRATHCLYDE

Biggar (Lanark)

Biggar Gasworks Museum The gasworks were built in 1839 and worked until 1973. They are now preserved and contain retorts, two gas holders and working steam engine.

Bonawe (Argyll)

Bonawe Furnace (SDD) Ironworks established in 1762. Restored remains of charcoal blast furnace and other buildings beside loch. (NN 009 318)

Glasgow (Lanark)

Museum of Transport, 25 Albert Drive. Museum covering land and water transport, with important collection of ship models.

People's Palace, Glasgow Green. Social history museum, including history of local tobacco industry. See also Templeton Carpet Factory on Glasgow Green – polychrome building in style of Doge's Palace, Venice.

P.S. Waverley Last sea-going paddle steamer in the world. Regular sailings from Stobcross Quay.

High Blantyre (Lanark)

The David Livingstone Centre Late eighteenth-century cotton mill complex, including mill cottages, one of which, the birthplace of the explorer Livingstone, is preserved. Adjoining north-west Hamilton.

Islay (Argyll)

Islay Woollen Mill, Bridgend. A water-powered tweed mill of 1883 restored

as working museum, manufacturing cloth from fleece to finished product. Early machines include jennies, piecing machine and slubbing billy.

Kilbarchan (Renfrew)

Weaver's Cottage (NTS) Eighteenth-century weaver's cottage with period furnishings and loom. Off A737.

Kirkintilloch (Dunbarton)

Auld Kirk Museum, Cowgate. Local history museum with sections on weaving, mining, iron founding and shipbuilding.

New Lanark (Lanark)

Built as a mill town for workers of the cotton mill established in 1785, later made famous by Robert Owen's social experiments. Mill and town remain.

Oban (Argyll)

Macdonald's Mill, Soroba Road. Exhibition of spinning and weaving history. Working machinery includes handloom and spinning jenny.

TAYSIDE

Aberfeldy (Perth)

McKerchar and MacNaughton, Mill Street. Water-powered oatmeal mill of 1826, with kiln.

See also General Wade's bridge of 1733, designed by the architect William Adam.

The weaver's cottage at Kilbarchan (NTS). Handloom weavers lived and wove here until 1940.

Auchterarder (Perth)

Glenruthven Weaving Mill, Abbey Road. Woollen mill built in 1877, with preserved horizontal tandem compound steam engine.

Blair Atholl (Perth)

Water mill on Atholl estate. The mill is seventeenth century, the attached kiln and granary *c.* 1800. Produces oatmeal and flour.

Brechin (Angus)

Balbirnie Mill Water-powered meal mill of *c.* 1850 with double kilns.

Comrie (Perth)

Museum of Scottish Tartans, Drummond Street. Demonstrations of spinning, weaving and dyeing in eighteenth-century weaving shed.

Perth (Perth)

The Round House, Marshall Place. Part of Perth City Waterworks of 1832, now Tourist Information Centre.

WESTERN ISLES

Shawbost

Shawbost Folk Museum, Lewis. Restored Norse mill. An oval stone building with thatched roof.

WALES

CLWYD

Glyn Ceiriog
Chwarel Wynne Slate mine and museum with remains of tramway linking mine to Llangollen Canal. On the B4500 6 miles from Chirk.

Holywell
Holywell Woollen Mill Built 1777 and still working. Large-scale mill originally built for cotton spinning.

Llangollen
Canal Exhibition Centre, The Wharf. Canal museum housed in old warehouse. Also horsedrawn boat to Pontcysyllte aqueduct.
Llangollen Railway Society, The Station. Collection of industrial locomotives and rolling stock; occasional steamings.

Wrexham
Erddig House (NT) Estate buildings include sawmill and smithy. Agricultural museum in former corn mill lies on the route of the Bersham industrial trail which leads to remains of John Wilkinson's ironworks.

DYFED

Aberystwyth
Aberystwyth Cliff Railway, Cliff Terrace. Funicular railway completed in 1896. Passengers travel 798 feet up Constitution Hill in original cars.
Vale of Rheidol Light Railway, Aberystwyth Station. British Rail's last remaining regular steam passenger service. A narrow-gauge (1 foot 11½ inch) line running 11½ miles to Devil's Bridge.

Ambleston
Wallis Woollen Mill Woollen mill of *c.* 1800. Three looms at work, restored turbine and flannel press. 8 miles north-east of Haverfordwest on B4329.

Bronwydd Arms
Gwili Steam Railway, Bronwydd Arms Station. Standard-gauge railway running steam-hauled passenger service on 3 mile journey. 2 miles north of Carmarthen, on A484.

Canaston Bridge
Blackpool Mill Large water-powered grain mill built in 1803 and refitted 1901, still at work. Display of mill documents.

Capel Dewi
Rock Mills Late nineteenth-century water-powered woollen spinning mill. 2 miles north-east of Llandyssul, off B4459.

Carew
Carew French Mill Restored tide mill beside Carew Castle.

Cwmduad
Cwmduad Woollen Mill Water-powered woollen mill of 1840, now housing small museum. 9 miles north of Carmarthen on A484.

Drefach Felindre
Museum of the Woollen Industry A branch museum of the National Museum of Wales with a collection of textile machinery housed in part of a working woollen mill. South of the A484, 3 miles east of Newcastle Emlyn.

Eglwysfach
Dyfi Furnace (WO) Eighteenth-century blast furnace for iron production, recently restored. Originally a silver-refining site.

Llanelli
Parc Howard Museum, Parc Howard Avenue. Museum housed in former master's home has displays of tinplating processes. Off A476.
Trostre Tinplate Works Museum, British Steel Corporation. Museum devoted to history of tinplating. Visits by arrangement with BSC manager. South of A484, 1 mile east of town.

Maesllyn
Maesllyn Mill Museum A working museum housed in a woollen mill of 1881 with machinery covering all aspects of production from carding to weaving and finishing. Water-powered by three Pelton wheels. West of A486, 4 miles north of Llandyssul.

Newcastle Emlyn
Felin Geri Mill, Cwm Cou. Seventeenth-century water-powered mill still producing flour. Also mill museum and water-powered saw mill. 2 miles north of Newcastle Emlyn, east of B4333.

Ponterwyd
Llywernog Silver-Lead Mine Restored as museum to show working methods, the large site has underground section and working machines including ore crusher, jigger and horse gin.

Pumpsaint
Dolaucothi Gold Mine (NT) The site was originally worked by Romans. Remains show both open-cast and drift mines and site of Roman aqueduct.

Treffgarne
Nant-y-Coy Mill and Museum Nineteenth-century mill with restored water wheel.

GWENT

Abersychan
Cwmbyrgwm Balance Pit Head Gear Water balance winding gear preserved as industrial monument. Last example left in situ. To be found at Cwmbyrgwm, west of town. (SO 251 033)

Blaenafon
The Big Pit Based on Big Pit Colliery. Underground visits.
Blaenafon Ironworks, North Street. Spectacular remains of eighteenth-century ironworks with blast furnace bank, water balance tower and workers' houses.

Cwmafon
Forge Row Twelve ironworkers' cottages of 1804. 2 miles south-east of Blaenafon on A4043.

Pontypool
Junction Cottage, Pontymoel. Canal toll-keeper's cottage with canal exhibition.

Tredegar
Sirhowy Ironworks Early nineteenth-century ironworks. Four blast furnaces recently excavated.

GWYNEDD

Bangor
Penrhyn Castle Industrial Railway Museum (NT) Museum of slate-

working and exhibition of loco-motives, including *Fire Queen* of 1848, and quarry rolling stock. 1 mile east of Bangor between A5 and coast.

Beaumaris, Anglesey
Beaumaris Gaol Contains a treadmill used to power water pumps.

Betws-y-coed
Conwy Valley Museum, Old Goods Yard. Collection of locomotives and rolling stock.
Cyffty Lead Mine Trail Trail includes surface remains and powder house. 3 miles west of town on A5.
See also Waterloo Bridge by Telford, completed in 1815.

Blaenau Ffestiniog
Ffestiniog Railway See **Porthmadog** below.
Gloddfa Ganol Slate museum based on huge slate mine and quarry with inclined planes and numerous buildings.
Llechwedd Slate Caverns Slate mine with underground railway and museum complex.
Narrow-Gauge Railway Centre

Collection of over seventy narrow-gauge locomotives covering a hundred years of development. $\frac{1}{2}$ mile north of town.

Bontddu
Clogau Gold Mine Working mine with interpretative display.

Caernarvon
Caernarvon Maritime Museum, Victoria Dock. New museum featuring *Seiont II*, a coal-fired steam dredger.

Corris
Corris Railway Society Museum, Corris Station Yard. Small, developing railway museum.

Dinas Mawddwy
Meirion Mill Water-powered woollen mill still at work. Also preserved pack-horse bridge and walk along track bed of Mawddwy Railway.

Fairbourne
Fairbourne Railway, Beach Road. Narrow-gauge (15 inch) railway providing steam-hauled passenger service on 2 mile track to Barmouth. See also Barmouth wooden viaduct.

Harlech
Old Llanfair Quarry Slate Caverns Slate mine with conducted tours through extensive underground workings. 1 mile south of Harlech off A496.

Llanberis
Llanberis Lake Railway Former narrow-gauge (1 foot $11\frac{1}{2}$ inch) slate railway now has regular steam-hauled passenger service along shore of Llyn Padarn.
Snowdon Mountain Railway Narrow-gauge (2 foot $7\frac{1}{2}$ inch) rack and pinion railway to summit of Snowdon, constructed in 1890s. Regular steam-hauled passenger service.
Vivian Quarry Trail On shore of Llyn Padarn. A short trail around part of former Dinorwic Quarry system.

The vast Dinorwic slate quarry, Llanberis. Wales had such a huge slate industry because its slate was cheap to extract and could be cleaved to make thin, light slates.

Welsh Slate Museum (WO) The museum is housed in the former workshops of the Dinorwic Slate Quarry. The 50-foot diameter water wheel that powered the workshops still survives. Workshops include foundry and pattern making.

Llansantffraid Glan Conway
Felin Isaf Mill Seventeenth-century water-powered grain mill, still at work.

Llanuwchllyn
Bala Lake Railway Narrow-gauge (1 foot 11⅝ inch) railway with steam-hauled passenger trains along former GWR line beside Bala Lake.

Penmachno
Woollen Mill The original seventeenth-century mill was a fulling mill but was changed to weaving with the introduction of power looms in the nineteenth century. Still makes cloth.

Porthmadog
Ffestiniog Railway Narrow-gauge (1 foot 11½ inch) railway giving steam-hauled passenger rides on 14 mile track to Blaenau Ffestiniog. Ffestiniog Railway Museum at Porthmadog Harbour Station.
Gwynedd Maritime Museum Museum housed in former slate warehouse on quay. Alongside is the restored 1909 ketch *Garlandstone*.
Welsh Highland Railway Narrow-gauge (1 foot 11½ inch) railway with steam-hauled passenger service to Pen-y-Mount (¾ mile).

Tan-y-grisiau
Moelwyn Mill Water-powered fulling mill of early eighteenth century, now containing industrial museum. Original machinery being restored. (By Ffestiniog Railway station.)

Trefriw
Trefriw Woollen Mill The 1859 mill demonstrates all aspects of cloth manufacture from the blending of the wool through spinning and dyeing to weaving.

Tywyn
Talyllyn Railway Former narrow-gauge (2 foot 3 inch) slate railway now provides steam-hauled passenger service on 7½ mile jour-

ney. Also Narrow-Gauge Railway Museum at the station.

MID GLAMORGAN

Aberdare
Dare Valley Country Park Industrial trail takes in Dare Valley Railway and coal mining remains.

Caerphilly
Caerphilly Railway Society, Harold Wilson Industrial Estate. Collection of locomotives and rolling stock.

Gilfach Goch
Industrial trail with descriptive panels tracing coal-mining history of region. 2 miles north-west of Tonyrefail, off A4093.

Merthyr Tydfil
Brecon Mountain Railway, Pontsticill Station. Narrow-gauge (1 foot 11¾ inch) railway offering steam-hauled passenger rides.

New Tredegar
Elliot Colliery Contains steam winding engine of 1891. Can be viewed by arrangement with National Museum of Wales.

POWYS

Church Stoke
Bacheldre Mill Restored seventeenth-century water-powered grain mill.

Llanfair Caereinion
Welshpool and Llanfair Light Railway Narrow-gauge (2 foot 6 inch) railway offers steam-hauled passenger service on 5½ mile line. Rolling stock includes European and African coaches.

Llanidloes
Bryntail Lead Mine (WO) The surface remains of a small lead mine can be seen at the foot of the massive Clywedog Reservoir. 3½ miles north-west of Llanidloes on B4518.
Museum of Local History and Industry, Old Market Hall. Relics of local flannel industry and the Van Lead Mines.

Newtown
Newtown Textile Museum, Commercial Street. Museum of the woollen industry, housed in handloom weaver's house and workshop.

SOUTH GLAMORGAN

Cardiff
Melingriffith Tinplate Works, Ty Mawr Road. The water pump which pumped water from the works back to the canal has been restored.
Welsh Industrial and Maritime Museum, Bute Street. Museum housed in new building next to Bute Dock. Important industrial collection together with open-air exhibits including steam tug and Bristol pilot cutter. Replica of Trevithick locomotive regularly steamed.

St Fagans
Welsh Folk Museum Large open-air museum with buildings re-erected in grounds of St Fagan's Castle, including water-powered fulling mill, tannery and quarryman's cottage.

WEST GLAMORGAN

Aberdulais
Aberdulais Falls (NT) Remains of Mines Royal Company where copper smelting began in the 1580s.

Crynant
Cefn Coed Coal and Steam Centre Preserved steam winding engine, colliery buildings and simulated mine.

Cymmer
Welsh Miner's Museum and Afan Argoed Country Park Museum with simulated coal faces and demonstrations of early mining machinery.

Resolven
Canalside Walk Industrial Park 4½ mile walk along Neath Canal, now disused but retaining several features including iron aqueducts.

Swansea
Maritime and Industrial Museum, South Dock. Contains complete working woollen mill and other industrial exhibits housed in nineteenth-century warehouse.

Further Reading

There are two major series of guides to industrial remains, organized on a regional basis: the first, edited by E.R.R. Green, under the series title *The Industrial Archaeology of Great Britain* (David & Charles) and the second, edited by Keith Falconer, under the series title *The Industrial Archaeology of the British Isles* (Batsford). Many local societies produce their own regional guides. The following are recommended as general introductions to the subject:

BRACEGIRDLE, BRIAN *The Archaeology of the Industrial Revolution* (Heinemann, 1973)

BUCHANAN, R.A. *Industrial Archaeology in Britain* (Penguin, 1972)

BURTON, ANTHONY *Remains of a Revolution* (André Deutsch, 1974)

BURTON, ANTHONY *The Past at Work* (André Deutsch and BBC, 1980)

BUTT, JOHN and DONACHIE, IAN *Industrial Archaeology in the British Isles* (Elek, 1979)

COSSONS, NEIL *The BP Book of Industrial Archaeology* (David & Charles, 1975)

MAJOR, J.K. *Fieldwork in Industrial Archaeology* (Batsford, 1975)

PANNELL, J.P.M. *Techniques of Industrial Archaeology* (David & Charles, 1966)

The following give more detailed accounts of the industries described in the main text:

Chapter 1 Natural Power

REYNOLDS, JOHN *Windmills and Watermills* (Evelyn, 1970)

WAILES, REX *The English Windmill* (Routledge, 1954)

WEST, JENNY *Windmills and Watermills Open to View* (Society for the Protection of Ancient Buildings, 1981)

Chapter 2 Wealth from Underground

ASHTON, T.S. and SYKES, J. *The Coal Industry of the Eighteenth Century* (Manchester, 1929)

ATKINSON, FRANK *The Great Northern Coalfield* (Durham County Local History Society, 1966)

BOWDEN, COLIN, COOPER, GEORGE and McAVOY, TED *Stationary Steam Engines in Great Britain* (Bowden, 1979)

BUCHANAN, R.A. and WATKINS, G. *The Industrial Archaeology of the Stationary Steam Engine* (Allen Lane, 1976)

BURTON, ANTHONY *The Miners* (André Deutsch, 1976)

DUCKHAM, B.F. *A History of the Scottish Coal Industry* (David & Charles, 1970)

GRIFFIN, A.R. *Coalmining* (Longman, 1971)

NEF, J.U. *The Rise of the British Coal Industry* (Routledge, 1932)

Chapter 3 Warp and Weft

BYTHELL, DUNCAN *The Handloom Weavers* (Cambridge University Press, 1969)

CHAPMAN, STANLEY D. *The Early Factory Masters* (David & Charles, 1967)

CHAPMAN, STANLEY D. *The Cotton Industry in the Industrial Revolution* (Macmillan, 1972)

FITTON, R.S. and WADSWORTH, A.P. *The Strutts and the Arkwrights* (Manchester University Press, 1958)

MANN, J. DE L. *The Cloth Industry in the West of England* (Oxford University Press, 1971)

TANN, JENNIFER *Gloucestershire Woollen Mills* (David & Charles, 1967)

TANN, JENNIFER *The Development of the Factory* (Cornmarket, 1970)

WADSWORTH, A.P. and MANN, J. *The Cotton Trade and Industrial Lancashire* (Manchester University Press, 1931)

Chapter 4 The Metals

ASHTON, T.S. *Iron and Steel in the Industrial Revolution* (Manchester University Press, 1924)

BARTON, D.B. *A History of Tin Mining and Smelting in Cornwall* (Barton, 1967)

BARTON, D.B. *A History of Copper Mining in Cornwall and Devon* (Barton, 1968, second edition)

GALE, W.K.V. *Iron and Steel* (Longman, 1977)

RAISTRICK, ARTHUR *Dynasty of Ironfounders* (David & Charles, 1970)

RAISTRICK, ARTHUR and JENNINGS, B. *A History of Lead Mining in the Pennines* (Longman, 1965)

Chapter 5 On the Road

ALBERT, WILLIAM *The Turnpike Road System in England* (Cambridge University Press, 1971)

BIRD, ANTHONY *Roads and Vehicles* (Longman, 1969)

COPELAND, JOHN *Roads and Their Traffic* (David & Charles, 1968)

HALDANE, A.R.B. *New Ways Through the Glens* (David & Charles, 1962)

MARÉ, ERIC DE *The Bridges of Britain* (Batsford, 1954)

SMITH, PETER *The Turnpike Age* (Luton Museum, 1970)

TAYLOR, CHRISTOPHER *Roads and Tracks in Britain* (Dent, 1979)

Chapter 6 **Goods by Water**

BURTON, ANTHONY *The Canal Builders* (Eyre Methuen, 1981, second edition)

BURTON, ANTHONY and PRATT, DEREK *Canal* (David & Charles, 1976)

HADFIELD, CHARLES *British Canals* (David & Charles, 1974, sixth edition)

HADFIELD, CHARLES *The Canal Age* (David & Charles, 1968)

HANSON, HARRY *The Canal Boatmen* (Manchester University Press, 1975)

HARRIS, ROBERT *Canals and Their Architecture* (Evelyn, 1969)

RANSOM, P.J.G. *The Archaeology of Canals* (World's Work, 1979)

ROLT, L.T.C. *Navigable Waterways* (Longman, 1969)

Chapter 7 **Iron Rails and Steam**

BAXTER, B. *Stone Blocks and Iron Rails* (David & Charles, 1966)

BINNEY, MARCUS and PEARCE, DAVID *Railway Architecture* (Orbis, 1979)

ELLIS, HAMILTON *British Railway History* (2 vols) (Allen and Unwin, 1954 and 1959)

MORGAN, BRYAN *Civil Engineering: Railways* (Longman, 1971)

REED, BRIAN *150 Years of British Steam Locomotives* (David & Charles, 1975)

SNELL, J.B. *Mechanical Engineering: Railways* (Longman, 1971)

RANSOM, P.J.G. *Archaeology of Railways* (World's Work, 1981)

Chapter 8 **Pro Bono Publico**

DUNSHEATH, P.A. *A History of Electrical Engineering* (Faber, 1962)

PARSONS, R.H. *The Early Days of the Power Station Industry* (Cambridge University Press, 1939)

ROLT, L.T.C. *Victorian Engineering* (Penguin, 1970)

STEWARD, E.C. *Town Gas* (Science Museum, 1958)

Chapter 9 **Back to Basics**

BARKER, T.C. *The Glassmakers* (Weidenfeld & Nicolson, 1977)

HUDSON, KENNETH *The History of English China Clays* (David & Charles, 1969)

LINDSAY, JEAN *A History of the North Wales Slate Industry* (David & Charles, 1969)

MATHIAS, P. *The Brewing Industry in England* (Cambridge University Press, 1959)

THOMAS, J. *The Rise of the Staffordshire Potteries* (Adams & Dart, 1971)

Maps of the British Isles

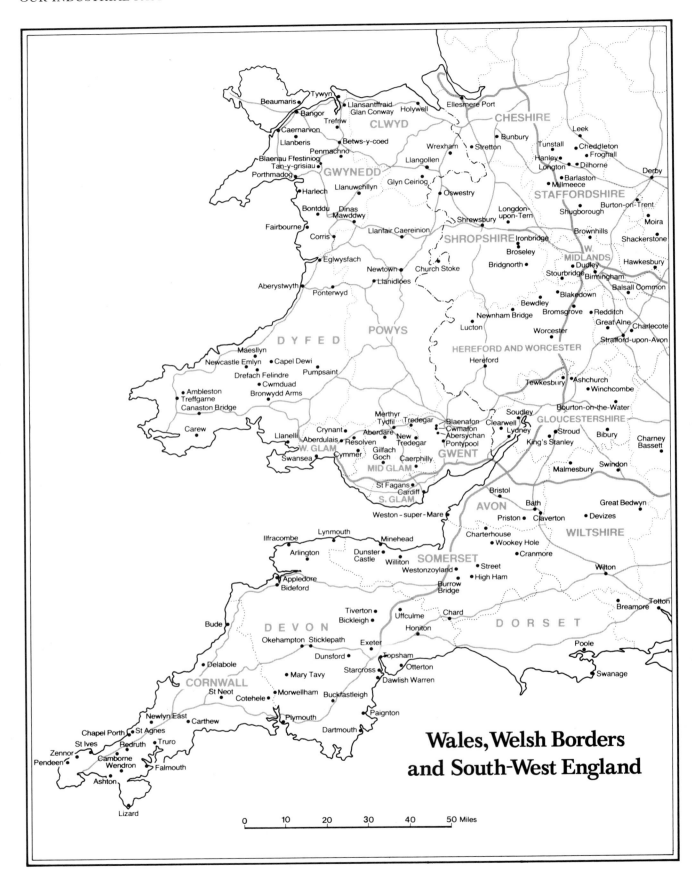

Beaumaris
Tywyn
Bangor
Trefriw
Caernarvon
Llanberis
Penmachno
Betws-y-coed
Blaenau Ffestiniog
Tan-y-grisiau
Porthmadog
Harlech
Llanuwchllyn
Bontddu
Dinas
Mawddwy
Fairbourne
Corris
Eglwysfach
Newtown
Aberystwyth
Ponterwyd
Llanidloes

Llansantffraid
Glan Conway
Holywell
Trefriw
CLWYD
Wrexham
Llangollen
Glyn Ceiriog
Oswestry
Llanfair Caereinion
Church Stoke

Ellesmere Port
CHESHIRE
Bunbury
Stretton
GWYNEDD
Shrewsbury
SHROPSHIRE
Ironbridge
Broseley
Bridgnorth
POWYS
DYFED

Leek
Tunstall
Cheddleton
Froghall
Hanley
Dilhorne
Longton
Derby
Barlaston
Millmeece
STAFFORDSHIRE
Burton-on-Trent
Longdon-upon-Tern
Shugborough
Moira
Brownhills
Shackerstone
W. MIDLANDS
Dudley
Hawkesbury
Stourbridge
Birmingham
Balsall Common
Blakedown
Bewdley
Bromsgrove
Redditch
Newnham Bridge
Great Alne
Charlecote
Lucton
Worcester
Stratford-upon-Avon
HEREFORD AND WORCESTER
Hereford
Tewkesbury
Ashchurch
Winchcombe

Maesllyn
Newcastle Emlyn
Capel Dewi
Pumpsaint
Drefach Felindre
Cwmduad
Bronwydd Arms
Ambleston
Treffgarne
Canaston Bridge
Carew
Llanelli
Crynant
Aberdulais
Resolven
Swansea
Cymmer
W. GLAM
MID GLAM

Merthyr
Tydfil
Tredegar
Aberdare
New
Tredegar
Gilfach
Goch
Caerphilly
St Fagans
Cardiff
S. GLAM
Blaenafon
Cwmafon
Abersychan
Pontypool
GWENT
Clearwell
Lydney
King's Stanley
Soudley
Bourton-on-the-Water
GLOUCESTERSHIRE
Stroud
Bibury
Charney Bassett
Malmesbury
Swindon

Weston-super-Mare
Bristol
AVON
Bath
Priston
Claverton
Charterhouse
Wookey Hole
Great Bedwyn
Devizes
WILTSHIRE

Ilfracombe
Lynmouth
Minehead
Arlington
Dunster Castle
Williton
SOMERSET
Westonzoyland
Street
High Ham
Cranmore
Wilton
Appledore
Bideford
Burrow Bridge
Tiverton
Bickleigh
Uffculme
Chard
Honiton
DORSET
Totton
Breamore
Bude
DEVON
Okehampton
Sticklepath
Dunsford
Exeter
Starcross
Topsham
Poole
Delabole
Mary Tavy
Otterton
Dawlish Warren
Swanage
CORNWALL
St Neot
Cotehele
Morwellham
Buckfastleigh
Newlyn East
Carthew
Plymouth
Paignton
Chapel Porth
St Agnes
Dartmouth
Zennor
St Ives
Redruth
Truro
Pendeen
Camborne
Wendron
Falmouth
Ashton
Lizard

Wales, Welsh Borders and South-West England

0   10   20   30   40   50 Miles

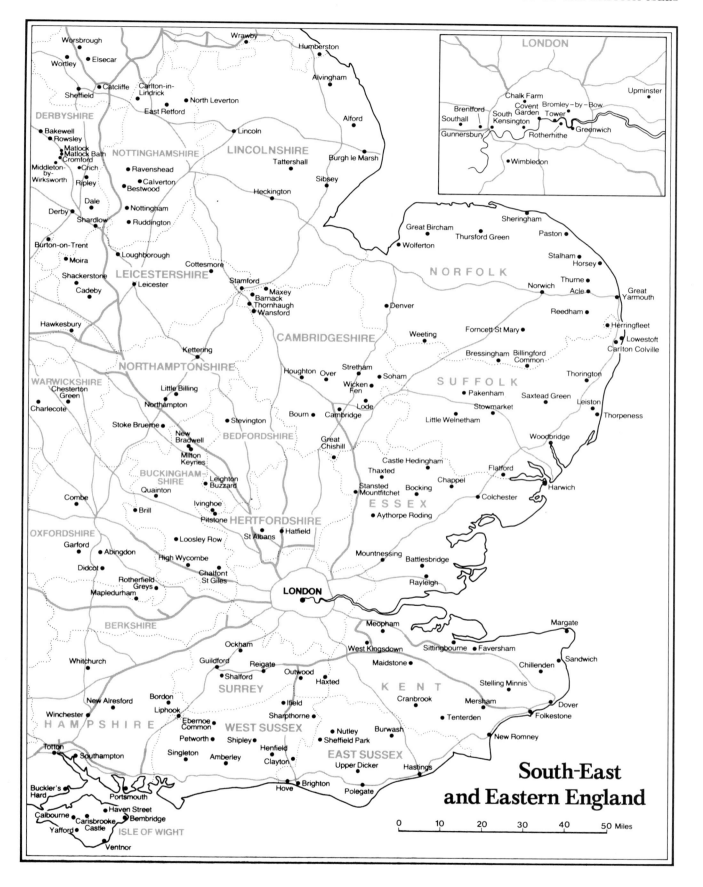

South-East and Eastern England

LONDON

Chalk Farm
Covent Garden
Brentford
South Kensington
Southall
Gunnersbury
Wimbledon
Bromley – by – Bow
Tower
Rotherhithe
Greenwich
Upminster

Worsbrough
Wortley
Elsecar
Catcliffe
Sheffield
Carlton-in-Lindrick
East Retford
North Leverton
Wrawby
Humberston
Alvingham
Alford
Lincoln
Burgh le Marsh

DERBYSHIRE
Bakewell
Rowsley
Matlock
Matlock Bath
Cromford
Middleton-by-Wirksworth
Crich
Ripley
Dale
Derby
Shardlow
Burton-on-Trent
Moira
Shackerstone
Cadeby

NOTTINGHAMSHIRE
Ravenshead
Calverton
Bestwood
Nottingham
Ruddington
Loughborough

LINCOLNSHIRE
Tattershall
Sibsey
Heckington

LEICESTERSHIRE
Leicester
Cottesmore
Stamford
Maxey
Barnack
Thornhaugh
Wansford

Hawkesbury

NORTHAMPTONSHIRE
Kettering
Little Billing
Northampton
Stoke Bruerne
New Bradwell
Milton Keynes

WARWICKSHIRE
Chesterton Green
Charlecote

Stevington

BEDFORDSHIRE
Great Chishill
Bourn
Cambridge
Houghton
Over
Stretham
Wicken Fen
Lode
Soham

CAMBRIDGESHIRE
Denver
Weeting

NORFOLK
Great Bircham
Wolferton
Thursford Green
Paston
Sheringham
Stalham
Horsey
Thurne
Acle
Norwich
Reedham
Great Yarmouth
Herringfleet
Lowestoft
Carlton Colville
Forncett St Mary
Bressingham
Billingford Common
Thorington

SUFFOLK
Pakenham
Stowmarket
Little Welnetham
Saxtead Green
Leiston
Thorpeness
Woodbridge

Castle Hedingham
Thaxted
Chappel
Flatford
Bocking
Harwich
Stansted Mountfitchet
Colchester

ESSEX
Aythorpe Roding

BUCKINGHAMSHIRE
Quainton
Leighton Buzzard
Ivinghoe
Pitstone
Brill
Combe

HERTFORDSHIRE
Loosley Row
St Albans
Hatfield

OXFORDSHIRE
Garford
Abingdon
High Wycombe
Didcot
Rotherfield Greys
Chalfont St Giles
Mapledurham

Mountnessing
Battlesbridge
Rayleigh

BERKSHIRE
Whitchurch
Ockham
Guildford
Reigate
Shalford
Outwood
Haxted

Meopham
West Kingsdown
Sittingbourne
Faversham
Margate
Sandwich
Chillenden

KENT
Maidstone
Stelling Minnis
Mersham
Dover
Folkestone

SURREY
New Alresford
Bordon
Liphook
Ebernoe Common
Petworth
Shipley
Singleton
Amberley

Cranbrook
Tenterden
New Romney

Ifield
Sharpthorne
Henfield
Clayton
Nutley
Sheffield Park
Burwash
Upper Dicker
Hastings

WEST SUSSEX

EAST SUSSEX

HAMPSHIRE
Winchester
Totton
Southampton
Buckler's Hard
Portsmouth
Calbourne
Haven Street
Carisbrooke Castle
Bembridge
Yafford
Ventnor

ISLE OF WIGHT

Brighton
Hove
Polegate

0   10   20   30   40   50 Miles

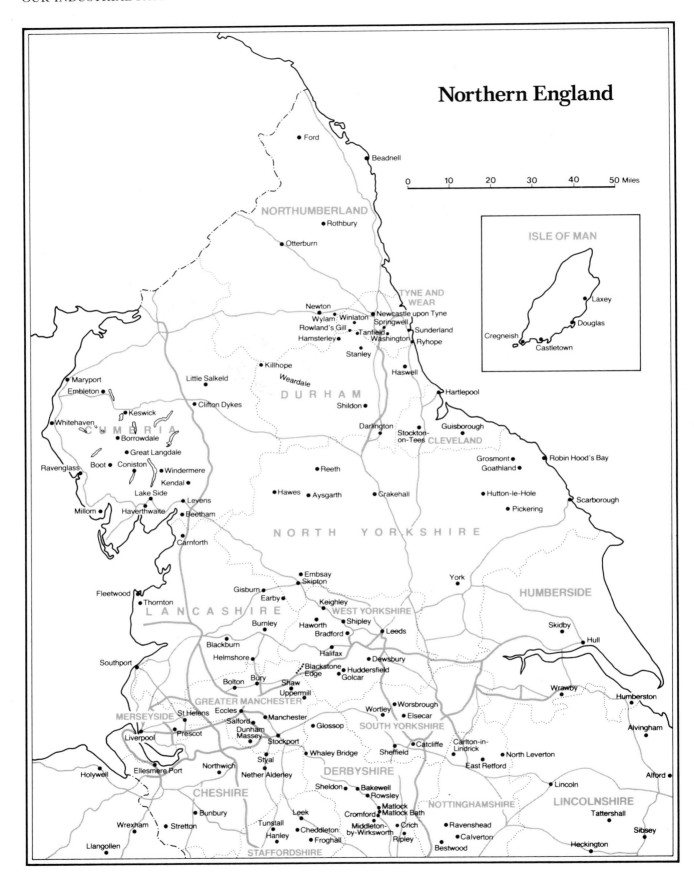

Northern England

ISLE OF MAN

0 10 20 30 40 50 Miles

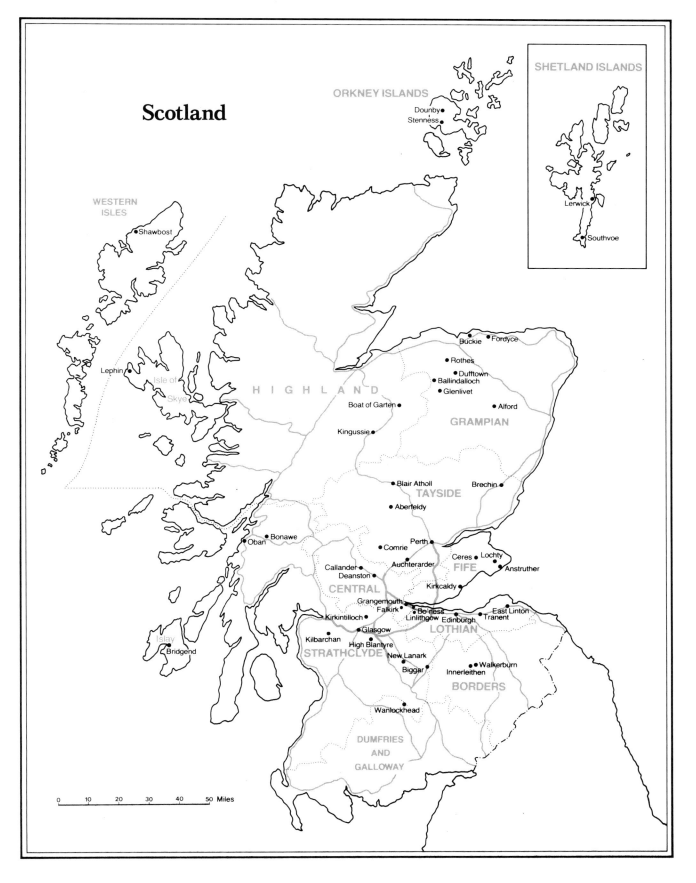

Scotland

SHETLAND ISLANDS

Lerwick
Southvoe

ORKNEY ISLANDS
Dounby
Stenness

WESTERN ISLES
Shawbost

Lephin

Isle of Skye

HIGHLAND

Buckie Fordyce
Rothes
Dufftown
Ballindalloch
Glenlivet
Boat of Garten
Alford

GRAMPIAN

Kingussie

Blair Atholl
Brechin

TAYSIDE

Aberfeldy

Oban Bonawe

Perth
Comrie

Ceres Lochty
Auchterarder
FIFE
Anstruther

Callander
Deanston

Kirkcaldy

CENTRAL

Grangemouth
Falkirk Bo'ness
Kirkintilloch Linlithgow Edinburgh East Linton
Tranent
Glasgow LOTHIAN
Kilbarchan
High Blantyre
New Lanark
STRATHCLYDE Biggar Innerleithen Walkerburn

BORDERS

Islay
Bridgend

Wanlockhead

DUMFRIES
AND
GALLOWAY

0 10 20 30 40 50 Miles

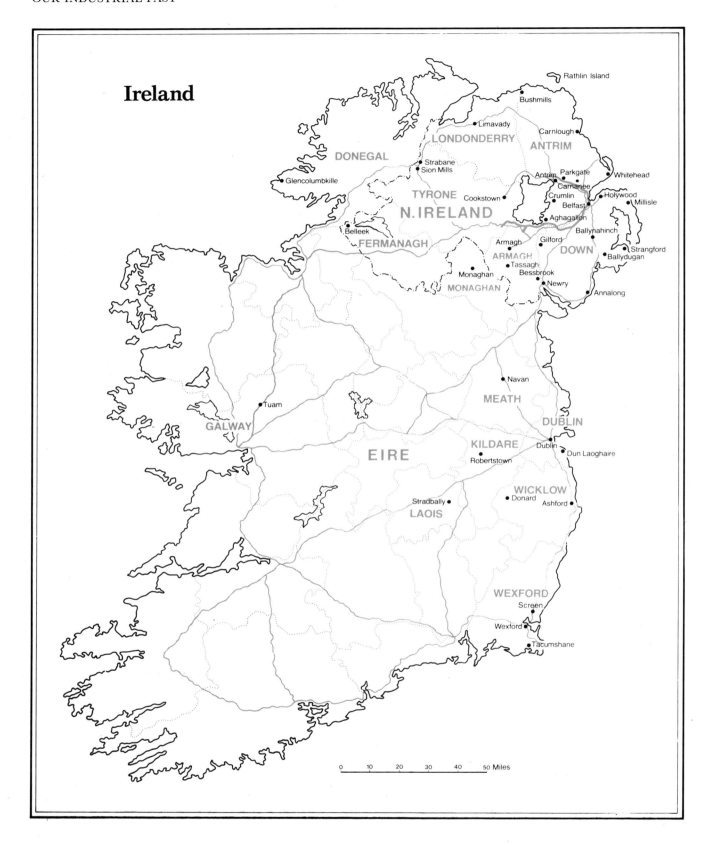

Ireland

Rathlin Island
Bushmills
Limavady
Carnlough
LONDONDERRY
ANTRIM
DONEGAL
Strabane
Sion Mills
Antrim Parkgate
Whitehead
Carnanee
Glencolumbkille
TYRONE
Cookstown
Crumlin
Holywood
N.IRELAND
Belfast
Millisle
Belleek
Aghagallon
FERMANAGH
Ballynahinch
Armagh
Gilford
DOWN
Strangford
ARMAGH
Ballydugan
Tassagh
Monaghan
Bessbrook
Newry
MONAGHAN
Annalong

Navan
MEATH
Tuam
DUBLIN
GALWAY
KILDARE
Dublin
EIRE
Robertstown
Dun Laoghaire

WICKLOW
Stradbally
Donard
Ashford
LAOIS

WEXFORD
Screen
Wexford
Tacumshane

0 10 20 30 40 50 Miles

Index